Praise for *Savvy Woman In 5 Minutes a Day*

"*Savvy Woman in 5 Minutes a Day* takes one through the entire year. With fun and verve, Moira shares through stories and examples how one can achieve success at a high level in business and life. It isn't just for CEOs!"

Karen Briscoe, author, *Real Estate Success in 5 Minutes a Day*
and host of the podcast "5 Minute Success"

"This book provides the key to living a balanced life, with increased health, well-being, and productivity, even in the most hectic occupations. Everybody can find guidance through her easy to understand and deeply enriching writing."

Amy Dufrane, Ed.D, SPHR, CAE
CEO, HRCI

"Moira successfully influences any person, from any walk of life, to reexamine their mental habits and to act in order to change their life for the better. The book is practical and fun to read, all the while helping the reader to achieve their goals."

Robin Camille Dennis, LMT, NCTMB
Owner, FitPro Massage

"Have you ever strived to live a more balanced life? Have you ever felt stuck in a particular mindset, seemingly unable to experience clarity or direction? This book is your answer to all of your woes. It's fast and easy to read and jam-packed with guidance to enrich your life. Pick this book up and you will be forever benefited because of it."

Amy Clay, LPC
Owner, Sunstone Counseling

"Just like a daily motivational or spiritual devotional, *Savvy Woman in 5 Minutes a Day* readings are full of inspiration and information. Invest just five minutes a day to achieve success at a higher level in business and life. Use it to help create the life of your dreams while you live your best life now."

Christy Mistr, JD, CPA, CFP
Owner, Dominion Financial Consultants

SECRETS OF A TOP CEO

Savvy Woman

IN 5 MINUTES A DAY

Make Time for a Life That Matters

MOIRA LETHBRIDGE, M.Ed.

ISBN 978-1-936961-38-2

Books are available for special promotions and premiums.

For details, contact:
specialmarkets@savvywomanbook.com

Published by linx

DEDICATION

To Stevie and Patrick—I am the luckiest mom in the world.

And to all the women who are holding my hand
on this amazing journey.

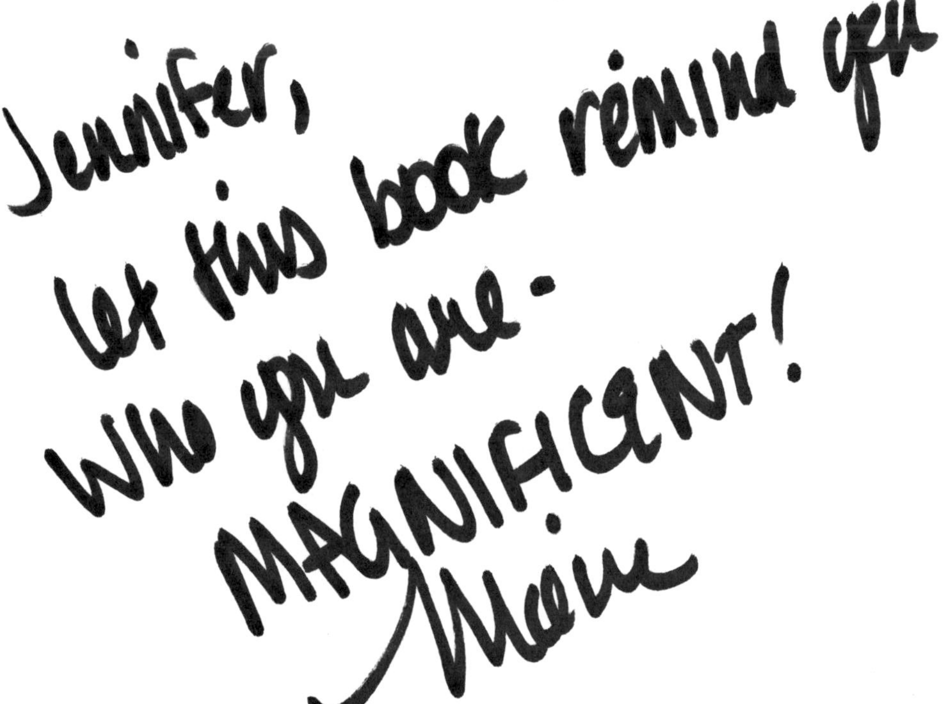

TABLE OF CONTENTS

JANUARY

FEBRUARY

MARCH

APRIL

MAY

JUNE

JULY

AUGUST

SEPTEMBER

OCTOBER

NOVEMBER

DECEMBER

INTRODUCTION

Six years ago, I was uncomfortably stuck—making fear-based decisions, I was stressed, anxious, unhappy, and wasn't sleeping. I was the president and CEO of a professional services firm and the company was growing and bringing in more revenue than ever before. Everything should have been great, but personally, I was struggling—really struggling.

I didn't think I had a choice but to stay where I was. I was miserable, but I couldn't imagine walking away. I ignored my inner guidance and took a practical path. Everyone else was telling me that this was major success, but I kept thinking, *Is there something more than this?*

I had a bad case of the "shoulds." "I should be happy, but I'm not. I should be grateful, but I'm not. I should know what I want and how to get it, but I don't." I don't want to ask for help. I hate bothering others. If everyone else says I have a normal life, then what's wrong with me?

I couldn't see any choices.

- My husband was a stay-at-home dad for the past sixteen years.
  He can't go out and get a job.
- Nobody will pay me what I'm making here.
- I've haven't looked for a new job in twenty years.
- I don't know how to start a business.

I was completely out of balance and disconnected. My limiting beliefs were drowning out the voice inside of me, and I continued to make compromises that made me feel increasingly numb.

I was really stuck.

The company I worked for went up for sale and I experienced a Harajuku Moment. This phrase, coined by author Malcolm Gladwell, refers to a time when something nice to do becomes something necessary to do. Before the company went up for sale, I thought it would be nice to leave. Now it was necessary. **It was my time.** I had spent twenty years growing a business and now I was taking the leap of my life. It was the change I was starving for, and it was scary. I struck out on my own. The first gift I gave myself was time off, which was something

I struggle accepting. My fear-based thought said, "Any time off is not productive and not revenue-generating."

I went to Rehoboth Beach, Delaware and stopped in a Walmart for supplies. Before taking the leap, I raced into grocery stores, wearing my black suit and talking on my phone while grabbing a microwavable meal. The customers in Rehoboth were not wearing business suits or on their phones making "important calls." I realized this was my new life. The contrast between the two worlds hit me. My hands shook. I broke out in a sweat and my chest felt constricted and painful. I had a full-blown anxiety attack. I rushed outside and sat on the curb with my head between my knees.

What have I just done?

I realized I had lost my identity. I had always believed I am what I do, and now it was gone. I had no idea what to do next. It was a horrible feeling.

In that moment, I made a promise to myself: **figure out how to live the life and have the business of my dreams.**

Here's what I did.

- I took an online course on how to teach others, despite feeling stupid.
- I coached a business for free when I first launched my business.
- I joined an online entrepreneur group.
- I attended a women's entrepreneur conference.
- I admitted what I really wanted to do for work and turned down work that didn't fit that description.
- I let go of relationships that no longer served me, even though I thought I was too old to make new friends.
- I learned how to use my reset button several times a day.
- I learned how to ask for help by joining a mastermind group and taking an online marketing course.
- I allowed myself to be seen by posting a sixty-second video on YouTube for a contest to participate in a live webcast with Tim Ferriss, author of *The Four-Hour Work Week, The Four-Hour Chef, and The Four-Hour Body*, and was selected from hundreds of entries. I was also the oldest person selected.
- I failed several times: by offering a women's leadership workshop that nobody signed up for, offering a workshop on overcoming gender stereotypes in the workplace that nobody signed up for, presenting The Seven Ingredients of Collaborative Innovation to several CEO and COO groups and nobody bought in to it.
- I succeeded by increasing my coaching business, conducting weekend retreats for women and offering seminars on effective leadership and mindfulness.
- I read tons of books on change, mindfulness, transformation, and success.

- I learned how to practice yoga and meditate to reconnect to my body and to the present moment.
- I took time to discover myself, even when my inner critic told me it was selfish.
- I changed my thoughts and beliefs about work and my worth.
- I redefined success on my terms.

I dug myself in the trenches and did the hard work so now I can teach others how to get there in a quick, straightforward way.

Here's what it led to in my life:

- I'm calmer and I finally sleep really well.
- I've lost weight.
- I've created my own successful business.
- I'm helping people change their lives.
- I'm spending my days doing what I love.
- I've got more time in my life.
- I'm making money helping other people do what I've done.
- I'm happier and at peace with myself.
- I accomplish my goals faster, easier, and have fun doing it.
- I love my life. I couldn't say that six years ago.

I learned what is my work to do, what my purpose is, and where I belong in this world. Now I am happy, free and successful.

Some of the key lessons I learned became the foundation of everything I do and teach.

Our thoughts and beliefs create our experiences, and by changing our thinking and our belief system, we can profoundly change our lives for the better and have amazing lives.

- I realized that everything in my life—my achievements, lifestyle, relationships, health, is based on my thoughts and beliefs.
- I recognized I do have a choice in everything, but some of my thoughts and beliefs were blocking my choices.
- I learned how to change my thoughts and beliefs to create a life and business I love.

Most people don't even know what thoughts and beliefs get in the way of having an amazing life, and they don't know how to question their thoughts and beliefs in order to create the change that would make them happy. The impact is significant: staying in crappy jobs and relationships, hurting your body and relationships, engaging in compulsive behaviors, doubting yourself, and shrinking your world. And not creating the change you want in your life.

By practicing the exercises in this book, you will:

- Accomplish what you want faster and easier.
- Have less wear and tear on yourself and your psyche.
- Increase your self-confidence and happiness.

Why am I sharing this with you?

I found out it doesn't have to be hard or take a long time to see results. And that change is not only possible, but also inevitable with my method and approach.

I want you to feel as excited when you get up in the morning as I do.

I want you to remember who you are and forget what you are not.

Love,
Moira

How Savvy Woman in 5 Minutes a Day Can Help You Achieve Your Sweet Spot of Success

The Sweet Spot of Success is the overlap of three areas of your life: self, relationships, and work. It is the balance of health, well-being, and productivity in each area that allows you to experience clarity, direction, and peace of mind.

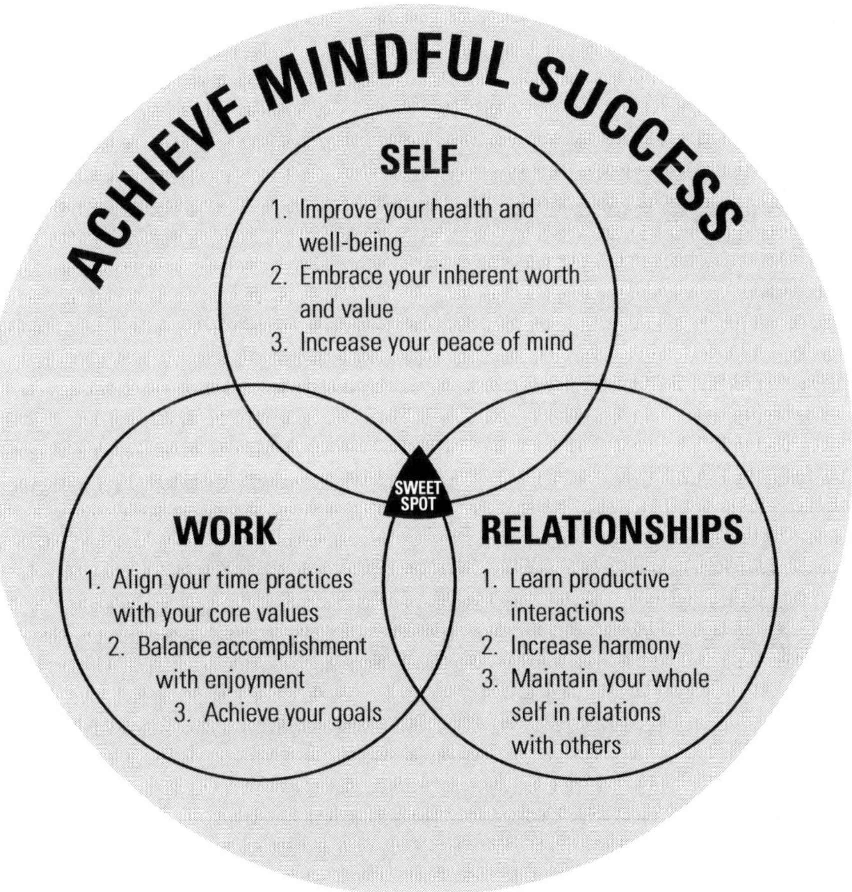

The Sweet Spot of Success is the intersection of all the best practices included in *Savvy Woman in 5 Minutes a Day: Make Time for a Life That Matters*. Enjoy reading one story each day. Use these practical methods to achieve mindful success.

Mindful success is intentionally choosing your thoughts and actions every day. It is consciously choosing to have more faith in abundance and worthiness than in scarcity and unworthiness.

HOW TO USE THIS BOOK

STEP 1: Take 5 minutes every day for success—ideally, first thing each morning.

STEP 2: Read the daily entry in *Savvy Woman in 5 Minutes a Day: Make Time for a Life That Matters.*

STEP 3: Apply the technique during the day and share your results with a friend.

Write Your Look-Back Intentions

Setting your intention for the year tells your unconscious mind what to look for and make happen. Imagine you are on a ship, and you see an iceberg jetting out of the water, bright blue and white. The part of the iceberg that you can see is only about 5 percent. This is your conscious mind. The other 95 percent is your unconscious mind, or the rest of the iceberg under the water. It is your supercomputer that can access tons of information and share it with your conscious mind. The way to access it is through journaling.

Put pen to paper and write down everything you want to be, do, or have. This clarifies your thinking and helps you get to know yourself, putting you in touch with your inner world. Journaling reduces stress and is an effective way to retain new information, helping you connect knowledge in new ways.

So often, we block what we want to achieve and experience because of past disappointments, failures, and fear. Suspend judgment so you can access your heart's desire.

Write a letter to yourself in the present tense, dated December 31, describing everything you achieved throughout the year. Do not edit yourself by saying, "This is stupid. It won't work. It's not realistic." Give yourself permission to want what you want. In the letter, describe what it **feels** like now that you have achieved what you want. Describing your feelings of receiving what you want is key to this exercise.

Journaling Date: December 31, ______

Dear _________________,

I am so happy and grateful now that__________________________.

It's OK to want what you want. Write it down and see how the Universe rushes in to support you.

Journal to access your heart's desire.

Choose Love

You were born into a thought system of fear. Choose the thought system of love.

The world believes in the thought system of scarcity and unworthiness. Advertising has perfected it through quantity-related scarcity: only two seats left and the last day to buy.

Booking.com shows: "booked twenty-six times today." Amazon lists: only two left in stock. The Bumble dating app has a countdown timer: you have twenty-four hours to respond to a prospective date or the match disappears.

It plays on the fear of missing out (FOMO). When you operate from this thought system, you neglect your needs, overwork, overfunction, and are not in the present moment.

Choose the thought system of love. It is the belief in abundance and worthiness.

"Because I believe in my inherent worth and value, and that I live in a friendly universe, I practice mindful success every day, and I need never worry again."

Mindful success is intentionally choosing your thoughts and actions every day. It is consciously choosing to have more faith in abundance and worthiness than in scarcity and unworthiness.

This thought system leads to the freedom to choose balance in giving and receiving, between work, family, and self-maintenance, between being and doing, and increased present-moment awareness—increased tolerance with the unknown, increased curiosity, and decreased judgment.

Practice the exercises in this book. They will strengthen your ability to choose love more often than not.

Remember who you are and forget what you are not.

Successful Women Ask for and Accept Support

Whether it's hiring a cleaning service, a dog walker, personal assistant, or asking friends for help, support is essential for you to thrive and achieve your goals.

I'm going to fail at this again. Why bother? Nadia chided herself. She huffed and shook her head. *How do I follow through on eating healthfully and exercising?* Every January she wrote a vision for the year ahead, and exercise and eating right were always on it.

She owned her own business and loved the service she provided her clients. It brought her joy and fulfillment. She had the flexibility to structure her day to support her goal. Yet when it came to spending time on her health—exercise, buying groceries, and making healthy lunches—she always put work ahead of it. "I'll do it tomorrow."

The biggest obstacle is not information, knowledge, money, or time. It's support. She needed support to make her health a priority.

Identify friends and colleagues to support you for thirty days.

Tell them to text you encouraging phrases on specific days and times.

Don't believe that you can do it on your own or that you just need more willpower. If this were true, you would have already done it.

Expect to feel uncomfortable and vulnerable when you ask for support. This is normal and to be expected.

Nadia asked Beverly: "Text me on Tuesday at noon to support my fifteen-minute walk outside. Tell me I deserve this time."

She asked Denise: "Text me on Sunday by 1:00 p.m. to remind me about grocery shopping. Say, 'Successful entrepreneurs make their health a priority, and you are a successful entrepreneur.'"

Put a support team around you to help you make change stick.

Teach Others How to Support You

People aren't mind readers. They need help to know what supportive word or phrase works for you.

Isabelle blurted out, "I want support, but don't know how to ask for it." She had tried to get support from her friends, but ended up feeling worse than before.

"You're not alone. I wanted support from friends too. I didn't know what to ask for, so I listed what I didn't want to hear. This helped me identify what I did want to hear," Holly explained.

Write down phrases that are not supportive for you. Then write the opposite of them. Tweak them until you have supportive phrases that work for you. Share them with others.

Holly showed Isabelle her two lists.

"I don't want to hear: Suck it up. Count your blessings. Just do it. Stop blowing it off. You're so lucky you even have time to do that activity. These phrases feel supportive: I believe in you. You deserve this time. You always persevere, even when you are frustrated. Your effort and attitude are excellent."

Holly continued, "My friends were relieved. It made supporting me easier because before they didn't know what to say."

Take the time to discover the words and phrases that feel supportive to you.

Carpool Karaoke Cranks Out Joy

James Corden is an English comedian, actor, and TV host of the *Late Late Night Show* on CBS. One of his sketches is called Carpool Karaoke. Musical stars join Cordon for his car ride to work so he can use the express lanes. He puts on various songs from the artists and then films them singing together.

When Corden was asked where the idea for Carpool Karaoke came from, he said that it was inspired by a British television sketch in which he drove around London and sang songs with pop star George Michael. Cordon said in an interview that he "always thought there was something very joyful about someone very, very famous singing their songs in an ordinary situation."

He has hosted artists such as Elton John, Selena Gomez, Harry Styles, and former first lady Michelle Obama. His joyful, humorous car ride won an Emmy and in 2016 Apple bought sharing rights to produce a television show.

Add joy to your day. Watch Carpool Karaoke YouTube videos. Sing along with Stevie Wonder, Adele, Bruno Mars, or your favorite artist. You too will crank out the tunes and feel the joy.

Make time to sing and laugh.

A Good Laugh Heals a Lot of Hurts

Take a break from intense life experiences.

"I can't spend another Friday night alone," Velma mumbled into the phone as she searched for more tissues. It was six months since the divorce, and her pain felt most intense on the weekends.

Sadie insisted that Velma allow her to bring dinner and a movie on Friday nights for a month. "I want to do this. Please accept this gift of love from me. I want to spend time with you."

Velma's chest constricted. "I have to call you back." She sank to the floor and sobbed. Completely wrung out, she rested on the couch until she was awakened by the doorbell. Sadie stood there with food and a movie. "I made our favorite," she gushed. "Meatloaf, baked potatoes, broccoli, and chocolate-chip cookies."

"What movie did you bring?" Velma asked, grateful to see her friend.

"*Dumb and Dumber.*"

Laughter brings people together and establishes connection. It reduces stress hormone levels, which in turn cuts anxiety and stress that impacts the body. When you go through challenging times—a divorce, death, or job loss—take breaks from the intensity with laughter.

As Sadie got the movie ready, Velma settled onto the couch with a blanket, tea, and her dog, Parker. "Thank you," Velma whispered.

Identify what makes you laugh and add it to your daily routine.

Let Your Light Shine

The world needs you.

The following quote is from an article, "Rich Generosity," written by Master Sheng-Yen.

"When out of gratitude we use our candle to light other people's candles, the whole room gets brighter. This is why we transfer merit to others. This kind of light is continuous and inexhaustible."

Journal on the following questions:

- If I allowed myself to acknowledge my gifts, what would they be?
- How would I share them with myself?

Once you have identified your gifts and how you would share them with yourself, block time over the next week to practice giving them to yourself. You will experience how good it feels to receive them. Only then do you give them to others.

Share your gifts with yourself.

Beginner's Mind Brings Relief

The Zen principle of Shoshin, or Beginner's Mind, is when the mind of the beginner is empty, free of the habits of the expert, is open to all possibilities, and can see things as they are.

A professor decided he wanted to learn something new, so he went to visit a Zen master. While the master served tea, the professor talked about all he knew about Zen. The master poured the professor's cup full and continued pouring to overflowing. The professor yelled, "It's overflowing, and no more will go in the cup!" The Zen master responded, "You are like this cup. How can I show you Zen unless you first empty your cup?"

Remember when you first started your career. Were you excited to learn? Did you expect to know everything? Did you ask a ton of questions? This is the practice of beginner's mind.

Watch a child learn a new skill. They don't expect to know how to play the piano or hit a baseball, and yet we expect ourselves to know everything.

Our natural tendency is to plow ahead, doing what we've always done and rarely stepping back to question whether we're on the right path. Feeling compelled to believe "I should already know this" can make us less curious and less open to new ideas and possibilities. It leads us to asking fewer questions.

Practicing Beginner's Mind takes a willingness to act as if you don't know why anything is happening, what anything means, or its purpose and reason. It means releasing all expectations and attachments to outcomes.

Say the Set-Aside Prayer: *Help me let go of everything I know and how I think things should turn out.* Act as if you believe this will help you see more opportunities and experience more moments of serendipity—a fortuitous meshing of events.

Remember a time when you were excited to learn a new skill.
Step into that attitude and apply it to your day.

SELF-CARE

Celebrate Clean Off Your Desk Day

The second Monday of January is celebrated as Clean Off Your Desk Day. It's not an official holiday; nonetheless, it encourages you to focus on starting the New Year with a clutter-free, organized work space.

A clean work space conveys a professional and personal image. It increases efficiency and reduces distractions and the stress of trying to locate a document from an unruly pile of papers, wrappers, and sticky notes.

Whatever method you choose to organize your workspace, do this one action first: Clean your computer keyboard.

Studies show that keyboards can be up to five times dirtier than the average toilet seat. Read your owner's manual for product-specific cleaning instructions. Shut down your computer and unplug it. Use an air duster to blow off crumbs. Turn the keyboard upside down and shake it to remove any remaining morsels. Moisten a link-free cloth with isopropyl alcohol and gently wipe across the keyboard.

It's not the most exciting task, but it will keep you healthy so you can do other fun things like take a well day. Or you can go with this quote from A.A. Milne, author of *Winnie the Pooh*: "One of the advantages of being disorderly is that one is constantly making exciting discoveries."

Clean your keyboard and stay healthy.

Interrupt Distressing Thoughts with Deep Breathing

The breath can be used to directly influence the body's response to stress.

Brenda grabbed her coat as she sprinted for the front door. "Do you have your keys?" Tom yelled from the top of the stairs. Her body halted, as if she hit a brick wall. Her ashen face told the truth. She turned toward the stairs. Tears rolled down her cheeks. "I'm pathetic," she groaned.

Stressful thoughts can cause shallow breathing, which in turn triggers a fight-or-flight response. Deep abdominal breathing slows your heartbeat and quiets your stress response.

Place one hand on your chest and the other on your abdomen. Take a deep breath in. The hand on your abdomen should rise higher than the one on your chest. It indicates that your diaphragm is pulling air into the lower lobes of your lungs, where the greatest amount of blood flows. Exhale twice as long as you inhale.

"Honey, breathe. I'll help you locate them." Tom sat on the steps with Brenda and modeled deep breathing. After a few minutes, she joined him.

Teach others how to breathe deeply.

Assume You Did Something Right

"I need an appointment to talk with you," her boss, Ken, said to Zoey.

"OK. Let me get my calendar." Zoey raced back to her office.

She reviewed her to-do list, ticking off the tasks that had been completed and sent to her boss. She searched through her piles of paper, spreading them out over her desk. "I haven't looked through this pile in a week. Email. Check your unread emails. What is my client status? Is Josh angry with me again?"

Zoey jumped when her boss entered her office. "Zoey, what's wrong?"

She sputtered, "Nothing. I'm just reviewing my to-do list to see what needs to get done next."

Identify if you have the habitual response to authority figures: "What did I do wrong?" It can trigger you into a fight-or-flight response. This is a physiological reaction to a perceived harmful attack, event, or threat to survival.

Instead, assume you did something right. You aren't guilty. Think of all the things you do well. It's time for you to accept, appreciate, and express your talents.

"OK," Ken continued. "Let's set up a time to talk about you. I want to do it as soon as possible, so I can submit your bonus paperwork."

Stop being surprised by your talents. Claim them.

Don't Let Others Live Rent-Free in Your Head

The hurt you have experienced by others, although painful, is now just a thought you carry around inside you. Anger, resentment, and hatred take up space in your mind and drain your energy.

"I have a right to be upset with my daughter. Did you hear how she spoke to me?" Ella jammed the dishes into the dishwasher and slammed it shut. She stared out the kitchen window, wringing out the sponge.

"You've hit your quota on how many times you can tell me the same story. It must give you a buzz, but it's a real buzz killer," Melinda said as she wrapped her hands around her teacup.

The ticking of the clock on the oven resounded. Music blared from a passing car. Ella's sigh broke the silence.

Melinda leaned forward. "Are you going to talk to me or keep killing that sponge?"

Holding on to resentment and hurt ties you to the pain of the past. When you've been slighted or confronted, release resentments and discouraging memories. Identify your payoff for holding on:

- I don't have to change.
- I don't have to learn a new behavior.
- I don't have to take personal accountability.
- I don't have to make a choice.

Choose to let go of this story and identify what you have to change.

Ella described the fear of learning a different way of connecting with her daughter. "If I let this go, I don't know how to relate to her. This makes me feel really stupid. My mom didn't know how to relate to me, either, and I don't want her to experience this pain too."

Ask yourself, "Do I want to be right or to be at peace?"

Listen to Your Still, Small Voice

Thursday night I drove to meet a friend for dinner. I noticed a state police car behind me. No big deal. I was going the speed limit. He hit his lights and pulled me over. The good news was, I didn't feel nervous at all. No sinking feeling. No color draining out of my face.

"Ma'am, do you know your registration has expired?"

I had no clue. "Is that what I pay in October to the county?"

"No ma'am. That's your property tax."

"Hmmmm."

"Here's your summons. This is what you do so you don't have to pay the fine. Carry this ticket in your car until you get your registration paid. That way, if you get pulled over again, you can show them this." I went on to dinner. I was so grateful to have time with my friend that I forgot about the ticket.

I brought the ticket inside on Friday morning to remind me to pay it. I went to work and forgot about it again.

Saturday morning I looked for the ticket. It wasn't in my office, the kitchen, or on the foyer table. "Maybe I left it in the car. I'll look for it when I go to the gym." The ticket was not in my car.

The weather was frigid: low 20s. It had snowed during the night. I returned from the gym and remembered that I was responsible for shoveling the part of the sidewalk in front of my house. My sons were away, so I couldn't ask them. "Ugh. I don't want to go out and shovel. I need to look for my ticket."

Shovel the walkway, I heard inside my head.

"Fine. I'll shovel it." I went out to the garage and grabbed a shovel. After I was done, I went to put the shovel back in the garage. I walked in a different way—a way I never do because the location of the shovels is on the other side of the garage. As I bent down to move a box to make space for the shovel, I saw a yellow piece of paper underneath one of the storage racks. My ticket. I must have dropped it on my way into the house.

I never would have found that ticket if I didn't listen to that still, small voice. It's always looking out for me. It's the voice for love. It is gentle, kind, and patient.

Pause. Still your mind. Take five deep breaths. Write down what you hear. Check it out with a trusted friend. Act on what you think is the next right thing to do. It's probably the thing you don't want to do. Following it will save you time and wear and tear on yourself.

Make friends with your intuition.

Be Curious Like a Four-Year-Old

You were born to inquire. Now it's time to relearn this valuable skill.

Do you know what age we peak at questioning? Four. The average four-year-old girl asks her mom 390 questions a day. Boys ask a few less.

You don't ask questions like you did at four for many reasons. You may have gotten into trouble in school or at work for asking questions, and it made you feel isolated and insecure and unsafe to be who you are.

- Questioning is underappreciated in work, undertaught in schools, and underutilized in your everyday life.
- Information overload leads to an inability to separate what's relevant or reliable from what's not.
- Questioning is not rewarded.

You get caught up in the cycle of your daily to-do list. You don't spend any time thinking about whether you are happy or could be happier.

In order to handle the constant conditions of the new, the unfamiliar, and the unknown, you need to maintain a sense of wonder, curiosity, and willingness to try new things—just like you did as a child.

Practice being neotenous. *Neoteny* is a biological term that describes the retention of childlike attributes in adulthood.

Find a picture of yourself as a child. Every morning, ask her, "How are we going to be curious today?"

Ask, "What would a four-year-old do in this situation?"

Say No in the Name of Love

I believe that unarmed truth and unconditional love will have the final word.

—Martin Luther King Jr.

Martin Luther King Jr. was a Baptist minister and leader in the civil rights movement. He was inspired by the nonviolent activism of Mahatma Ghandhi and led the advancement of civil rights using the same tactics. He received the Nobel Peace Prize for combating racial inequality through nonviolent resistance. He said no from a place of love.

If you are in a helping role, you are more prone to losing yourself in the needs of others, especially those who are overly needy and rarely reciprocate. You give and give and give, which leads to overworking, overfunctioning, and neglecting your own needs.

You may think saying no means you are selfish, bad, undeserving, or unlovable.

Change the meaning of no.

Ask yourself if you wish to continue to believe that saying no is bad or selfish. Would you teach your children or friends that it's OK to protect themselves from exploitation? How often do you allow others the opportunity to be givers?

Practice saying no with the following phrases: "That doesn't work for me." "I'd love to say yes, but I cannot." "It's hard to say no, but I must."

Replace the limiting belief that saying no is selfish and replace it with the empowering belief: for me is not against you.

Love yourself through the power of saying no.

Answer Your Call to Adventure

What does *The Wizard of Oz*, *Buffy the Vampire Slayer*, and the novel *Wicked* by Gregory Maguire, which became the basis for the Broadway musical *Wicked*, all have in common?

They portray the Heroine's Journey. Based on the work by Joseph Campbell, (*The Hero's Journey*), it is the journey where you make long-lasting changes and return with gifts of increased happiness and peace of mind.

The heroine goes on an adventure, faces and overcomes a crisis, and returns home transformed.

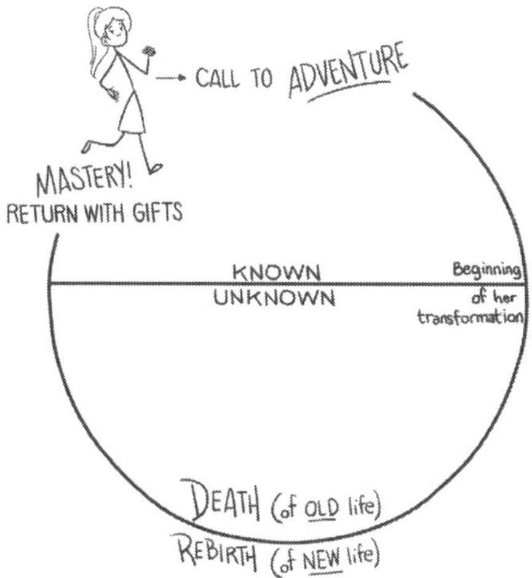

In *The Wizard of Oz*, Dorothy goes on an adventure to get back to Kansas after being swept away by a tornado. Landing in the magical land of Oz, she encounters helpers—the Scarecrow, Cowardly Lion, and Tin Man—who provide her with support along the way. Throughout, she is guided by Glenda, the Good Witch of the North. She faces several tests and trials. She defeats the Wicked Witch of the West, unmasks the Great Wizard of Oz as a fraud, and is granted a reward for her efforts in the knowledge that clicking her heels will return her to Kansas. Dorothy awakens from this dream with a renewed appreciation for her family and her life.

Each day you are called to an adventure. Answer the call. Go into the unknown with friends. Accept support from your guides. Come back with treasures.

Journal to Solve Problems

When you find yourself in circumstances that are draining you emotionally, physically, or spiritually, you may try unskillful ways to lessen the pain in an attempt to endure the situation. Choose to heal instead.

Lia's career had been stellar. She consistently exceeded her sales goals and was awarded top salesperson in her region. Her kids were doing well in school, and her husband was very supportive of her career. But for the last two years, she had been uncomfortably stuck. She was anxious and unhappy. She woke up regularly in the middle of the night, unable to fall back to sleep. Everything should have been great, but personally she struggled. She continued to ignore her inner guidance and stayed on her current path.

At wit's end, she took a much-needed break and hibernated for a weekend at a local hotel—alone. She ordered room service, worked out at the gym, and binge-watched Netflix. She also journaled.

"Is there something more than this? I should be happy, but I'm not. I should be grateful, but I'm not. I should know what I want and how to get it, but I don't. I don't want to ask for help. I hate bothering others. If everyone else says I have a normal life, then what's wrong with me? If my daughter was in my situation, what would I tell her?" She experienced a Harajuku Moment.

Harajuku Moment is a phrase coined by author Malcolm Gladwell. It is when something nice to have becomes something necessary. Journaling helps you unblock emotions and translate experiences to make them understandable. It is a route to healing.

Tears stained her page. Her hand moved furiously to capture her aha moment. She wiped her nose on her shirt as words flew across the page.

"I would tell her that it's OK not to know what you want next, to ask for help when making changes in your career, to admit that your family and marriage are suffering because you put your work first often."

Discover your Harajuku Moment.

PROFESSIONAL ACCOUNTABILITY

Accountability Is Ownership

There is the mistaken belief that accountability is something that can and must be imposed on others. This is not accountability; it's consequences.

The vice president, program director, and the accounting manager named Bridget wrapped up a meeting. Bridget promised the vice president, "You'll have the financial reports by Friday at 1:00 p.m." The program director wrote down the date and time. The vice president did not.

"Aren't you going to write that down and hold Bridget accountable?" the program director asked.

"I've worked with Bridget for over two years. She is as good as her word." Bridget consistently acted in an accountable manner.

The belief that you have to hold people accountable is the very thing that keeps you from experiencing what you want—other people owning what is theirs to do.

Change how you look at accountability. Instead of equating it with poor performance and negative consequences, view it as a person's ownership of their decisions, work, and results. Start with the premise that each person has freedom of choice, and accountability is ownership of those choices.

The only person who can hold you accountable is you.

See it. Own it. Solve it. Do it.

Post a Quote

In 1939, England and France declared war on Germany and World War II began. The British government ordered posters to convey a message to strengthen the morale of their citizens: "Keep Calm and Carry On."

The poster never made it out of the warehouse. The government commissioned other posters that did. "Freedom Is in Peril. Your Courage, Your Cheerfulness, Your Resolution Will Bring Us Victory."

In 2000, an English bookseller bought boxes of books at an auction. Inside the boxes he discovered posters with the message, "Keep Calm and Carry On." He hung one in his store window. Customers asked to buy it. By 2005, the poster was included in the Christmas special of a national newspaper.

Phrases inspire, motivate, and encourage. Choose quotes you want to stick in your brain:

- One year = 365 opportunities.
- She believed she could, so she did.
- Life is not about waiting for the storm to pass, but learning to dance in the rain.
- When you think about quitting, remember why you started.
- Just because your path is different doesn't mean you're lost.

Remind yourself what's important in life.

You Have the Right to Be Happy Without Feeling Guilty

These five areas are examples of misplaced guilt.

1. Being emotional.

Have you ever been called too sensitive or emotional? Or told that your emotions make other people uncomfortable? Emotions help you become aware of your needs and set boundaries. They help you pay attention, so you can respond to what is happening around you.

2. Making your needs clear.

If you ask for what you need and feel like a nuisance, you were probably taught as a child not to be a "pain." You have needs; journal to discover what they are.

3. Being happy.

Your friend is having a bad day. Empathize and sympathize, but do not take on their bad day. You have a right to be happy.

4. Taking time to be alone.

Alone time is a way to gain clarity, make better decisions, and get in touch with your values and purpose. When your friends or family want you to go out or there is a pile of laundry to be washed, you do not have to feel guilty for saying no.

5. Putting yourself first.

Women commonly feel guilty for taking care of their own needs first. There are millions of overt and covert messages that encourage you to minimize your own needs and feel guilty when you engage in self-care. "If you take care of yourself, you have less time and energy for others." Reframe how you view self-care to other-care. Practicing self-care helps you help others more effectively.

It's OK to live a life others don't understand.

Take time to discover yourself.

What You Do Demonstrates Your Values

Fun is a process, not a result. It is when you enjoy what you are doing, no matter what others think or what your inner critic tells you.

"Show me your calendar," Darcy insisted.

"Why?" Aria's eyes narrowed as she crossed her arms.

"Because I want to see if your actions mirror your intentions."

"What does that mean?" Aria blurted.

"Show me your calendar, and I'll tell you what's important to you."

Aria had committed to do fun things, such as go for a walk and read. Every time Darcy asked about her fun commitment, Aria came back with an excuse for why she didn't do it.

Productivity and accomplishments are important. Work can be all-consuming, especially when you love what you do. Work-life balance is the proper prioritization between work and your health and well-being. Balancing achievement with enjoyment helps you avoid the "As Soon As" trap. This is the mind-numbing habit of postponing fun until "as soon as" you finish everything else.

Block time for fun. Treat it as important as sleep, eating healthfully, and work.

Aria added a column, Have Fun, to her weekly to-do list. She got a kick checking items off her list: knit (check), read (check).

Change the way you look at fun. It is the idea that life is to be enjoyed.

An Expectation Is a Resentment Waiting to Happen

An expectation is a belief about what will happen in the future. Expectations frequently guide your behavior.

Your expectations shape your reality. Be aware of the following common unrealistic expectations that set you up for negative emotional reactions:

- Life should be fair.
- Opportunities will fall into your lap.
- Everyone should like you.
- People should agree with you.
- People should understand what you're trying to say.
- You should be perfect.
- Things and people will make you happy.
- You can change another person.

Examples are, "If my marriage were good, then it would be easy." "I should get straight As in school or an outstanding performance review."

Unrealistic expectations assume a level of control that you don't actually have in a situation. They give you a false sense of protection. You may believe that if you loosen your expectations, other people will take advantage of you. Instead, focus on how people treat you in the present moment. This gives you more information about your safety than unrealistic expectations do.

Develop comeback statements for your expectations. When you think, *If my marriage were good, then it would be easy*, respond to yourself: "Relationships take effort, lots of communication, and compromises to work." When you make a mistake, say, "Everybody makes mistakes. Welcome to humanity."

Expectations are part of the human experience. Be patient with yourself as you learn how to wear life like a loose garment.

Don't let unrealistic expectations prevent you from enjoying your experiences.

Your Values Are Your North Star

The North Star is an analogy to describe what someone uses as a guiding light.

The term North Star comes from a time when sailors would use Polaris as the constant to navigate the ship to safe ports. It was the brightest star in the night sky, so it could always be found. If you knew where the North Star was, you could use it as a reference point to plot your course.

Your values are the North Star that keeps you on course. As your guiding light, you count on it to correct and guide you in everything you do. If you go off course in the way you do things, it is only by your North Star that you can get back on course.

Values are the principles that you believe are important in the way you live and work. They are the measures to tell if your life is going in the right direction.

When you act in a way that matches your values, life goes smoother, and you are more content. When your actions don't match your values, life feels "wrong."

If you value time with your family but work eighty hours a week, there is a disconnect between your actions and your values. If you value a healthy mind and body, but spend no time exercising or meditating, you have a disconnect with your values.

- Identify the times when you were happiest. What were you doing, who were you with?
- Identify the times when you were most proud. What factors contributed to your feelings of pride?
- Identify the times when you were most fulfilled.

List your top three values. Faith, family, love, serenity, service, excellence, balance, and curiosity are some examples. Post them where you can see them daily.

Decide what is most important in life and act in alignment with your values.

Know Your Inner Operating System

Your values are the heart of your inner operating system. They guide your thoughts, decisions, and behaviors.

Computers have operating systems (OS) that run its software and hardware. Think Linux, Mac OS, and Microsoft Windows. Without it, a computer would be useless. The companies that make them offer constant upgrades to improve their efficiency and effectiveness. Your values provide upgrades and improvements to your happiness and satisfaction.

Consider values and thoughts.

If you think, *I have to keep working, even though I'm really sick*, pause and check in with your values. Does this thought contradict your values of balance, compassion, or inner harmony?

Consider values and decisions.

Sometimes you have to choose between two good things. Use your values to guide you. When you have to choose between two job offers, check which one is closer in line with your values.

Consider values and behaviors.

Determine what you value most. The ice cream cone or fitting in your jeans. Staying up to watch another TV show or getting more sleep. Time with your partner or time spent to get a promotion.

It's not always easy in the moment, when many options are reasonable. Values point you in the right direction.

Use your values as a guide to make the best choices in all situations.

It's OK to Be Sick

Justine is a successful project director. She is admired and respected by her colleagues and employees. She loves her job. One morning she woke up with a high fever and nausea. "I can't cancel my appointments. I don't want to inconvenience my clients. I'm not that sick. I'm exaggerating how badly I feel."

Her inner critic continued, "You're going to lose clients if you take sick time. They need you. They depend on you. You're being selfish. You're already behind. Taking a day off will only put you further behind and increase your stress and anxiety." Taking time off felt completely wrong.

To sort through the internal conflict she felt, Justine sat down and journaled for five minutes to discover why she felt that it was unacceptable to admit that she was too sick to work. She wrote: "I have to make up for the lost time. These are tasks that only I can do. I'll be replaced and won't make money. Others will see me as needy. Being sick is a sign of weakness, it's inconvenient, makes me feel vulnerable, and people leave you when you are needy."

Her internal conflict made more sense after reading the journal entry that she had just written. Justine discovered that she was afraid to take a day off because it had not been OK to be sick as a child. What she had learned when she was young was now controlling how she responded as an adult.

Her writing provided the clarity she needed. She cancelled her appointments and went back to bed. The next day she felt better and realized, "Taking time off to recover from illness isn't as scary as I thought."

See and hear what sickness is teaching you.
Time off is a necessary part of life.

What Forgiveness Is and Is Not

Forgiveness is difficult because it is often misunderstood.

Forgiveness is not forgetting. It is being mindfully aware of what has happened and its value in your life. To forget injuries may mean you pass up a learning opportunity. Forgiveness is only possible when the pain that once controlled you is gone. The memory may last.

Forgiveness is the vehicle for correcting your misperceptions and for letting go of fear, condemning judgments, and grievances. Forgiveness releases you from all thoughts that seem to separate you from yourself and from others.

Define what forgiveness means to you.

It's Better to Give a Resentment Than to Get One

By dwelling on your resentment, you keep it alive and keep yourself in a mental prison.

Mark Cuban is an American businessman, investor, author, TV personality, and philanthropist. He owns the NBA's Dallas Mavericks. He started his first company, MicroSolutions, after getting fired. He was twenty-five years old, had no money, and slept on a couch. After he became somewhat successful, his secretary, Renee Hardy, embezzled $83,000 of the company's $85,000.

Cuban had good reason to spend time resenting her and seeking revenge. Instead, he studied PC software and coding to gain on his competition. He sold his company to H&R Block for $6 million in 1990.

Holding on to resentments harms your health. It acts as a chronic stressor. Each time you revisit your resentment, you get a burst of the stress hormone cortisol. Ruminating on it raises your blood pressure. Long term, it can make you vulnerable to disease and keeps you out of the present moment.

Identify your resentment and the reason it upsets you. Express your emotions. Get them out of your body. Journal. Talk to someone. Go to a batting cage and hit balls, punch pillows, do a strenuous cardio workout. Accept that this experience happened and it cannot be changed. You don't have to like it or let the person back in your life. After you identify, express, and accept, be willing to forgive. This is a choice to release the old pain that keeps you stuck.

Forgiveness is a deeply personal decision. The payoff is worth the emotional work.

Spend the time to release resentments to make space for success.

Take Time to Grieve Unmet Needs

Abraham Maslow created a hierarchy of needs and demonstrated the importance of meeting human needs. When these needs are not met, we feel a sense of lack and loss.

Evy struggled to know what was going on inside her. "I'm so discouraged, overwhelmed, and tired. What's wrong with me?" She pulled out her journal and started writing.

It surfaced that her one-time best friend Clare had recently come back into her life. Clare had sent Evy an email saying, "Hi. I heard our favorite author is coming to town to promote her new book, and it made me think of you."

Evy poured her anger onto the pages. "How dare you disappear with some flimsy reason and then just pop back in like nothing happened. We did everything together. How could you just walk away? You're so selfish." Evy's eyes reddened with tears. She bowed her face into her hands. Her shoulders bobbed with each sob she released.

Journal to identify what's going on inside you. Five to fifteen minutes is enough time for whatever's going on to surface.

"I'm sad because my need for connection, empathy, and understanding were not met by you," she wrote. "Why did you leave me? Why don't you love me? What did I do to make you walk away?"

For Evy, relief came in the form of tears and exhaustion. She felt an internal shift. She accepted that Clare would never meet her needs.

Journal to identify unmet needs and give yourself space to grieve the loss.

BREATHE

Inhale and Stick Your Belly Out

Increased awareness of your breathing improves your health, confidence, and stress level.

According to the Marketdata Enterprises, Inc. study and report, "The U.S. Weight Loss and Diet Control Market," the value of this market is $66.3 billion. Meal replacements, obesity drugs, and weight-loss surgeries are all driven by the desire for a quick fix. The flat-belly craze taps into this desire, selling special shakes, teas, fasting, even stomach vacuuming.

The good news is that deep breathing rewards sticking your belly out.

Lie on your back. Put a light object on your belly: a box of tissues, an empty bowl, or a toy. Inhale and watch the object rise. If it doesn't, you are inflating your chest. Concentrate on pushing your breath into your belly. Imagine your breath dropping into your abdomen. This practice fills the lower part of your lungs, where the blood is the richest with oxygen. With practice, you'll see the object riding the breath wave.

You breathe 18 times a minute, 1,080 times an hour, and 25,920 times a day. When you breathe correctly, you have better digestion, improved balance, and optimum posture.

Stop taking sips of breath.

Open Up to Experience Miracles

The mastermind group gathered in the community center conference room, where they met monthly. Seven women participated to achieve their personal and professional goals.

Karen marched into the room, propped a picture against a chair and announced, "I suck at art, but you all asked me to share the picture I painted at Paint Nite, so here it is." She fell into a seat, crossed her arms, and looked down. Bracing herself, she thought, *There's an artist in this group. She'll definitely tell me it's pathetic.*

The group facilitator broke the silence and reflected back to her. "Karen, you just told yourself you suck at art. Can you say more about this?"

Her face flushed. She sighed and balled her hands into fists. "I'm not creative. I never have been. I had to go to speech class instead of art class as a kid." She described how painful it was to be pulled out of art class to take speech lessons. She struggled with a speech impediment, and the only time slot the speech therapist was available was during art class. She told herself the story, "I suck at art," for decades.

Be vulnerable with safe people. Open up a little at a time.

Member after member gave her similar feedback. "I like your picture. I want to paint my own picture. Karen, will you go to Paint Nite with me? I haven't painted since I was a kid."

The artist in the group finally spoke. "I have lots of my students start with Paint Nite. It is a safe way to open up their creative channel. They have a lot of fun painting with their friends. Doing my creative activities is much easier after they've spent time there."

Their words embraced her like a hug. Karen let out a sigh of relief. Her willingness to open up allowed her to release the story of being bad at art and tapped into a creative vein that had been dormant.

Ask your inner child what she would like you to share with a safe person. Then do it.

You Are an Eagle—So Fly

You are here to achieve your highest potential. Let this knowledge free you to be who you were born to be.

A baby eagle was abandoned by its mother. It was not yet able to fly when a farmer found him and placed him in the care of his chickens. He grew up thinking he was a chicken. He flew a few feet like the other chickens, but was told he could not fly. One day, as he scratched the ground for grubs, another eagle flew into the barnyard and said to him, "Hey, eagle. What are you doing? Don't you know you can fly?"

The eagle had to face his deepest fear: "What is my chicken family going to think of me when I fly the coop?"

You may have been told things that limited your understanding of your potential. It takes courage to embrace your skills and talents and to soar to your next level.

Reframe your beliefs about moving forward. All people are naturally creative, resourceful, and whole. This means that as you succeed, they have the choice to succeed too. You model how to move forward and allow others the dignity to choose to do this too . . . or not.

Don't waste another second fretting about what others will think of you when you succeed.

The Only Person in Your Way Is You

I'm so tired of chasing my dreams that I've decided to ask them where they are going and I'll meet them there.

—Sam Kinesan, comedian

Belinda sighed and slumped farther in her chair.

"Are you listening to me?" Fran asked her.

"Of course I am. It's just that you've told me why you can't go for that job you want a million times, and it's wearing me down."

Fran face went ashen. She sighed as her eyes stung with tears. "I want to go after that job, but I'm still grieving the loss of my marriage."

"I know you are grieving. But it's been a year, and you're still complaining about it."

Imagine that not another person, place, or thing holds power over you:

1. Identify the story you are telling yourself and others that keeps you stuck.
2. Decide that it has served its time and let it go.
3. Replace it with a new story.

Fran rewrote her story. She realized she'd rather blame her ex-husband than to admit she was afraid to try again because she might fail. She replaced her story with a new one: "Successful women try again and again, ask for and accept help, and expect bumps along the road, and I'm a successful woman." She transformed her story from a stumbling block to a stepping stone.

Identify one story you tell yourself about why you can't do something. Rewrite it.

What's Your Groundhog Day Shadow?

In the movie *Groundhog Day*, Bill Murray plays a weatherman who is forced to live the same day, February 2, over and over again, until he learns his life lesson.

A Groundhog Day Shadow is something you keep doing over and over again, even when you don't want to do it. You can't see any other choices. This can be staying in a relationship, staying out of a relationship, not writing that book, being overly responsible, saying yes, saying no. It's feeling trapped in the routine of a job you don't like or a relationship that isn't working. You repeat the same day over and over and feel unfulfilled.

The message of *Groundhog Day* is that you have choices to improve your life.

Identify your payoffs for staying stuck:

- I don't have to change.
- I don't have to learn a new behavior.
- I don't have to take personal accountability.
- I don't have to make a choice.

Stop making compromises that make you feel increasingly numb.

Ask for and accept help from a friend or loved one to take action to get unstuck.

Breathe Deeply

In honor of World Breathing Day, practice the Buddha belly breathing technique. Named after depictions of the potbellied Chinese folkloric deity Budai, it is a technique that pushes your belly out to support optimal breathing. It relaxes the mind and body and eases physical and mental tension.

In 2012, Susanne Hovenas, a Swedish health journalist, initiated World Breathing Day to inspire and share practical tips about breathing to strengthen your health and well-being. Several studies show the effectiveness of deep breathing techniques in preventing and reducing stress. Proper breathing increases concentration and productivity.

Place one hand on your solar plexus, located just below the base of the breast bone. Consciously breathe into your hand. Pay attention to your hand rising and falling. Fill your lungs to capacity and release the breath over four to six seconds. Do this for five to fifteen breaths. Release any tension in your jaw, eyes, and neck.

There are several deep-breathing apps available to guide you through breathing exercises to keep you energized, focused, and productive.

Make a conscious decision to focus on your breath for a part of each day.

The One Ingredient to Making Change Stick

Having support helps you move faster and easier through the changes you want to make.

Only 8 percent of us keep our New Year's resolutions, according to the University of Scranton. That's a lot of people getting stuck in making long-lasting changes. About 40 to 45 percent of American adults make one or more resolutions each year. The top three New Year's resolutions are weight loss, exercising, and stopping smoking.

What people most commonly tell themselves when they have tried to make changes and have failed:

- "I don't have enough willpower."
- "I need to work harder."
- "I'm lazy."
- "I need more self-discipline."
- "It was an unrealistic goal anyway."

What's the reason people succeed in making long-lasting changes?

Alan Deutschman, an organizational development specialist and consultant, decided to study how individuals and organizations are successful at making changes. He studied a group of people with life-threatening illnesses—heart-bypass patients—who literally had to change or die.

The results were shocking. Nine out of ten patients did not make the changes necessary to get better.

He went on a quest to find a solution, and he found a program developed by a doctor in San Francisco. Patients in this program had to make radical changes: eating a vegetarian diet, doing yoga, and practicing meditation. Eight out of ten made these major changes and maintained them for years after they left the program.

Alan figured it out. The number-one reason people succeed in making long-lasting changes is through a relationship with a person or a group that shows them the way, inspires hope and belief, and makes them say, "If she can do it, I can do it too."

According to Deutschman, the key to the program's success is the relationships those type-A workaholics and steak eaters develop with other type-A workaholics and steak eaters; when they see that their peers are chanting "ohm" or eating kale, they realize it can be done.

They lost weight, lowered their cholesterol, achieved a 91 percent decrease in the frequency of chest pains in the first month, and avoided further surgery.

Making changes has less to do with willpower and self-discipline, and more with surrounding yourself with a person or group that inspires hope and belief and makes you say, "If she can do it, I can do it too."

Have you ever dreamed about taking a trip by yourself, or of starting ballet as an adult, or writing a book, or starting your own business?

Have you ever dreamed of running a marathon, or getting into a relationship, or saying no to people in your family?

Do you ever wish you had the kind of job that you were excited to go to every day?

Do you ever wish you didn't compare yourself, your body, your partner, your job, your home, to others?

Studies have found that social support is the strongest single predictor of happiness.

Find a group to support you in making changes you tried to do alone but couldn't.

MASTER YOUR CHANGE CURVE—PART 1 OF 5

Understand the Four Stages of Change

When you understand the four stages of making a change, you can make them stick faster and easier.

Think of change as following the Change Curve (below): a box divided into four squares with a U that is drawn from the top left hand corner, down, across, and up to the other side.

It starts with business as usual at the top left. When the change begins, there is a turn downward into a trough that consists of stress, uncertainty, upheaval, and diminished productivity (resistance). As acceptance of the change takes place, there is a climb up the other side of the curve as you regain your sense of direction, learn new skills and roles, and begin to work in a new way (exploration and commitment).

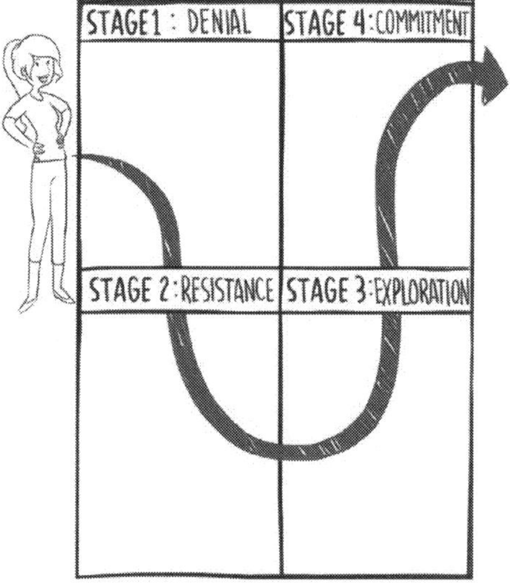

The Change Curve has four stages: denial, resistance, exploration, and commitment. You may move slowly or more quickly through change. Sometimes people move back to a previous phase or get stuck in one phase.

In *denial*, the reality of the change does not sink in, and you act as if it will blow over.

The *resistance* phase is the "stuck phase," which is where most women get hung up. It's when you realize the change will happen and experience uncertainty and self-doubt.

In the *exploration* phase, you begin to take action, learn new ways of being, and decide how you will respond to the change.

The *commitment* phase is when your productivity returns and you master new behaviors.

There are two types of change:

1. The change you are facing right now. For instance, my contract is ending, my husband lost his job, my son is leaving for college.
2. The change you want to make. For instance, I want to get a new job, lose ten pounds, learn yoga, be more organized.

Complete the following sentences:

The change I am facing right now is ______________________________.

The change I want to make is ____________________________________.

The Change Curve is a powerful model that shows you how to succeed in making long-lasting changes and experience intentional success.

Use the Change Curve model in all areas of your life, whether the change is to go after a new career, start a new relationship, or take more downtime.

MASTER YOUR CHANGE CURVE—PART 2 OF 5

What to Expect When You Make Changes

Here is a framework that explains what you may say, do, or feel as you go through the four stages of change.

STAGE 1 : DENIAL	STAGE 4 : COMMITMENT
SAY "IT'S NOT HAPPENING TO ME." "I DON'T HAVE TO DO THIS." "I'M SURE IT WILL BLOW OVER." DO • BLAME OTHERS • AVOID FEEL • NUMB	SAY • "I'VE REALLY COME A LONG WAY WITH THIS CHANGE." • "THIS IS A BETTER WAY." DO • PRACTICE • TEACH OTHERS FEEL • POWERFUL!!
STAGE 2 : RESISTANCE	**STAGE 3 : EXPLORATION**
SAY "NO WAY THIS WILL WORK FOR ME." "I'LL JUST GO BACK TO THE OLD WAY AND REDECORATE HELL." DO • CRITICIZE THE CHANGE • DOUBT YOUR ABILITY TO CHANGE FEEL • ANXIOUS • ANGRY • IRRITABLE • "OFF"	SAY "OK. MAYBE THIS CAN WORK." "THERE MIGHT BE A WAY." DO • TRY NEW BEHAVIORS FEEL • EXCITED • OPTIMISTIC • ORGANIZED

The change Marissa wants to make is getting into a loving relationship. Here's an example of what she may say, do, and feel in the resistance phase. Marissa's marriage had been falling apart for a long time. She was stuck and believed she couldn't leave for many reasons. "I don't know how to be on my own. Nobody else will want me. I'm exaggerating how bad it is. I'm not that lonely." She was continuing to live in misery rather than risking change. She used her excuses to mask that she felt she was unworthy of a loving relationship.

Understanding the predictable patterns of what you say, do, and feel while moving through the Change Curve helps reduce the negative thoughts like, *What's wrong with me?*

Understand that there are universal stages of change. When you know them, the process of change goes faster.

MASTER YOUR CHANGE CURVE–PART 3 OF 5

Tools to Move through the Resistance Stage of the Change Curve

These tools help you move through the resistance stage of the Change Curve. When you are in the resistance stage of change, you will experience self-doubt and believe that staying stuck is better than facing uncertainty. There are two tools that can help you move from resistance to exploration: identify missing knowledge, skills, and abilities; and identify your payoff for staying stuck.

Using the example of Marissa's marriage falling apart, she was stuck and believed she couldn't leave for many reasons. "I don't know how to be on my own. Nobody else will want me. I'm exaggerating how bad it is. I'm not that lonely."

She asked herself, "What knowledge, skills, or abilities do I need in order to live on my own?" She wrote a list—learn how to pay bills online, find a car mechanic, get my own credit card. Once the list was complete, she felt relief. She knew what she needed to learn.

The second tool to help move through resistance is asking yourself, "What's my payoff for staying stuck?" There are four payoffs.

Marissa asked herself, "If I hold on to my belief that I can't take care of myself, what payoff do I get?"

- I don't have to change.
- I don't have to learn a new behavior.
- I don't have to take personally accountability.
- I don't have to make a choice.

She used her excuses to mask that she felt she was unworthy of a loving relationship and she was afraid to learn a new behavior. Once she identified her payoff, she was able to move into the exploration phase and ask her best friend for help.

The goal is to help bring you through your own Change Curve by understanding which phase you are in and also what support tools you need to transition through and embrace the new change.

Stop redecorating hell by saying, "It's not that bad." Move out of resistance and into exploration.

MASTER YOUR CHANGE CURVE—PART 4 OF 5

Tools to Move through Exploration: Bookending

Bookending helps you move through the exploration stage of the Change Curve.

Belinda's workshops weren't filling up. She was frustrated and getting depressed. She was ready to hang it up and quit. "Why bother trying again? I can't stand failing. What will my family and friends think of me?" She believed she didn't deserve another shot at her business.

She identified her payoff: "I don't want to have to learn something new. I'm afraid I won't get it."

She listed the skill she needed to learn: social media marketing.

Belinda asked two friends to help her learn how to use social media to market her workshops. They gave her several resources—people, online webinars, and apps. She committed to bookend her action steps.

Bookending is a technique to help you complete tasks. Think of bookends. They sit on two ends of a row of books, holding them up. Bookending is when you call, email, or text another person, and tell them about the task you are committing to complete. Follow up with them after you completed it.

Use bookending whenever you feel stuck, need someone to support and hear you as you take action, or are nervous about taking the next step. The results are accomplishing tasks that you haven't been able to on your own.

Bookending is a form of accountability. You tell someone you are going to take an action, you do the action, you tell them you did the action. You will only hold yourself accountable for goals that others know about.

Belinda was inspired and applied their suggestions, and felt optimistic that she could build her new social media marketing muscle.

Bookend to move forward.

MASTER YOUR CHANGE CURVE–PART 5 OF 5

Tools to Move Through Commitment: Start Small and Build Up

The tools in the commitment phase are all about practicing new knowledge, skills, and abilities. This is done by integrating and sustaining them by:

- Deciding when and where you are going to do the new behavior
- Starting small and building up
- Anchoring new behaviors to existing ones

Select the new behaviors you want to integrate and maintain. For example, "I want to change jobs, exercise more often than not, and learn negotiation skills."

For each new behavior, decide ahead of time, "How am I going to keep this going?"

1. Decide ***when*** you're going to do this. Example: Monday and Friday
2. Decide ***where*** you're going to do this. Example: every time I sit down to eat

The reason this is important is that your actions are ten times more effective when you decide on them ahead of time. Studies show that the more we can do the thinking up front, the more likely we are willing to take the action.

Start small and build up. The number-one mistake people make is not going small enough. Define what is starting small for you. If you find it not working, go smaller again.

Let's use an example of jogging. A small step is to put on your running shoes after you turn on your coffee pot. No jogging; just put your running shoes on for five days straight.

Anchor your new small step to a current habit or behavior. Using the example of the running shoes, you put them on after you push the "on" button on your coffee pot. The habit of pushing the "on" button is something you already do every day. Identify and anchor putting on your running shoes to that action.

Starting small and building up increases your confidence and refuels your confidence in your ability to master change.

Develop and implement your action plan to maintain long-lasting changes. This is what separates a New Year's resolution from a lasting, powerful new habit!

I.A.L.A.C.: I Am Lovable And Capable

The acronym I.A.L.A.C. stands for "I am lovable and capable." Imagine the infinity symbol: the left circle of the infinity symbol represents "I am lovable" and the right circle represents "I am capable."

Most women crank on "I am capable" and starve the "I am lovable" side. The limiting belief is to value only those things that are productive and revenue-generating. This leads to overworking, overfunctioning, neglecting self-maintenance, and not being present.

Jessica was a dedicated and dependable employee. She prided herself on being reliable. She got sick with a fever and cough. "I'm not that sick. I'll go into work, and if I'm not feeling better by noon, I'll go home." Her "capable" muscle was overdeveloped. She believed that a sick day was not productive.

I asked her, "What do you tell your children when they are sick and can't go to basketball practice?"

She said, "Your body needs to rest in order to get better. Your team needs you healthy."

She faced her fear, acted as if she believed she was lovable, stayed home, and rested.

In order to achieve happiness and success, balance "I am capable" with "I am lovable."

Time Block to Accomplish Your Priorities

Time blocking is an effective strategy to use time wisely and achieve greater productivity and results. Blocking out time for specific activities allows you to focus on one task at a time and limits distractions, procrastination, and stress.

Marta wanted to start exercising again. She had all the equipment she needed and still found herself distracted by other tasks. She felt disappointed every time she promised herself to exercise and didn't. Then she stuffed her disappointment with extra work. She continued this cycle over and over again.

Time-blocking steps:

1. Pick your highest energy times to do the tasks that require the most concentration.
2. Identify your top priority. What's the one thing that, when tackled, will make everything else you have to do easier or unnecessary? Design your time block around doing that one thing.
3. Blocked times should scream out at you when you look at your day planner, online calendar, or task management solution. If you use paper, use a different color pen or write in capital letters to make them stand out among your other items. You need to make sure that your eyes don't miss them.
4. Stick to the blocked times for thirty days. In order to make this a habit, you need to repeat it thirty times. The blocked times become part of the flow of your week, and you will figure out how much time you really need.

Marta blocked time for her important work tasks and experienced pressure relief and clarity. She got the important things done and felt excited to exercise. Her "aha" moment was when she realized she was skipping exercising because she felt perpetually behind at work. Time blocking helped her feel less behind. She now exercises three times a week.

Identify your priority and block your highest energy time to complete it.

Limit Activities that Interfere with Your Time-Blocking Goals

My client Jane wanted to start painting again, but was too tired after working all week. She decided to hire a cleaning service to free up the time and energy she spent doing this chore. She was ready to paint.

Limit activities that interfere with your time-blocking goals:

- Avoid checking email, answering the phone, or texting. Focus your attention only on the task that you blocked off the time to complete. Let your calls go to voicemail or turn off your phone, and sign out of your email account.
- Eliminate unproductive activities. During the block of time, avoid unnecessary television watching or Internet surfing.
- Notify others that you will be unavailable. If working at home, explain your time-blocking strategy to family members so that they will refrain from interrupting you. In an office setting, limit interruptions from co-workers by suggesting that they join you in time-blocking activities.

Jane blocked time to paint on the weekend. She looked at her typical weekend calendar and decided:

- She's a morning person and enjoyed going to the farmer's market on Saturday, so she blocked Sunday mornings as paint time.
- She let her family know and asked them to come into her painting area only if there was a true emergency.
- She turned her phone off.
- She left her laptop in another room.
- She started small and built up. The first time, she spent fifteen minutes setting up her painting area. The second time, she painted for fifteen minutes, and the third time for thirty minutes. This ensured she would be more successful.
- She shared her success with her girlfriends. She had been complaining to them for years about her desire to paint, but she didn't have the energy or time to do it. They were relieved to hear this.

Limit distractions and focus on one task at a time.

Surprise Someone Today

The Pay It Forward Foundation is a nonprofit organization that inspires the growth of the pay-it-forward philosophy: through acts of kindness, we all foster a more caring society.

One way to do this is by surprising others. Surprises are the small gestures that bring delight into our lives, and that others don't expect.

- Write a heartfelt thank-you note to someone you admire.
- Pick flowers from your garden and give them to your neighbor.
- Fill plastic eggs with candy and place them around the office.
- Leave a generous tip for your restaurant server.
- Pay for the coffee for the person behind you.

You don't have to wait for a birthday or anniversary. It's better to do it when there is no special occasion. Surprises increase engagement and productivity and show appreciation in an unexpected way.

Surprise someone today. It will make their day and yours.

Lookin' for Love

Johnny Lee recorded the song "Lookin' for Love" in 1980 as part of the film soundtrack for the movie *Urban Cowboy.*

The chorus:

> *I was lookin' for love in all the wrong places*
>
> *Lookin' for love in too many faces*

You hold the key to your happiness. Take responsibility for your life. Do not blame anyone else for your circumstances. Decide whether you want to lift yourself up or put yourself down. Are you for or against yourself? Do you choose those things that give you pain or joy?

To change the way you look at yourself, you have to look into yourself. Identify the ways you pull yourself down. Do you look for love from a job, an unavailable person, or food?

Give as much attention to your successes as you do to your problems. Do not dismiss your accomplishments. Identify one complimentary statement you would like to hear. Say it to yourself. Say it until you believe it. Your ego will fight you on it. This is normal and to be expected.

Look for love in the place where it is limitless—yourself.

Wear Life Like a Loose Garment

Under the Tuscan Sun is a movie about a recently divorced writer whose life has been turned upside down. The main character, Frances Mayes, finds her husband cheating on her, gets writer's block, and sinks into depression. Her friends give her an airline ticket to Italy. While there, Frances buys a villa in Tuscany, in hopes it will change her life.

Her dream is to have a wedding, family, and love in the house. She goes on a roller-coaster ride of emotions, experiences, and unexpected encounters. She fumbles often, doubts herself constantly and, in the end, discovers life gives her second, third, and fourth chances. She does get the three things she wished for, just not in the way she expected.

Acceptance of *what is* helps you move forward in your life. The opposite is when you think, *I want my life to be different than how it is.*

Practice acceptance. For ten minutes, notice how many times your judge yourself and your life. Judging statements keep you stuck. Curiosity moves you forward.

What if, just for today, you wore the world like a loose garment, didn't judge anything that happened, and were curious?

Manage your expectations of how you think your life should be.

Self-Awareness Is the Single Most Important Skill You Can Develop

Every human has four endowments: self-awareness, conscience, independent will, and creative imagination. These give us the ultimate human freedom . . . the power to choose, to respond, to change.

—Stephen Covey, author, *The 7 Habits of Highly Effective People: Powerful Lessons in Personal Change*

Self-awareness is the ability to notice your thoughts, emotions, reactions, and your physical responses, and how you may be perceived by others.

Julia met with her team to review progress on the company's annual goals and any emerging opportunities. She asked for any new goals to be considered.

Bonnie said, "We need better collaboration across departments."

"Can you elaborate?"

"My employee had a video chat session with a client at 8:00 a.m. and the software was not working. Nobody from IT was in the office."

"That sounds like an operational issue, not a collaboration issue," said Julia.

Bonnie fidgeted in her seat and sighed. "It's their job to be available, and they aren't working with my team."

Joe from IT spoke up. "Maybe if you asked for support, we could help you."

Her eyes darted back and forth from Julia to Joe. She dug her nails into her palms and pursed her lips. "See! He isn't collaborating. How am I supposed to hit my goals when IT doesn't support me?"

"Time out. This meeting is about reviewing our annual goals. Your issue is about coordinating support. Table it for another time."

Bonnie continued to bring it up throughout the meeting, until Julia called a break and pulled her aside. "Do you see what you're doing? You aren't letting this IT issue go and it's affecting our productivity."

"I don't understand. I did let it go," Bonnie replied.

Bonnie was not aware that her emotions were negatively impacting others.

Awareness is the capacity to notice things. You may notice that you are late for an appointment or that it's cloudy outside, and you grab an umbrella. Self-awareness is the capacity to notice yourself.

Ask trusted friends to tell you how you come across to others. Give them permission to be candid and direct. Take their feedback and implement it.

Self-awareness is the key to changing patterns and behaviors that do not serve you. It allows you to make conscious choices that lead to positive changes.

FORGIVENESS

FEB 17

FORGIVENESS IS A PROCESS–PART 1 OF 5

Stage One: Claim the Hurt

You generally go through five stages in the forgiveness process: claim the hurt, guilt, victim, anger, and wholeness. Understanding this process can help you make sense of where you are in the forgiveness process and that it's normal and to be expected.

The first stage is to claim the hurt. Admit that it is yours, what it has done to your life, and what it may continue to do if it is not healed.

Write a letter to the person who harmed you. Include how it felt then and now, how your life has been influenced by it then and now. Identify your feelings, and the reasons it's hard to forgive them.

Write a second letter to yourself, pretending to be the person who hurt you. This is their apology letter to you that explains why they did it and how they wish to make it right.

Do not judge or edit what your write. This exercise is for you. Burn or shred what you've written, releasing it.

This is the first step to release you from the burdens you no longer need to carry.

Start from where you are.

FORGIVENESS IS A PROCESS–PART 2 OF 5

Stage Two: Guilt

The five stages in the forgiveness process are claiming the hurt, guilt, victim, anger, and wholeness.

"Why? Why did she do that? What did I do to cause her to hurt me?"

This is the normal and natural response to hurt. You want to make sense out of it and you naturally turn to something over which you have control: yourself. If only you could have said or done something different, they would not have left you, fired you, or abandoned you. Personal responsibility is exaggerated in this stage. It is also a cop-out. If you blame yourself, you don't have to forgive others. You can stay stuck.

Self-blame leads to unskillful reactions: perfectionism in your next job so no one can find fault with you, isolation, overeating, or overworking so you are not available to find another partner.

Recognize you're in this stage. Move immediately to inner compassion. Do kind acts for yourself: call a friend and ask her to tell you three things she admires about you, go to a movie or for a walk, take a bath. Compassion moves you out of guilt and into your inherent worth and value.

Do not accept unearned guilt.

FORGIVENESS IS A PROCESS–PART 3 OF 5

Stage Three: Victim

The five stages in the forgiveness process are claiming the hurt, guilt, victim, anger, and wholeness.

The victim stage is when the hurt turns to bitterness, depression, and apathy. You are identified with your wounds. Behaviors include lashing out at others and passive-aggressive behaviors like forgetting a commitment, being late, shopping for things you don't need, or isolating through TV or alcohol.

This stage serves a purpose. It is a cry for comfort, consolation, and sympathy. It allows you to express your hurt and anger when you could not at the time the hurt was inflicted on you. It is a way of getting the sympathy you deserved at the time of the hurt.

Ask for and accept help. If you just divorced, look for a support group of others going through this experience. If your parents abused and neglected you as a child, seek counseling or support groups for adult children.

Victim is a stage to pass through, not make your permanent residence.

Take responsibility for your choices and actions.

FORGIVENESS IS A PROCESS—PART 4 OF 5

Stage Four: Anger

The five stages in the forgiveness process are claiming the hurt, guilt, victim, anger, and wholeness.

"I'm mad as hell and I'm not going to take it anymore!" raged news anchor Howard Beale in the 1975 movie classic *Network*. It's a fitting description of the type of anger in this stage. It's focused on getting ahead, not on getting back at the person who hurt you. Use this energy to move you forward in your healing process.

Get the energy out. Take a tennis racket to a pillow, pull weeds, scream into a pillow or in your car. Express how you truly feel.

Put an end to the victim stage. Exclaim, "Never again!"

Use anger as a motivating force for positive change.

FORGIVENESS IS A PROCESS–PART 5 OF 5

Stage Five: Wholeness

The five stages in the forgiveness process are claiming the hurt, guilt, victim, anger, and wholeness.

Accept what happened in the past. You did suffer. Look for any benefits you can gain from it. Move forward. It is not your identity anymore.

Now, experience a spaciousness and deliciousness in knowing yourself and the gifts you bring from walking through the hurt, guilt, victimization, and anger. Your experience will also help others.

Welcome to yourself.

All forgiveness heals your wounds.

Hands-On-Heart (H.O.H.)– The Fastest Way to Make Progress

Using the H.O.H. technique is one of the most powerful tools to help increase your happiness and contentment.

Most women are brutal with themselves. "I should be further along, I should know this, I shouldn't have said that, I should be thinner." Fill in the blank. We react to these limiting beliefs by overworking, overeating, or neglecting self-care like sleep or healthful eating. Nobody is meaner to me than I am to myself, and I found this to be true for the women I coach.

H.O.H. is a self-compassion practice that creates a caring space within you that is free of judgment, that sees your hurt and failures, and applies kindness to these experiences. It is a mental state that strengthens with practice.

Put both hands on your heart and say, "I deeply and completely love and accept myself as I am." Use H.O.H. anywhere and everywhere—when you're in a boring meeting, or when you feel badly about something you said or did.

When you've just yelled at your child: "I deeply and completely love and accept myself as I am, even if I yelled at my child."

When you've behaved poorly: "I deeply and completely love and accept myself as I am. Even if I blew my diet, told myself I'm a loser, or cut that old lady off in traffic."

Every woman I've taught this to has said, "Puck! Is there any other tool besides this one?" They felt selfish, stupid, and uncomfortable.

I recently taught this technique to a group and received this email within twenty-four hours: "OK. I know I didn't really buy into the Hands-On-Heart exercise, but I practiced. I've used it several times today. What I found is that it was a way of setting an intention for my day—to practice compassion with myself—and I have to admit it worked. I can look back on the day and see that I was clear about choices I made throughout the day—even the ones I might have liked to do a bit differently—it's OK. I made the choice, and it was a conscious decision, not just done out of habit. So, Hands-On-Heart: I love myself deeply and completely, just as I am right now, along with all the choices I made today."

The results other women have experienced when they practiced H.O.H. include a sense of security, calming their minds and nervous systems, reducing their anxiety, increasing their happiness and contentment, and increasing their courage. It also lowers cortisol, the stress hormone.

Practicing H.O.H. moves you through difficult emotions faster, so you can spend more time on actions that move you toward your heart's desire.

Place your Hands-On-Heart to lower your cortisol
and increase your happiness.

EMOTIONAL TRIGGERS–PART 1 OF 2

Identify Your Triggers

Emotional triggers consist of thoughts, feelings, and events that seem to "trigger" an automatic response. Your reaction occurs automatically. You become acutely sensitive to situations that may not have bothered you had you been emotionally stable.

They produce feelings of guilt, shame, insecurity, jealousy, anger, resentment, or withdrawal.

If not managed, emotional triggers can cause acute stress, discontent, and interpersonal conflict. Triggers can also prevent you from having the types of relationships and careers you really want. You can take control of your emotional triggers by increasing your awareness of them and developing new ways of responding.

Examples of triggers:

- Someone offers to help you and you experience a shame attack and want to withdraw into yourself.
- You see a red sports car and want to cry because it reminds you of your ex-boyfriend.
- A song comes on the radio and reminds you of something you can't put your finger on, and you feel anxious.

When you feel triggered, come back to the here and now. Triggers are products of a past event.

- Remind yourself that the event is not happening now.
- Take several deep breaths.
- Put your hands on your heart and diaphragm. This signals your internal circuitry to balance.

Get to know your emotional triggers and learn to respond lovingly with yourself.

EMOTIONAL TRIGGERS–PART 2 OF 2

Manage Your Triggers

Emotional triggers drain us of energy, leaving us feeling helpless and vulnerable, confused, angry, or experiencing decreased productivity.

Follow these steps to manage triggers and learn more about yourself.

Name your trigger.

- "Feeling behind and needing to catch up."
- "Not knowing something I 'should' know."
- "Feeling unworthy and having to earn the air I breathe."

Anticipate them. Triggers may be situational or social.

- You may find yourself overeating during the holidays when you are around your family of origin, focusing on others at work during a stressful project, or reacting to someone else's anger.
- You may be triggered by an email. Get up and walk around for five minutes.

Accept your triggers. You are not doing anything wrong; they just happen.

See each trigger as an opportunity for personal growth. You can learn what brings you peace and happiness, what makes you uncomfortable, and what works to support your growth.

Use Self-Compassion to Reduce Emotional Triggers

Emotional triggers are people or events that set off intense, emotional reactions within us. Triggers happen in an instant. You become acutely sensitive to situations that may not have bothered you had you been emotionally stable. They produce feelings of guilt, shame, insecurity, jealousy, anger, resentment, or withdrawal.

I recently went to a chamber of commerce meeting with one hundred women. The speaker was an author who had written a book about women breaking the rules at work. Before the presentation, I was talking with another attendee who said, "Oh, you must be the speaker this morning."

I was triggered! I felt uncomfortable. My inner critic started yelling, "Moira, you should be doing this presentation. Moira, write your book!"

After the presentation, I spoke to the chairwoman responsible for booking speakers. I told her that I teach a complimentary method to the author's book and would love to do a presentation on it. She asked me to send a proposal. I was still in a triggered state. I hate feeling stupid and behind. I felt uncomfortable sharing my elevator pitch in a "corporate" environment. "They'll think I'm a loser. Who leaves a CEO job to do what I do? I should just give up and get a 'real' job."

Write down the one thought, story, idea, or belief that is causing you pain. This is the one that draws most of your energy.

In the example above, I felt unsure of my new business and capabilities, especially expressing them in a corporate setting. The story I told myself was, "Nobody who leaves the corporate world is ever successful."

I placed my hands on my heart (H.O.H.) and said, "Even if I've told myself this story that nobody leaving the corporate world is ever successful, I deeply and completely love and accept myself as I am."

H.O.H. is the fastest way to get to self-compassion and helps you connect with your intuition. It reduces the cortisol that keeps the triggered state going—short-circuiting the inner critic and moving faster to problem solving.

When I got home from the chamber meeting, I practiced the opposite of self-compassion—self-hate. I punished myself by overeating and overworking. "Who do you think you are?" "You're behind!" "You sounded stupid." Then I remembered to place my hand on my heart and say,

"Regardless of where I am in my business, I deeply and completely love and accept myself as I am." It broke the cycle of being triggered.

Emotional triggers can serve as mirrors for our own conscious and unconscious intentions and provide us with opportunities to see ourselves in new ways.

Address emotional triggers with self-compassion to increase self-awareness, self-acceptance, confidence, and self-trust.

PRESENT-MOMENT AWARENESS

Wonderful Surprises Happen in Silence

At a silent retreat, you're not "on." You don't have to make small talk and tell others about yourself. You are not being rude if you don't make eye contact.

You also have no distractions. At my first silent retreat, I found that I wanted to have my cell phone on for both comfort and distraction. I wanted to see if something "important" came in—any message to say, "Moira, you matter." A text, email, Facebook comment . . . anything to validate me.

I realized I use my phone to help me feel grounded and secure. If I can just know, manage, or control life, I'll feel better—more secure, loved, and safe. I use the phone as a way to get some ground under my feet. I'm looking for certainty in an uncertain and ever-changing world.

My phone is one way for me to escape uncomfortable feelings—both "good" ones and "bad" ones.

It's like having poison ivy. I have the itch (discomfort) and I scratch it (eat, check my phone, etc.). It's a way for me to escape feelings of restlessness, boredom, and irritability.

It feels good to scratch the poison ivy in that moment. The problem is that scratching it makes it worse and the discomfort escalates. The antidote for the poison ivy is staying present—without scratching the itch. This is why I meditate daily. It helps calm my mind and not scratch.

To get real learning, critical thinking, and change, you need to embrace discomfort. Discomfort is a normal experience, and it's going to happen. By embracing discomfort, you reduce anxiety, fear, and shame. If you are uncomfortable, you are growing.

By the end of the retreat weekend, I felt calmer, rested, and ready to talk! My inner thirst was quenched.

Spend five minutes in quiet reflection.

Receive the Gift

My second silent retreat experience was a weekend in northern Maryland. The setting was a large home surrounded by acres of woods and walking paths. People came for a respite from the hustle and noise of life to get quiet, reflect, and refresh.

The group gathered on Friday night and chatted a while before going into silence. I met Eileen, a tall Scotswoman, with a beautiful brogue. She told the story of meeting her birth mother's family three years earlier. She had always known she was adopted and had decided it was time to seek them out.

She worked with a social worker, discovered she had a brother, and made arrangements to meet him in her birth town of Glasgow, Scotland. She was scared to knock on the door. Would he be nice or mean? She discovered a group of nervous relatives who welcomed her into the family. She and her brother have reconnected several times since then, and he gave her one of their mother's brooches.

When the retreat group met for breakfast on Saturday, Eileen was wearing the brooch. I acknowledged it with a big smile, and I put my hands on my heart.

After breakfast, I sat in the main hall and pulled out my journal. I decided to write on a topic I teach regularly: the ability to receive. Women are great at giving, but struggle with receiving. We think giving is more valuable than receiving. I teach women the importance of balancing the two. After writing for a while, I got up to leave, and Eileen placed her mother's brooch in my hand and gave me a hug.

I was stunned. I didn't move for a few minutes. *OMG!* I thought. *She can't be serious. She can't give me her birth mother's brooch! I just wrote about the need for women to receive!*

On Sunday morning, we gathered to share about our experiences of being in silence for two days. I told the entire group this story. Eileen cried and hugged me. She told me she had been guided to give it to me. "Whenever two hearts are gathered, there is love."

Accept love.

It's Uncomfortable to Ask for Help

Requesting assistance is something many people have trouble doing. Doing so helps you and the other person.

Gwen sighed as she committed to thirty days of healthy eating. "I know what I need to do. Buy groceries on Sunday and make lunches. Eat breakfast at home instead of skipping it and foraging for food at work. Have two dinners a week out with friends. Yet I never seem to make it happen."

"What gets in the way?" Felicia asked.

"Work gets busy. I forget. I get frustrated after the first week and give up."

"Do you ask others to support you in making this change?"

Gwen shuffled in her seat. "Um, that seems kind of weird. Won't I be bothering them if I ask?"

Expect discomfort when you ask others for support. You may think:

- "I don't want to bother people."
- "My issue is not that important."
- "I don't want to appear like I don't have it all together."
- "I should be able to figure it out on my own."
- "I feel stupid asking for help."

Making changes has less to do with willpower or self-discipline and more with surrounding yourself with a person or group that inspires hope and belief in you.

To ease Gwen's discomfort, Felicia wrote three questions for her to ask her friends when she needs support to stay on track.

1. "__________ (friend's name), would you invest some of your time in my success?"
2. If they say yes, ask, "Am I inconveniencing you by asking for this support?"
3. If they say yes, ask, "Would you text me on (day of week/time of day) and encourage me to (buy groceries/eat breakfast at home/ask me out for dinner)."

Gwen squirmed. "It feels weird to ask for so much support."

Felicia calculated how much time each person would spend supporting her. It was less than ten minutes a month.

Don't assume you are bothering people when you ask for their support. Most people want to help and derive pleasure from it.

There Are Two Kinds of Beliefs

Most people don't know what thoughts and beliefs get in their way, let alone how to change them. You can learn how to identify, dispute, and revise limiting beliefs into empowering beliefs.

A *belief* is a state of mind; it is when you think something is reality. For example, kids believe in Santa Claus, and at one time people believed the world was flat.

There are two types of beliefs: limiting and empowering.

A *limiting belief* is a thought that constrains you in some way. It holds you back from your goals or detracts you from enjoying life. It creates a feeling of heaviness and constriction. For example, when you say, "I'm stuck" or "I should know the answer to this," how does it feel inside?

Empowering beliefs cause you to reach for your goals and enjoy a greater quality of life. You feel lighter and more optimistic.

Picture a tethered hot-air balloon. The hot-air balloon and its ability to fly to new heights is a symbol of your empowering beliefs. Limiting beliefs are the ropes that keep it tethered to the ground. A limiting belief, such as "I'm stuck," can be changed to "The way I'm feeling—off, frustrated, and uncertain about my ability to make this change—is normal. I'm going to ask for and accept help."

"I should know the answer to this" can be changed to "Questions I don't know the answer to lead me to new opportunities and discoveries!"

Here are some sample limiting beliefs. Check the ones that resonate with you:

- It's selfish to take time for myself.
- I better be good at something to earn my keep.
- I have to take care of others' needs first.
- I don't want to bother people.
- I tell myself I shouldn't feel this way and I should just "get over it."
- I can't say no to others.
- There's not enough time or money in the world, so I have to get what I can now—applying for a job I don't want, bidding on work I hate, having lunch with someone who is unsupportive.

- If I don't do (a task, taking a job I may not want) right now, it's never going to get done, or I'll never get another opportunity.

Notice when you feel irritable or restless. Write down what happened just before you felt that way. You will discover clues about your thoughts and beliefs.

You have a choice in what you believe.

Inner Compassion Helps You Change Faster

Inner compassion is a practice that helps you make changes faster.

My client Jane wanted to start painting again, but was too tired from working all week. I asked her, "Is there something you don't want to do anymore that could make space for painting?" She said, "I don't want to clean my house anymore."

She had the money to pay for a cleaning service. She believed she had to clean her house because her mother and grandmother were still cleaning their homes. She believed that cleaning her own home made her a "good" wife.

Practicing inner compassion makes the process of changing limiting beliefs go faster and easier. It lowers your anxiety and depression, and increases optimism and curiosity. Inner compassion is not a wishy-washy practice. It's a habit for those who want to have a great life and be successful in all areas—health, career, relationships.

Practice inner compassion:

- Ask for and accept help
- Take a bath
- Get a massage
- Play the piano or guitar
- Take a walk
- Take a nap

What inner compassion is NOT:

- Comparing yourself to others or punishing yourself. Our society has a limiting belief that self-criticism is a great motivator. It's not.
- Thinking that inner compassion is self-pitying, egocentric, or self-indulgent. It's not shirking responsibilities or being slothful. Rather, inner compassion focuses on alleviating suffering. From this perspective, you can consider whether something will hurt you in the long run.

Practice inner compassion for ten minutes today.

Dispute Limiting Beliefs

My client Julie was taught to always put other people's needs first. She did not know what she wanted in life, because she automatically went into caretaking mode. Because of this behavior, she was too tired to think about what she wanted. Her limiting beliefs were: "I don't deserve the time to figure out what I want. It's selfish to put my needs first. It's not that important."

Here's how you can dispute limiting beliefs. Take one of your limiting beliefs and ask these three questions:

1. "What is the evidence for my beliefs?" Show that it is factually incorrect. Julie told me, "My spouse tells me to take time to figure out what I want to do and my kids are off at college, so there's time in my life."
2. "What are the alternatives?" There are usually multiple causes, so why latch on to the worst one? Focus on the changeable, the specific, and the non-personal causes. Julie discovered that she had huge blocks of time now because her kids were in college. She had no idea what to do with all this time and felt guilty about it. Having free time can cause all sorts of reactions: guilt, anxiety, feeling lost, ungrounded, and undeserving.
3. "How useful are my beliefs? Do I or others get any benefits from holding on to them, or would we benefit more if we held other beliefs?" Julie was afraid to discover what she wanted. She had been taking care of others for so long, she was afraid that there was nothing left to discover. It was easier to stay stuck than to explore new possibilities. She was choosing unhappiness over uncertainty.

Another example is when someone gets upset because life isn't fair. The belief that life isn't fair may cause more grief than it's worth. What good does it do you to dwell on this?

- I don't have to figure out who I am.
- I don't have to get out of my comfort zone.

As you change your beliefs, choose the ones that take you closer, not further, from your goals.

By disputing limiting beliefs, you can change your customary reaction and remove the ropes that are tethering your hot-air balloon full of empowering beliefs!

Identify Your Limiting Beliefs to Create Empowering Beliefs

Identifying your limiting beliefs helps you change them into empowering beliefs. How do you determine what thoughts and beliefs are holding you back? Most people have no idea what their limiting beliefs are and how to change them.

Look at the following statements of limiting beliefs about asking a friend for help:

- "I don't want to appear needy."
- "Not knowing what I'm asking for or how to put it into words."
- "Thinking the other person is too busy and not interested. Interrupting."
- "Learning a totally new behavior and not quite knowing where to start."
- "Fear of rejection."
- "The 'thing' isn't important enough."
- "Appearing like I don't have it together."

You can also notice your behaviors and any negative impact or emotions they lead to.

My client Julie was taught to always put other people's needs first. She did not know what she wanted in life, because she automatically went into caretaking mode. She noticed that she made the meals, did the washing, cleaned the house, arranged all her husband's travel plans and often felt tired and resentful because no time was left for her. She noticed that she couldn't define what she wanted or what her dreams were and that made her feel sad and inadequate.

She realized that an underlying belief was, "I have to put others' needs first—others are more important than me."

Think of a recent situation when you wanted to do something for yourself but stopped. Identify your thoughts or beliefs that prevented you from taking action.

Spend More Time with the Right People

Performance, health, and happiness are grounded in the skillful management of energy.

— Jim Loehr, world-renown performance psychologist

The book *The Power of Full Engagement: Managing Energy, Not Time, Is the Key to High Performance and Personal Renewal*, by Jim Loehr and Tony Schwartz, is a practical, scientifically based approach to managing your energy more skillfully, both at work and in your personal life.

Think about your energy when you spend time with people you admire. You feel great when you are with them. Now think of people who drain your energy. I call them emotional vampires. They suck the lifeblood out of you. Spend less time with emotional vampires and more time with people who fill your tanks.

Make a list of the people who energize you and people who drain you. Write the reasons you spend time with energy drainers. For example, "She has nobody else to talk to. I said I would have lunch with her and don't want to cancel. I feel awkward saying no."

Replace these with the empowering belief: "People are naturally creative, resourceful, and whole." If you believe this, then your friend is capable of finding someone else to dump on or have lunch with, and will deal with your answer of no.

Maximize your energy throughout the day by expending more time with the right people.

Guilt Blocks You from Receiving Love

Luna asked Kay, "What happens if I go too far off the rails with this self-care stuff? I'm afraid I'm going to lose my edge. I'm already losing my edge because I'm so tired."

"Yes, you are going to lose your edge. Your bleeding edge," Kay declared.

Luna had made a decision to take better care of herself through regular exercise, time with friends, and rest. She worked diligently on changing her thoughts and beliefs about deserving time for these activities. Her friend Kay encouraged and supported her changes.

"I hear you," Kay continued. "It's going to feel uncomfortable to take time for yourself. That's normal. You weren't taught how to care for these needs. Resistance to building new habits is part of the process. Keep going."

Luna whispered, "I feel guilty taking time away from my family and work." Tears rolled down her cheeks.

Guilt is an emotion that follows a thought or belief. Luna thought, *You have to sacrifice your health and well-being to survive and succeed. Spending time on yourself is wrong and selfish. People will leave you.*

Expect resistance when you change your thoughts and beliefs. Guilt is a form of resistance. It sounds like this: "Oh my God, what and I doing? This is crazy. Nobody else is doing this. I have to change back. I can't stand the discomfort. This is crazy. I'm crazy. This new thought and belief is wrong. My old way isn't that bad. I'm not that tired. I'm going back to my old way. I'd rather be unhappy than uncertain. At least I know what to expect there. I feel like I'm losing control over myself, my situation, my circumstances. What happens if I start taking care of myself? Will I end up jobless, homeless, and relationship-less? What if it all falls apart? I caused it to fall apart because I'm being selfish and unreasonable. Who will take care of everything while I take care of myself? I'm afraid to slow down, even a little bit, because I may never get going again."

This inner dialog is normal and to be expected.

You are building new neural pathways in your brain. Your brain is wired to resist change. It sees change as a threat. Its positive intention is to keep you safe. That's why all that chatter of "change back" goes on.

Stop looking for evidence that you are guilty.

EMOTIONAL INTELLIGENCE

How to Make More Money

Increase your emotional intelligence.

Emotional intelligence is a set of emotional and social skills that establish how you perceive and express yourself, develop and maintain social relationships, cope with challenges, and use emotional information in a meaningful way. Unlike intelligence (IQ), emotional intelligence (Emotional Quotient or EQ) is not static. You can improve your emotional intelligence.

According to Talent Smart, the administrator of the emotional intelligence assessment (EQI 2.0), 90 percent of top performers have high EQ. EQ is responsible for 58 percent of job performance in all types of jobs. People with high EQ make $29,000 more annually than their low-EQ counterparts. The link between EQ and earnings is so direct that every point increase in EQ adds $1,300 to an annual salary.

Start with self-awareness. This is the ability to accurately identify your emotions when they happen. It is your ability to stay on top of your reactions to people, places, things, and events.

Stop labeling your emotions as good or bad. Judgment stops you from understanding what it is that you are feeling. Sit with an emotion. Remind yourself that the feeling is trying to give you important information.

Ask yourself the following questions:

- Am I comfortable communicating with others who have different opinions from my own?
- Am I aware of and comfortable talking about my strengths and limitations?
- Am I open to receiving feedback in areas where I need improvement?
- Am I aware of the impact my attitude and behavior has on me, others, and my performance?

If you answered YES to these questions, you have a strong sense of self-awareness. If you answered NO, you may need to work on becoming more self-aware.

Work to improve your emotional intelligence.

SELF

COMFORT AND DISCOMFORT

MAR 8

Credits Don't Transfer

If you want a breakthrough, you need to choose to walk through fear, discomfort, and uncertainty.

I love to ski. I started as a little girl and went once a year with my family to a local resort in Virginia. As an adult, I wanted to share this experience with my children. I started the tradition when my boys were four and seven. Once a year, we traveled out west to ski and snowboard. We talked regularly throughout the year about our favorite restaurant, slopes, and relaxing in the hot tub after a pounding day on the slopes. It was a magical time together, connecting with each other and nature.

January 2 rolled around. I booked our annual trip for March. My sons are now young adults and skilled skiers and snowboarders. They blew past my skill level a few years ago. I made the decision to get into the best shape I could so I would have every chance to keep up with them. Or at least to be only five minutes behind them. I had two months to achieve my goal. My mantra was: Kids, Cardio, Quads.

I blocked time on my calendar to attend a spin class twice a week and yoga once a week. The first spin class was at 6:00 a.m. I was excited to start. It was hard, but I was determined. It felt great afterward. I had more energy and focus throughout the day. When my alarm went off at 5:00 a.m. for the next spin class, I groaned. "Ugh. It's freezing outside. My bed is warm."

I discovered that credits don't transfer from one workout session to another. I faced resistance and discomfort every time the alarm went off at 5:00 a.m. I needed a compelling emotional stake to work through the resistance.

I created an image and feeling of being on top of the slope: the smells, sights, and feelings. Before I got out of bed, I played this image in my head. My emotional stake compelled me to move, grumbling the whole way to class.

Follow these four steps to work through resistance.

1. Decide: commit to one action that moves you forward
2. Block: time to work on it
3. Focus: on this one action for thirty days
4. Choose: to build your day around your focused activity

I stuck with my commitment to myself. I skied my heart out, kept up (sort of) with my sons, and experienced profound joy.

What you do demonstrates your values.

VISION

Discover by Doing

Effective execution happens when you have a strong emotional stake in the outcome.

To accomplish a goal requires you to take new actions, which in turn causes discomfort, fear, and uncertainty. You need a compelling reason to take uncomfortable actions. Create and maintain a compelling vision of the future.

Here is my compelling vision that helped me to get out of bed at 5:00 a.m. to go to a spin class to increase my cardio and quad strength so I would be in top shape for my ski vacation.

"I inhale deeply, savoring the smell of the outdoor fire pit roaring as my sons and I walk to the chair lift.

"I clip into my skis with power, as if I do it every day. We are swept up by the speed lift.

"I listen to the quiet of the mountain. The smell of the crisp air on the morning's first ride up and the scent of fresh snow.

"My heart fills with gratitude as I take in the mountain range. I swing my legs. My smile is hidden under my balaclava. Inside all I can hear is 'EEEEEH.'

"I stare down the slope, visualizing my S turns. I watch my sons take off. I charge the mountain.

"I feel each turn, poles planting, S turns matching the steepness of the slope, the rhythm of my S turns. The sound of my skis biting into the mountain.

"The final swoosh as I stop to enter the chair lift. My heart pounding. Total focus. Total present moment. Total gratitude.

"Skiing with my sons. What I look forward to every year."

Create your personal vision that drives your emotional stake in the ground to achieve your goal.

Tell Others What You Want and Need

Gloria fumed. Her jaw hurt from clenching her teeth. She tasted acid in the back of her throat.

"I give and give and give and now it's time to be selfish and take, take, take," she ranted. Gloria was tired of donating her time to school, church, and her family. She was angry that her family never pitched in, and the school asked her to do more than her fair share. The problem was that Gloria did not tell others what she wanted and needed. In her mind, she had plenty of conversations telling others this information.

When you don't tell others what you want and need, you feel frustrated, misunderstood, and unfulfilled. You don't get your relational needs met.

Candidly let others know what you need and want and how you feel. This demonstrates self-trust, self-respect, and increases self-confidence. Start small and build up. Instead of saying, "I don't care where we eat," say, "I want to try the new Thai restaurant."

Use phrases. When the school calls to ask for more of your time, say, "That doesn't work for me." Repeat this phrase over and over if the other person is persistent in asking you to volunteer.

Think of the one area you want help with at home. If it is cooking, ask your family to make one meal a week. Then add a second meal after they are routinely making one meal.

When you make changes, you may experience push-back from others. Just because someone has strong negative emotions toward you because you ask for what you want and need doesn't mean you did anything wrong.

You matter. Your point of view, needs, and feelings matter and deserve to be taken seriously.

Identify one area that you can ask for and accept help.
Ask. See what happens.

Strengthen Your Four EQ Muscles

Emotional intelligence (EQ) consists of four fundamental capabilities, each described with their key skills: self-awareness, self-management, social awareness, and relationship management.

Self-Awareness is the ability to read and understand your emotions, as well as recognize their impact on work performance and relationships. This includes an understanding of your strengths and weaknesses and knowing what motivates you to succeed.

Action: It's easier to start this process when you identify other people's feelings first. Emotions contain important information about people and the environment. Once you've identified their emotions, compare them to your emotions about the same situation.

Self-Management is the ability to effectively manage your emotions in a healthy way and keep disruptive emotions and impulses under control.

Action: Look at your thoughts about the other person's emotions. Emotions influence how you think, and your thoughts influence how you handle situations.

Social Awareness is the sensing of other people's emotions, understanding their beliefs, their perspectives, and needs. You know how to pick up on emotional cues, recognize different dynamics at work, and adapt to various social situations.

Action: Ask, "What may have caused that person to feel that way?" "What caused me to feel the way I do?"

Relationship Management is the ability to develop and maintain good relationships, communicate clearly, work well with others, and effectively manage conflict.

Action: Use your self-awareness, self-management, and social awareness to enhance your natural communication style. On the top of a blank page, write what your style is: direct, indirect, comfortable, entertaining, discreet, controlled, intense. On the left side of the paper, write the pros to your style. On the right side, the cons. Choose three from the pro column and use them more often. Choose three from the con list and intentionally eliminate, downplay, or improve them.

Stay on top of your reactions to people, places, things, and events.

Use Extreme Listening to Improve Other People's Thinking and Problem-Solving Skills

Give a man a fish and you feed him for a day; teach a man to fish and you feed him for a lifetime.

—Proverb

Darcy clicks her pen repeatedly as she listens to Jeff explain the results of her suggestions. "I tried what you told me, and it didn't work," he said.

"Have you tried the other three approaches I suggested?"

Jeff fumbled with papers and sighed. He stared down at the list Darcy has scribbled for him to follow.

"I've tried everything to fix the situation for you. I've given you so many ideas. Why don't you use any of them?" Darcy asked. Her lips pursed, she gripped her pen and wrote three more suggestions. "Follow these and come back with the results."

When an employee comes to you with an issue, let them talk without interruption. It's called *extreme listening,* and it helps others think clearly and take initiative.

Instead of giving them suggestions, which usually makes the other person feel unsupported, create a space for the other person to think effectively about their problem.

Extreme listening does two things:

1. Increases the person's feelings of autonomy and competence, which keeps them in curiosity mode; and
2. Encourages them to stop and reflect.

These two things improve critical thinking and increase performance.

Here's how to do it:

1. Listen only. Do not make comments or think of solutions. Save this for another time.
2. Allow the other person to set the topic. If they are not sure, ask, "What would you find helpful to talk through with me?"

3. Do not interrupt. Allow them to talk at least for five minutes. Nod your head. Make eye contact.
4. Encourage them to keep talking. Ask, "Is there anything else you're thinking about this?" If they are done talking, ask, "What do you think you'll do now?"

Darcy called Jeff into her office and explained that she was trying a different approach to problem solving, called extreme listening. She listened, nodded, and smiled as Jeff came up with solutions that even amazed himself.

You don't have to solve other people's problems all the time. It is not the best way to support your colleagues.

Practice extreme listening with one person. Explain the new approach you are using. Watch how people are naturally creative, resourceful, and whole.

A Nap Is a Self-Improvement Tool

Napping Day is an unofficial holiday that falls on the first Monday after Daylight Savings Time. It was created as a way to compensate for the hour lost due to the time change.

Sara Mednick, PhD, wrote the book *Take a Nap! Change Your Life. The Scientific Plan to Make You Smarter, Healthier, and More Productive.* In it, she shares how we are the only species that tries to get its sleep needs met in one long session. And this is a recent development. For most of our history, a rest during the day was considered as necessary a component of human existence as sleeping at night. Napping is a tool as old as time itself.

Science has proven that naps are helpful. Her book answers, based on scientific research, the more technical questions such as how duration, timing, and quality affect the benefits derived from a nap and how you can gain those benefits.

The benefits of napping:

- Increases your alertness
- Improves your accuracy
- Helps you make better decisions
- Improves your perception
- Preserves your youthful looks
- Improves your sex life
- Helps you lose weight
- Reduces the risk of heart attack and strokes
- Reduces stress

Mednick's book includes directions on how to customize the perfect nap for you. There's one to increase your creativity, another to retain a lot of content you just learned, and one to repair your body.

You can now make peace with something you shunned as a kid.

Give yourself permission to nap. Your success depends on it.

When You Point One Finger, There Are Three Fingers Pointing Back at You

Instead of getting caught up in anger and blame, pause and take a look at what is going on inside you and respond instead of react.

Emotional intelligence, or EQ, is the ability to identify your emotions and the emotions of those around you and respond to them appropriately and effectively.

EQ impacts your career and work life. Competencies such as the ability to listen and communicate effectively, persevere, maintain self-control, be flexible, and get along with others are all qualities of emotional intelligence, and what employers want. The World Economic Forum projects that emotional intelligence will be one of the top ten skills for employment by 2020.

Emotional intelligence consists of the ability to:

- Recognize your own feelings
- Recognize other people's feelings
- Identify one feeling from another
- Name feelings appropriately
- Discriminate among emotions and use the information to guide your thinking and actions
- Manage your emotions when the environment calls for it

When you get caught up in emotions or unskillful behaviors, you lose time and perspective that could help you create a fulfilling work experience. Emotional intelligence is the way you manage your emotions to better yourself in the workplace.

Increase your emotional intelligence. It's a sound career strategy.

What Gets Measured Improves

Alan Mulally was the CEO of Ford Motor Company from 2006 until he retired in 2014. *Fortune* magazine ranked him as one of the top three greatest leaders in the world, behind Pope Francis and Angela Merkel.

The year Alan arrived at Ford, the company had posted a record $12.7 billion loss. He used structure as one key element to turn it around. He instituted a weekly Business Plan Review (BPR) meeting with his top sixteen executives. His rules were simple: mandatory attendance, no side discussions, no joking at the expense of others, no phones, and each executive was responsible for developing their own presentation—no delegating it.

He started each meeting the same way, and he asked leaders to follow his format. "My name is Alan Mulally. I am the CEO of the Ford Motor Company." Then he reviewed the company's strategic plan, forecast, and his top five areas that needed focus, using a green-yellow-red scorecard to represent the status of each: good, concerned, and poor.

Each executive was required to use the green-yellow-red scorecard. They listed their top five priorities and graded their performance for the previous week. Most of them agreed and followed the structure. A few did not and eventually left the company.

Just as checklists help surgeons remember to wash their hands, structure such as the green-yellow-red scorecard helped executives be transparent and honest with themselves and their colleagues. This visibility encouraged everyone to take responsibility and accountability.

Under his leadership, Ford was the only American major car manufacturer to avoid a bailout fund provided by the government. Ford came back even stronger, profitable, and recaptured its position as the number-two automaker, in terms of US sales, from Toyota.

Create your own BPR:

- List your top five priorities
- Grade yourself at the end of each day
- Share your week's results with another person
- Practice this for thirty days

Your relentless focus, visibility, and accountability get you the results you want.

Identify one behavior you want to be accountable for.
Ask one person to join you in this exercise.

Worrying Is Like a Rocking Chair: It Gives You Something to Do, But Gets You Nowhere

Worrying is a mental habit. Habits can be changed.

Connie's parents lived 600 miles away. Connie worried about her dad's drinking and her mom not getting out of the house much anymore.

"Dennis could help Mom by putting a car service app on her phone. Maybe he could drive her. He's her son, for crying out loud. Mom hates spending money, but she has enough for these services. She should just spend it. She's so stubborn. I could order groceries online for her and have them delivered. Why doesn't Mom accept help? I'll call Aunt Mimi and have her go over there. No. I'll call Uncle Burt. He's more level-headed. And look on Craigslist for help. I don't want to overlook anything. Maybe their next-door neighbor would be willing to help. I don't want a surprise call and have to go up there to fix a crisis. I can figure this out."

Worrying temporarily reduces your anxiety. Thinking about a problem distracts you from your emotions and makes you feel like you're accomplishing something. Worrying, however, is not problem solving. Worrying keeps you in your head, thinking about how to solve a problem, rather than allowing yourself to feel the underlying emotions.

Learn how to feel your emotions. Identify your limiting beliefs that stop you from allowing your emotions to come up. "If I start, I'll never stop. I'm doing something wrong if I feel this emotion. These feelings aren't rational. I'll lose control. Good girls don't get angry."

List three ways these limiting beliefs hold you back. "I hide behind a suit of armor so I don't get hurt. I don't socialize. My husband thinks I'm rigid."

State an empowering belief: "I accept that feelings are a part of being human. Successful women make space for emotions to come up, and I'm a successful woman."

Connie was afraid to feel the grief that comes with aging parents. She had convinced herself that it was stupid to feel sad, that aging was just part of life, and she should just get over it.

Experience all your emotions to reduce worrying.

Determine If Your Worry Is Solvable or Unsolvable

When you have a worrisome thought, ask the following questions:

- Is this problem something you're currently facing or is it an imaginary what-if scenario?
- If the problem is an imaginary what-if, how likely is it to happen?
- Is there something you can do to solve the problem or prepare for it, or is it out of your control?

Solvable worries are those you can take action on immediately. If you are worried you are going to lose your job, ask your boss how your performance is, update your resumé and LinkedIn profile, and attend a networking event.

Unsolvable worries are, "What if my husband gets cancer, or my son gets in an accident?"

Worrying is a form of control and an unskillful way to deal with uncertainty. It is the illusion that if you can figure out what's going to happen in the future, you can mitigate bad outcomes. Focusing on worst-case scenarios takes you out of the present moment, where you can enjoy life.

Find a more positive, realistic way of looking at situations.

WORRYING IS A HABIT—PART 1 OF 3

Identify the Cue

Most habits have been around for so long, you don't pay attention to what causes them anymore.

Shirley wiped the counter down for the third time. "I said I loved him before he left. Yes. Yes, I did. He's fine. He's been driving for two years now." The sink sparkled like the sun as she rescrubbed every inch of it. "Check the traffic. Maybe it's slow traffic on the highway. I'm sure that's it. Did I have him check the tire pressure?"

To change a habit, according to Charles Duhigg, author of *The Power of Habit: Why We Do What We Do in Life and Business*, break it down into its component parts. Identify the three parts of a habit loop: cue, routine, and reward.

The *cue* is the trigger that tells your brain to go into automatic mode and which habit to use.

Shirley's cue to worry was her son driving back to college.

Notice your *routine*. It can be physical, mental, or emotional.

Shirley cleans.

List the *reward*. Rewards help your brain determine if this habit loop is worth remembering for the future.

Shirley gets immediate gratification from having a clean home. It burns off the cortisol rush.

Worry cues can be a certain look, tone of voice, the phone ringing, hearing stories on the news, or the smell of fresh-baked cookies. Write them down for one week.

Shirley was surprised to discover her cues for worrying: certain songs, her friends bragging about their kids, her husband's grumpy stare, and anything to do with her kid's safety.

Commit the time to change the habit of worrying. It didn't form overnight, and it won't change overnight.

WORRYING IS A HABIT—PART 2 OF 3

Notice Your Routine

Once you have identified the cues of your worry, notice your routines and replace them with new ones.

The brain is dependent on routines. They help you remember how to drive a car after a vacation, tie your shoes, or do laundry. Routines can be complex or simple.

In yesterday's story, Shirley worried about her son's safety driving to college. She identified her worry cues: kid's safety, songs, husband's glare, friends bragging about their children. The cue is the trigger that tells your brain to go into automatic mode and which habit to use.

Step two to change a habit is to notice your routine. It can be physical, mental, or emotional. This is the behavior you want to change.

Shirley's routine was to clean and pray the rosary when she was worried.

Replace your routine. There is nothing wrong with prayer or cleaning. However, Shirley used them as a way to avoid her feelings. She felt vulnerable and out of control when her son drove to college. She avoided feeling them through controlling behaviors, instead of sitting with her emotions, allowing them to surface, feeling them, and letting them pass. There are other routines she could choose: call a friend, take a hot bath, or go out for tea.

List five ways you can change a routine response to worrying.

WORRYING IS A HABIT—PART 3 OF 3

Identify Your Reward

Habits create neurological cravings. You associate cues with certain rewards. Rewards help your brain figure out if the habit loop is worth remembering for the future.

Rewards can be physical, mental, or emotional, such as food or feeling proud for doing something. Rewards satisfy cravings. Shirley craved connection with other mothers. She wanted someone to hear her need to keep her son safe, to hear how she worries as a way to do something that can stop something bad from happening, and to give her comfort.

Become aware of the cravings that drive your behaviors. Experiment with different rewards to determine which craving is driving your routine. Shirley got immediate gratification from having a clean home. Instead, she could go out for tea, get a massage, or go to a movie with a friend.

The reward may be a sense of completion and a clean house, receiving spiritual benefits from praying, or connecting with other parents and support to deal with uncertainty.

Identify the reward you get after the cue and routine.

All Together Now: Cue-Routine-Reward

Apply the cue-routine-reward framework to understand how habits works and as a guide to changing them.

Step 1: Identify the cue. Cues fall into five categories: location, time, emotional state, other people, or an immediately preceding action. Write these five things down the moment the urge to worry hits.

Shirley wanted to stop her habit of worrying. She answered:

1. Where am I? Kitchen.
2. What time is it? 10:30 a.m.
3. What is my emotional state? Worried.
4. Who else is around? Nobody.
5. What action preceded the urge? Son left for college.

Step 2: Have a plan. Once you identify your cue, develop a plan for a new routine. Shirley decided to meet with a friend outside the house as soon as she knew what day her son would be returning to college. In anticipation of her husband's grumpy glare, she planned to go to the bathroom and read something inspirational. She put daily readers under the sink.

You can choose your habits once you know how. The goal is to raise your awareness of your habitual urges, to remember what you were thinking and feeling at the precise instant, and to choose again.

Decide to change an unskillful habit. You have control and the responsibility to change it. Act as if you believe this.

The Story of Shirley

My mother, Shirley, was born on March 22, 1924. She grew up very poor in a small town in South Dakota. Her older brother paid for her to go to Duke University for nursing school. After graduation, she moved to Washington, DC, and lived with her older sister until she met my father, Tim Kelly. She had eight kids in thirteen years.

Growing up, we always had a clean home. I still marvel at how she was able to do that with my five brothers, two sisters, and one dog.

She worried all the time. She said the rosary whenever the kids left the house. We joked about her burning through several rosary beads. She also cleaned when she worried. This is why we had a clean house.

At the end of her life, she asked me to promise to keep her final wishes. I begged her to change one wish that she was adamant about. She wouldn't budge. Maybe her wish had to do with her great sense of humor. I relented, agreed, and followed through with her wish.

My father and two brothers had already passed away and were buried together. Each one had a bible quote on their headstone: My brother Kevin: "This is my beloved son in whom I am well pleased." My brother Michael. "Saints are persons who make it easier for others to believe in God." My father: "The father to the children shall make known the truth."

My mother's headstone reads: "She was a fairly good housekeeper."

My heart aches when I think about this. It's the reason why I wrote this book, why I chose the work I do. The vision for my business is to put the light back in women's eyes. I never want another woman to believe her value and worth are from something she does. Your worth and value are inherent.

Don't let worrying stop you from living a full, delicious, and messy life.

You Talk Too Much!

You know who they are. The people who talk *at* you, not *with* you. It's called "Broadcast Only."

Here are signs of someone who is in Broadcast Only mode:

- Hardly lets you get in a word
- When you do make a comment or start a different conversation, they bring it back to themselves
- They interrupt you

They may not be interested or don't know how to have a two-way conversation. It may be a compulsion, a nervous habit, or they're just not aware of it being a problem.

Often you can address the behavior, as with a child or a direct report. If you can't talk with them about it, limit your time with them. Someone else's word quota is not your problem.

Make a list of people who are set on "Broadcast Only." Choose how often and how long you will listen to them.

Emotions Can Drive Thinking and Behavior

The Disney Pixar movie *Inside Out* is a film that shows how everyday living is filled with emotions. It is a great example to explain the concept of emotional intelligence.

Emotional intelligence (EQ) is a set of skills that allows you to recognize, process, and use emotions to guide your thinking, decision-making, and behavior.

In the movie, which takes place in the mind of a young girl named Riley, five personified emotions—joy, sadness, anger, fear, and disgust, which represent the core human emotions—try to lead Riley through life as her parents move from Minnesota to California and she has to adjust to her new home, school, and friends. The fundamental point of the film is to show viewers that emotions can drive thinking and behavior.

Watch the movie *Inside Out* and write down your answers to these questions:

1. Notice your emotion. Observe its presence.
2. Experience your emotion fully. Think of an emotion as a wave, coming and going. Do not try to block it away (sadness), keep it around (happiness), or increase it (anger).
3. Remember, you are not your emotion. Describe the emotion as, "I have the feeling of _________(emotion)" rather than "I am ____________ (emotion)."
4. Accept, respect, and be willing to experience your emotion.

At the end of the movie, Riley's emotions all work together, allowing her to lead a more emotionally complex life.

Use emotions. Don't be used by them.

DELEGATE

MAR 25

Successful Leaders Delegate More Often Than Not

There are many reasons leaders do not delegate: they don't know how, their attitude toward their employees, reluctance, not enough time, or they tried it before and it didn't work.

Lacy struggled with delegation. Her business was growing, and she continued to have too much on her plate. She became the bottleneck in her own company. She wanted to grow her business and at the same time hesitated to delegate. Her employees grew frustrated with her delays in responding because she had too much of her own work. Lacy was in a highly regulated field and worried about the risks if one of her colleagues screwed up.

Identify the obstacles in your thoughts about delegating.

Reluctance

- "Nobody can do it as well as I can."
- "I'll just do it."
- "I can do it faster."
- "They'll screw it up."

All true. All possible. There is an element of risk in delegating. Your job is to teach, motivate, and provide feedback to ensure delegation works.

Not enough time to delegate

- If it is a one-time task, do not delegate.
- If it is a repeatable task, it's an investment to spend the time to document and teach the key steps.

Dump-and-run delegation, then take-it-back micromanagement

This approach is a result of not taking enough time to describe why you are delegating (big picture and context), vague instructions, unclear expectations and deadlines, and being unavailable to answers questions and provide feedback.

Practice the following four steps:

1. Pause
2. Ask, "Can this task be eliminated? If not, can it be automated?" If not, go to step 3.
3. Ask, "Who can do this?"
4. Set up a meeting to delegate it.
5. Communicate expectations of outcomes and results.

Delegation is a skill to learn and a habit to form. It takes practice.

Delegate one task today.

Women Who Quit Their Jobs to Follow Their Dreams

I had the privilege of being interviewed for an article in the *Huffington Post** as one of ten women who quit their jobs to follow their dreams.

Here's what I found to be true in following my passion, which is to put the light back in women's eyes:

- It feels really scary to take the leap and go after what you want.
- It's important to have a group of women to support you when you do. I call my support network my "angel tribe." They are there for me when I'm holding my breath and remind me to exhale. They hold me compassionately accountable so I don't hide under the bedcovers covers when fear grips me. They remind me to celebrate all my successes.
- Learn to listen to that still, small voice. It's the voice of wisdom, compassion, and direction. I've learned to trust myself by listening to this beautiful voice.
- The more I do what is mine to do, the more confident I feel . . . in all areas of my life.
- If I had the chance to do it over again, I would have done it sooner! It's worth walking through the fear and discomfort.

I help women forget what they are not and remember who they are.

Write down what you want. Share it with a trusted friend.
Make a decision to take one step toward it.

* http://www.huffingtonpost.com/brittany-policastro-/words-of-wisdom-from-10-women-who-quit-their-jobs-to-follow-their-dreams_b_9517382.html

Act As If

Mindful success is intentionally choosing your thoughts and actions every day. It is consciously choosing to have more faith in abundance and worthiness than in scarcity and unworthiness.

One way to practice mindful success is to act as if:

- You believe you were created worthy and valuable
- The Universe has your back
- The present moment is where the miracles are

Stop looking for evidence that you are guilty.

Act as if and practice the behaviors that help rewire your brain. This increases your happiness, gratitude, and peace of mind.

Act your way into right thinking.

There Are No Qualifiers to Worthiness

You push away your worthiness with "qualifiers." This is when you believe you can receive love, abundance, or sleep once you have a completed to-do list, lost five pounds, got a bonus, cleaned the house, volunteered at school, or made dinner.

Dr. Brené Brown understands qualifiers to worthiness. She is a shame and vulnerability researcher. "Most of us think, 'I'm pretty worthy of love and belonging. But I'd be super worthy if I lost fifteen pounds, or made partner, or my wife doesn't leave. Or I stay sober. Or whatever our thing is.'" She shares her experience in lectures on Oprah's Life Class.

"Worthiness is an as-is, here-and-now proposition. That's the definition of wholeheartedness. Wholeheartedness is about engaging with the world from a place of worthiness," she says.

Answer the following questions:

1. What would you do if you believed you were worthy of an amazing life?
2. What would you do if you were free from tension, stress, and worry?
3. What would you do if you believed everything you need is already given to you?

Recognize that your needs are worthwhile.

Flush It

A mistake ritual helps you perform better in the game of life.

Michael Jordan is a retired American professional basketball player. He is the principal owner and chairman of the Charlotte Hornets team and considered to be one of the greatest basketball players of all times.

He said, "I've missed more than 9,000 shots in my career. I've lost almost 300 games. Twenty-six times I've been trusted to take the game-winning shot and missed. I've failed over and over and over again in my life."

Basketball players need to recover quickly from mistakes. Each one develops their own mistake ritual that helps them quickly acknowledge a mistake and move beyond it. When you make a mistake, you are no longer in the moment. Your mind ruminates on the mistake you made. You are not ready for the next play at hand.

A mistake ritual is a gesture and statement used to ward off the fear of making mistakes so you can stay present and continue playing. It allows athletes to quickly reset and get ready for the next play or decision without wallowing in the past and berating themselves for having made a mistake.

Flush It is one of those quick-recovery techniques. It immediately rids your mind of the mistake.

When you make a mistake, put your hand above your shoulder and make a motion like you are flushing a toilet. Say, "It's OK _________ (your name). Flush it. Next play."

Michael Jordan accepted the fact that he made thousands of mistakes. He did not accept not trying.

Reduce your fear of making mistakes and use that energy to learn and grow.

Treat Your Mind Like a Frog on a Plate

Mary woke up at 3:00 a.m. Her brain raced with thoughts, and she had a pain in her chest. "What if I don't get my bonus? How will I pay for tuition? I can get a part-time job. I'll ask my boss for an advance. I wonder if I can get a line of credit?" She laid awake, worried and agitated, until it was time to get up for work.

She had been waking up in the middle of the night for months. Exhausted and overwhelmed, Mary decided to do something about her anxiety. She read about the practice of mindfulness and its benefits to reduce stress. Mindfulness is a mental state achieved by focusing one's awareness on the present moment, while acknowledging and accepting one's feelings, thoughts, and bodily sensations.

An example of mindfulness practice is to sit in a chair for five minutes, breathe deeply, and notice your thoughts and reactions. "I'm sitting and I'm bored, my knee hurts, I'm a little hungry, I'm anxious to look at my phone."

Mindfulness practice is similar to watching a frog. Frogs jump; that's their function. Minds think; that's their function. Your mind jumps from one thought to another and you have about 50,000 thoughts a day. Start your practice with the image of a frog on a plate. Every time you have a thought, imagine the frog jumping off the plate. Gently place it back on the plate.

Mary started her mindfulness practice with two minutes of deep breathing. Then she increased to five minutes, eventually working up to fifteen minutes. Every time she thought about her grocery list, problems at work, or paying for tuition, she imagined her frog jumping off the plate and she gently put it back. She experienced fewer sleepless nights, and her mind was less foggy. This allowed her to solve problems faster and easier.

Mindfulness is a method to bring you into the present moment. Whatever you are doing, be aware of it.

Take three deep breaths to calm your jumping mind.

Anything You Want

I recently read the book *Anything You Want, 40 Lessons for a New Kind of Entrepreneur*, by Derek Sivers. He is an American entrepreneur and musician who founded CD Baby and gifted the proceeds of the sale of the business, $22 million, to an independent musician's charity to support music education.

He shares his values and philosophy about success in business:

- If an activity or event doesn't make you say, "HELL YEAH," then say no.
- Most people don't know why they are doing what they are doing. They follow others, what society says is appropriate, and wake up one day having missed their own lives.
- Business is not about money. It's about making dreams come true for others and for yourself.
- Never do anything just for the money.
- Make yourself unnecessary to the running of your business.
- The real point of doing anything is to be happy, so do only what makes you happy.
- Set up your business like you don't need the money, and it will more likely come to you. People will be happier to pay you.

Learn what makes you happy and successful.

Plan for the Worst, Expect the Best

After stealing some paintings from the Louvre in Paris, a thief was caught when his getaway van ran out of fuel. Given bail at his first hearing, a reporter asked him on the steps of the courthouse how he had forgotten such a vital part of his plan.

"Simple," said the thief. "I had no Monet for Degas to make the Van Gogh."

Patient attention to details produces results. Take time to think through the resources needed to achieve the best outcomes.

ELIMINATE-AUTOMATE-DELEGATE—PART 1 OF 4

Use Eliminate-Automate-Delegate to Get Better Results

This technique helps you focus on the important tasks that move you closer to achieving your goals.

Here's the problem. You want to hit your end-of-year goals, or increase your satisfaction and productivity, or get a bonus, or just keep your job. You want to work on the right things to accomplish your goals. Instead, you get buried in emails, meetings, and conference calls that eat up all your time. So now the important stuff that will move you forward gets done after hours, after you put your kids to bed, after you make dinner, or at a time when you are fried.

The consequences are significant. You don't get enough sleep, you stop exercising, you miss out on family moments, like dinner with your family. Your relationships are negatively impacted.

How do you engage in work without getting lost in its relentless demands, hecticness, and speed?

The technique to help you focus on the important tasks is called "Eliminate-Automate-Delegate." It's a technique I learned from Tim Ferriss, author of *The 4-Hour Workweek: Escape 9-5, Live Anywhere, and Join the New Rich.* You do it in this order: eliminate, then automate, then delegate. Never delegate something that can be automated, and never automate something that can be eliminated.

Use Eliminate-Automate-Delegate to spend more time on tasks that will help you achieve your goals.

ELIMINATE-AUTOMATE-DELEGATE–PART 2 OF 4

Eliminate Tasks, Outgrown Habits, and Distractions to Increase Productivity

Use the Eliminate-Automate-Delegate tool to spend more time on the tasks needed to achieve your goals.

Step 1: Eliminate

Look for a discrete task in your day or week. For example, look at one weekly meeting, such as a business development conference call. Ask yourself, "Can I eliminate attending this call?"

One hundred percent of the time, people tell me, "I can't eliminate anything." This response is normal and to be expected.

If it is something you can't eliminate, identify the component parts of the conference call. Maybe you type up the meeting notes, and this is something you can eliminate, automate, or delegate. Most tasks you do are habitual. To change a habit, you have to know its component parts. Look for pieces around the call that you can eliminate.

Ask questions until you find a task to eliminate.

ELIMINATE-AUTOMATE-DELEGATE—PART 3 OF 4

Automate to Reduce Time Wasters

Use the Eliminate-Automate-Delegate tool to spend more time on the tasks needed to achieve your goals.

Step 2: Automate

Automate tasks to save time and focus on what's important. Let's look at the biggest time waster: email. We spend way too much time on emails. It's the black hole and the bane of my existence, and also the way I feel important. "Somebody needs me."

Think about how many times you look at your email, especially those you don't need to look at right away—conference announcements, chamber of commerce updates, or trade emails. Change your mailbox settings so that these types of emails are put into a folder called "Read Later." This can cut your email traffic by about 15–25 percent—time you can spend on those tasks related to your goals.

Never delegate something that can be automated, and never automate something that can be eliminated.

ELIMINATE-AUTOMATE-DELEGATE–PART 4 OF 4

Delegate What Others Can Do

Step 3: Delegate

The purpose of delegation is to further reduce the tasks that take you away from your primary goals. Unless something is well defined, specific, and important, no one should do it.

Look for a discrete task in your day or week. For example, one weekly meeting, such as a business development conference call. Identify the component parts of the conference call. Maybe you type the meeting notes and this is something you can delegate. Most tasks you do are habitual. In order to change a habit, identify its component parts. Look for pieces around the call that you can delegate.

Make sure you are specific in your delegation directions and that it's important they get done. If not, eliminate them.

Ask, "Am I the best person to do this task?" If not, delegate it to your supervisor, colleagues, employees, or other departments.

The Choice Is Yours

Gail woke up Monday morning angry and tired. Her husband had gone out of town for business and her dog was up in the middle of the night throwing up. She read her daily calendar while drinking her coffee, and it had a quote by Victor Frankl: "Between stimulus and response, there is a space. In that space is our power to choose our response. In our response lies our growth and our freedom."

She decided to write about this quote. "I want to call my husband and blame him for the dog getting sick. Then I want to punish myself for being tired by overeating." She discovered that she never paused long enough to choose her response.

"In my pause moment, I want to make a different choice. I choose to love myself by going for a run, which always makes me feel better. I'll go to bed early tonight and text my husband that I love him."

Her day went better than she could have imagined. Her run helped to clear her head, she got take-out dinner, and went to bed early. The next day, she received flowers delivered from her husband. Life is the sum of choices made, not ones we wish we had made.

Pause long enough between stimulus and response.
It gives you limitless choices.

Vulnerability Is a Sign of Strength

When others are vulnerable with you, you love it. When it's your turn, you hate it.

The belief that vulnerability is a sign of weakness stems from society's dislike for appearing emotional. As a child, you were taught to stop feeling the way you did, that your feelings were wrong. Many kids heard, "Stop being so dramatic. You're freaking out over nothing. You need to calm down. It's all in your head."

Vulnerability is an emotion. Emotions are a natural instinctive state of mind derived from your circumstances, mood, or relationships with others. They are a naturally occurring response to situations. They can be the result of your own evaluation or an automatic one, such as feeling angry when you get punched.

Reframe the way you view vulnerability. It is sharing your feelings and experiences with people who have earned your trust. Opening up connects you to others, to joy, and to opportunities. To feel is to be vulnerable.

Be intentionally vulnerable with a trusted friend.

EMOTIONAL INTELLIGENCE

APR

Successful Leaders Are Self-Aware

Emotional intelligence is key in the development of leadership skills.

Strong Leaders

Self-awareness means knowing and understanding

- Your values, beliefs, and principles
- Your emotions and thinking patterns
- What motivates or drives you
- Why you react to certain situations
- What you want out of life

Emotional intelligence is the ability to relate to others in effective ways, both personally and professionally, in a wide range of contexts and roles. At work it helps you manage stress and increase cooperation and collaboration.

Your ability to work with others is impacted by your emotions. Emotionally intelligent people understand and use emotions in positive ways to guide their thinking and actions. This leads to greater communication, increased empathy, and lower stress.

Increase your self-awareness through the following technique. Make a list of emotional triggers to better understand and predict your reactions to stressful situations and difficult people. These are the things that result in you losing behavioral control.

Use these stereotypes to help you identify the personalities that trigger you:

- Sniper: the person who comes out of nowhere and blindsides you with accusations or aggressive behavior.
- Passive-aggressive: hides their true feelings by pretending everything is OK when they are actually upset.
- Victim: constant complainer, attempts to draw you into their problems.
- Flyer: highly emotional person who flies off the handle and is emotionally reactive.

Understand how your emotions impact people at work.

There Are No Prerequisites to Worthiness

Receiving love, kindness, and compliments can be challenging. We think we have to earn them. We push them away. When someone says we look pretty in our dress, we respond, "Oh, this dress? I bought it used."

List your prerequisites to deserving. They are the thoughts and beliefs that get in the way of believing you deserve more time, sleep, fun, balance, money, or success. For example:

- It has to be hard.
- I should be afraid because the stock market is crashing and people are scared, and the politicians are crazy.
- I don't want to be disappointed if it doesn't work out.
- I don't want to feel bad.
- I don't want to fail.
- I have to earn the air I breathe, so I can't take any downtime.
- I don't trust it will work.
- I should already know this.
- It's a waste of time.
- I have to work harder.

Are you ready to engage with the world from a place of worthiness?

Accept a compliment today and say, "Thank you." Believe they meant it.

Do One Financial Task a Day

"Not again." Marta let out a long, heavy sigh. Her body felt heavy, as if her blood had turned to molasses. "I forgot to pay my credit card bill again. This time I'll set up autopay." She had forgotten to pay her bill before and felt stupid that she let it happen again.

She shoved the credit card statement in her top drawer and flipped open her laptop. "First, I need to check Facebook and my email, then I'll set up autopay for my credit card."

An hour later, Marta closed her laptop, feeling great about answering all her emails. She forgot all about setting up autopay. She left to meet with clients. The late fees increased.

Marta is a successful real estate agent. She is great with clients, takes care of all the transaction details of buying and selling homes, and consistently exceeds her sales goals. She also avoids her business and personal financial responsibilities, which makes her feel badly about herself.

To get clarity about your finances, do one financial task each day. Make a list of all money-related tasks. Take three deep breaths if you feel anxious.

- Open your mail
- Review your bank statement
- Schedule an appointment with your accountant
- Close an account you no longer use
- Ask for help

Over the next month, Marta completed one financial task a day. She felt both uncomfortable and inspired. Her clarity increased, along with her self confidence that she was learning how to be responsible for her financial well-being.

Complete one financial task today and increase your self-trust.

You're Going to Throw a Few Gutter Balls in Your Life

It was mid-June when Debbie finished with the spring real estate market. As a real estate agent, she had worked seven days a week for months. She received a commission check and decided to treat herself to a weekend at a spa retreat resort. She enjoyed massages, manicures, and fine dining.

She had not opened her mail for a few weeks because she had been so busy. When she did, she discovered a property tax bill she forgot was coming. It was more than her commission check.

She felt ashamed and angry at herself. "How could I forget this? I manage large financial transactions, and yet I can't remember my own. How will I pay this?"

Everyone makes financial mistakes. Some are small, like forgetting to pay your electric bill. Some are large, like not planning for recurring expenses such as life insurance or property taxes. The key to moving forward is to learn from your experience.

Answer the following questions.

1. What was I thinking about before I spent the money?
2. What were the consequences?
3. How did my choices make me feel?
4. If I had it to do over again, what would I do differently?
5. Have I given myself love and compassion about the choices I made?

Self-forgiveness and self-compassion help make life lessons stick. Learn the lesson, release it, and move on with your life. If you hold on to it, you'll get another opportunity to repeat the lesson.

Debbie journaled and realized she believed there was no time for self-maintenance activities, such as eating healthfully and opening her mail in a timely manner. She practiced Hands-On-Heart, called the county tax office, and got on a payment plan.

When you make a mistake, treat yourself the way you would treat a four-year-old who lost her favorite toy.

Don't Let Failure Define You

Failure is a part of success. Keep it right sized and move forward.

Four famous women failed before they succeeded.

Arianna Huffington is a Greek American author, syndicated columnist, and businesswoman. Her first book, *The Female Woman*, was well received. Her second book, *After Reason*, was rejected by thirty-six publishers. She has since written thirty-six books and has a net worth of $50 million.

J.K. Rowling is a British novelist and screenwriter. She was a single mother on welfare and her book was rejected by twelve publishers. She finally sold her first book, *Harry Potter and the Philosopher's Stone*, for $4,000. She is now worth $1 billion.

Vera Wang is a Chinese American fashion designer. She was a competitive figure skater and failed to make the Olympic skating team in 1968. She then took a job as an assistant at Vogue in 1971. She is now the most prominent designer of wedding dresses, with a net worth of $400 million.

Oprah Winfrey is an African American media proprietor, talk-show host, actress, producer, and philanthropist. She was demoted in one of her early jobs, from a co-anchor at Baltimore's WJZ-TV to morning cut-ins. This is when she met her best friend Gayle. She went on to create the highest-rated television talk show and is the richest African American, with a net worth of $3 billion.

Don't take failure personally. You are not your failures.

Redefine failure. F.A.I.L. = first attempt in learning.

Move a Muscle, Change a Thought

Paola is a successful attorney. She knows that her health is a key component to her success and working out provides immediate benefits. She committed to going to the gym on Friday morning. Her workload was light, and the kids were at school.

Her amygdala said, "You should keep working on this brief."

Her prefrontal cortex spoke up. "Go. You promised yourself you would go. Your thinking is clearer, and you have more stamina after a workout." She pushed through the amygdala's discomfort. "Ugh. OK."

Your brain is wired to resist change. The amygdala is the part of the brain that reacts negatively to uncertainty and risk. It's great in times of crisis, but lousy at supporting you taking new, positive actions. "If I do this behavior—take time to eat healthfully, exercise, go to the movies—I risk missing out on a business opportunity (safety and security). I may lose my job and end up on the streets."

The prefrontal cortex is the executive part of the brain. It counterbalances the amygdala. "Your clarity and confidence increase after a workout. You get great ideas walking on the treadmill. Successful leaders take the time to exercise regularly, and you're a successful leader."

Paola drove to the gym while her amygdala kept grumbling at her. "Are you sure you can afford this time away from work? You can go to the gym tomorrow. It seems a bit self-indulgent to go on a Friday morning. What if you see someone you know there?" She walked into a spin class and within two minutes was too busy trying to keep up that she forgot all about work and wasting time.

At the end of the class, she thought about her experience. "I guess my amygdala will always be uncomfortable doing this activity. Thank goodness for my prefrontal cortex."

Act on your commitment, not your feelings.

"Change Back!"

Afterburn is when you do something that is good for you—a new behavior, ending a relationship that has served its purpose, or stepping out of your comfort zone—and then you feel icky. Your inner critic says, "Change back!" "I shouldn't have done that!"

Growing pains are another way to describe afterburn.

Have you ever wanted to take an action to move you forward, but the feeling of discomfort comes up and you don't do it? Then you feel bad and angry with yourself. Did you turn these negative feelings on yourself by overeating or getting lost in Facebook or work?

Janice has her own business. She loves to paint when she's not working. She said, "I want to put one of my paintings on Facebook and see if anybody is interested in buying it."

Her inner critic started: "It's not that good. It's not that important. Who do you think you are?"

Her discomfort level was through the roof. Just thinking about posting one of her paintings made her want to crawl out of her skin. But she finally got up the courage and posted it. Then the afterburn kicked in.

You know what it's like when you post something on Facebook and you eagerly wait to hear the ping that somebody likes your post? She sat there waiting for the pings and nothing happened. No pings. She went down the shame spiral: "That was stupid. I can't believe I put my work out there. I should just take it down."

She decided to shut her laptop and go do the dishes. The dishwater was warm and the act of doing something that gave her instant results helped bring her back to the present moment. It interrupted her afterburn. She did something good for herself, even though her inner critic started screaming at her, "Change back! Take that picture down. Who do you think you are?"

She took a deep breath and sat back down at the computer. When she opened it up, she heard ping, ping, ping, ping. She sold the painting that day.

Afterburn is normal and to be expected when you are making positive changes.

Take one action that is outside your comfort zone.

EMPOWERING BELIEFS

Change Limiting Beliefs to Empowering Beliefs

Today is the day that many people struggle with limiting beliefs about money. Limiting beliefs are thoughts that constrain you in some way. They hold you back from your goals or detract from your enjoyment of life.

An example is, "I should know the answer to this."

An empowering belief causes you to reach for your goals and enjoy a greater quality of life. They have three qualities:

1. Give you strength in the moment
2. Have a lightness about them
3. Ring true to you

Practice changing limiting beliefs to empowering beliefs. For example, change "I should know the answer to this" to "Questions I don't know the answer to leads me to new opportunities and discoveries!"

LIMITING BELIEFS	EMPOWERING BELIEFS
"I'm terrible with numbers."	"I'm really good at sales, connecting with people, and learning new skills. Successful people embrace the discomfort that goes along with learning new skills, such as spending time understanding federal and state tax returns/process, and I'm a successful person."
"I'll never learn this tax software program."	"Lifelong learners are open to new ideas, learning new and different ways of making their lives easier, and I'm a lifelong learner."
"I can't ask for and accept help because I should know this."	"Successful women ask for and accept help, and I'm a successful woman."

Identify your limiting beliefs about money, filing tax returns, and worthiness. Change them to empowering beliefs and watch your productivity increase.

Be impeccable in your thoughts and words. Doing this helps you achieve greater success.

What Formula 409 and WD-40 Have in Common

There isn't any invention that didn't have a dozen—if not hundreds—of broken prototypes on its way to success.

It took researchers forty attempts to get the right solvent for WD-40™ and 409 attempts to create Formula 409®. What would our homes be like without the tenacity of those who failed all these times? Squeaky and dirty.

Failure is normal. Resisting the risk of failing gets in the way.

- You believe failure may hurt your credibility and chances for advancement at work and in your personal life, so you don't try.
- You limit yourself by using labels such as, "I'm being practical, realistic, and responsible."

The avoidance of failure becomes a barrier to going after what you want.

Most people see success and failure with success on one end and failure on the other. You do everything to move toward success and away from failure. But what if you reconfigured this model?

Instead of viewing failure as something to be avoided, turn it into a 'stepping-stone' on the path to success and gratification. In other words, success is the destination. Failure is how you get there.

Failure is how we learn. It is stigmatized, but anyone who has succeeded has failed first.

Rethink the way you look at failure–as a pathway to success.

Guilt Can Mask Feelings of Unworthiness

Joyce dumped her luggage at the front door, disheveled, feet aching, brain fried. She collapsed into a chair. She had just returned from a two-week business trip. All she wanted to do was take a hot bath and eat a home-cooked meal. She opened the refrigerator and saw a gallon of expired milk and old leftovers.

Dejected, she said, "I cannot drag myself out to the grocery store." Then an idea: "Wouldn't it be great to order groceries online?" "But no, I shouldn't spend money on this. I might need it for something else. I'm not that tired. I should be able to do my own grocery shopping."

Guilt kicked in. "I'm just being practical," says guilt. Think of another person in the same situation. Would you tell them to buy the groceries online and take a bath while waiting for the food to be delivered? If the answer is yes, do the same thing for yourself. You are worthy of a break, of support, of receiving.

Joyce ordered the groceries, enjoyed a hot bath, and made a delicious meal.

Revise your definition of guilt. Accept the support you deserve.

Change Limiting Beliefs to Empowering Beliefs The Forrest Gump Success Secret

Practicing present-moment awareness allows you to see and experience serendipity—a fortuitous meshing of events.

Forrest Gump is a movie about a man who faces many tribulations, but he never lets any of them interfere with his happiness. The main character, Forrest Gump, played by Tom Hanks, is an authentic and kind-hearted soul. He lives each moment from a place of integrity, loyalty, and present-moment awareness. This allows him to experience love, adventure, and great success.

His present–moment qualities included:

- No judgment—of his sweetheart Jenny, Captain Dan, himself, or from old experiences.
- Open minded—he was free from expectations. He inspired others to run, he started a successful shrimp business, and became a Ping-Pong champion.
- Spontaneous—he allowed new impulses to come in without criticism or suppressing them. He saved members of his platoon and was awarded the Medal of Honor by President Johnson.
- Free from worry—this allowed Forrest to keep his word to his friend Bubba, giving Bubba's profits from the shrimp business to Bubba's family.
- Fearless—he did not carry the regrets of the past or the wreckage of the future with him. Lieutenant
- Dan invested their profits from the shrimp business in Apple and they were financially secure for the rest of their lives.

Forrest Gump had a profound effect on others.

Practice one present-moment quality for five minutes today and notice the profound effects.

Comfort Is for Rejuvenation; Discomfort Is for Learning

Most people believe that being uncomfortable is a sign that something is wrong. Many equate comfort with happiness. We want to change, but don't want to be uncomfortable. We want to fit into our clothes, but don't want to exercise or eat less junk food.

It's vital to change your belief about discomfort. Being uncomfortable is a sign that you are stretching and growing, and becoming your best self. This is where your shifts happen and where you achieve your goals.

Look at the Comfort Zone Bull's-Eye Diagram below.

I'll use the example of learning to cook to explain how the diagram works.

***OVER-RATED !**

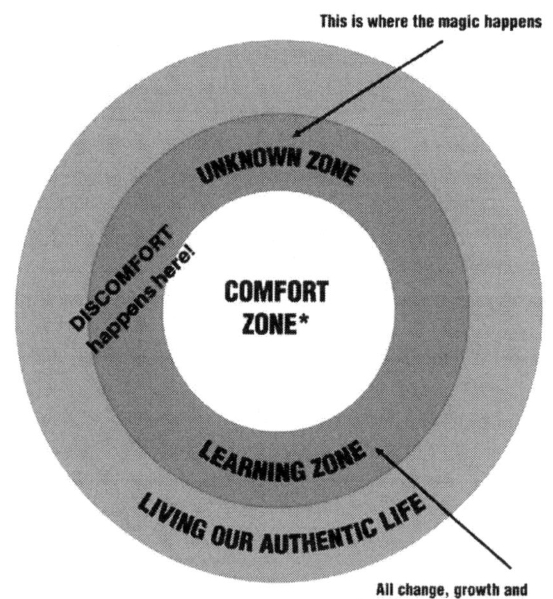

COMFORT IS FOR REJUVENATION.
DISCOMFORT IS FOR LIVING LIFE FULLY ALIVE AND AWAKE.

First, I get a cookbook and start with the basics: how to boil water and make eggs. As I spend time doing this, I hear my inner critic say, "This is stupid. You should already know this. What a waste of time. Why aren't you focused on generating revenue?"

It's the voice of discomfort. "Other women your age know how to cook. Stop now and save yourself the time and embarrassment."

I think, *I must be doing something wrong because I feel uncomfortable.*

I'm in the LEARNING ZONE of the diagram. It's where change happens and new habits are formed.

As I practice, I get better. Eventually I master how to cook. I move into the COMFORT ZONE. This is any behavior that keeps you at a low anxiety level. Your initial discomfort becomes your new normal. It expands your comfort zone wider.

Change your beliefs about comfort and discomfort.

- Stop equating comfort with happiness. Equate comfort with rejuvenation.
- Discomfort is for learning. It's where the gold is.

Accept that the most important actions are never comfortable.

Our Brains Are Wired to Resist Change

Uncertainty is uncomfortable. Certainty is ridiculous.

—Descartes

Our brains want to predict and control the future. This is our natural thinking process.

We are wired for certainty. Just like we are wired to crave food or sex, the desire to know what the future holds is a powerful motivator. This drive for certainty is a function of our nervous system. It has to do with our reptilian response; when we have a sense of uncertainty, the lizard brain goes into alert mode. Uncertainty feels like a threat to the brain. It is a basic human need to want the assurance of avoiding pain and gaining pleasure.

If we are wired for certainty and want to avoid uncertainty, then we have a good explanation of why change can be hard. Change involves uncertainty. It explains why we prefer things we know over risking the uncertainty of new ideas and solutions.

We react to uncertainty. We try to control everything around us—our work, our kids, our spouses, our weight. Are we effective? Not so much.

The solution is to stay in the present moment.

Ninety-nine percent of the time, we are either thinking of the regrets of the past or the wreckage of our future—or what I like to call *The Parade of Imaginary Horribles.*

We are not meant to suffer. We are meant to thrive. We suffer when we don't stay present.

When you have fearful thoughts come up, state the following: "I will not get caught in the melodrama of my mind." Put your concerns into an imaginary container. You can come back to them tomorrow (or never!).

Write down your fears and burn them. There is something liberating about watching them go up in smoke.

Expect resistance when you are making positive changes in your life.

The antidote for dealing with the uncertainty of change is to stay in the present moment.

Put Your Oxygen Mask on First and Thrive

Most women think that putting on their oxygen mask first is selfish.

Martina's throat tightened when her friend Paula asked, "Would you consider a job in another city and commute back and forth on the weekends?"

She'd asked herself this question 900 times before.

Martina rubbed her forehead to make the pain behind it go away. She answered, "I'd prefer to have a job with less travel."

Martina wanted a new job, one where her skills and talents would best serve the world. She had two children and travel put a huge strain on the family. She was not clear and direct with herself about what was acceptable in a new job, so she was sending mixed messages.

Paula watched her rub her forehead. "Is there something you're not telling me?"

"I'm confused about how much travel I want to do for a job."

"Let me ask the question another way. Is the amount of travel you do in your current job too little, just right, or too much?"

"Too much."

"What is the right percentage for you?"

"About zero to 20 percent."

Most of us have no frame of reference for what it means to put our oxygen mask on first. How you do it is to be clear and direct about what you want. "I'd prefer to have a job with less travel" is not clear and direct. Clear and direct sounds like this: "I'm looking for a job with travel from zero to 20 percent."

Martina felt guilty for not wanting to travel. She thought it was selfish to be clear and direct and ask for what she wants. She practiced restating her travel requirements with Paula until her throat opened up and her confidence increased.

Put on your own oxygen mask before helping those around you.

Earth Day

Earth Day is an annual event celebrated on April 22 worldwide. The first one was in 1970 and now there are events in more than 193 countries, showing support for protecting the environment.

Every day can be Earth Day. Here are a few ways to show gratitude for the place we call home:

- When you walk your dog, bring an extra bag and pick up trash.
- Switch from using disposable plastic bags to reusable grocery bags.
- Go meatless on Mondays.
- Switch from plastic water bottles to reusable ones.

Leave a legacy of compassion, responsibility, and an environment your great-great-great-grandchildren will love.

Reduce. Reuse. Recycle.

PRESENT-MOMENT AWARENESS

Practice Present-Moment-Awareness

Being present brings peacefulness into your life.

Shift from thinking to sensing: notice sounds, body sensations, thoughts, and breathing. Do not label or judge anything that happens.

Sounds. Focus on the most obvious sounds. As your concentration gets sharper, notice more subtle sounds, such as birdcalls and traffic.

Body sensations. Feel your arms resting on your lap, your legs on the chair. Feel your clothes against your skin. Notice any pains, muscle tightness, fluttering in your stomach, or anxious feelings. Watch how these sensations shift and change, letting go of them and becoming present to those that arise.

Thoughts. Watch your thoughts without getting caught up in them or feeling that you have to act on them. Some thoughts are nonsense; others are so compelling that you follow them.

Breathing. Watch the natural changes in your breathing as you become more relaxed. You might notice that your breath starts shallow and fast, then becomes deeper and more regular.

Say to yourself, "Now is the time to be aware of the present moment. I let go of the past and the future."

Allow the present moment to be as it is completely, and see what happens.

Persistence Pays Off

Ellen DeGeneres is an American comedian most commonly known from her TV talk show, *The Ellen DeGeneres Show*. She came out in 1997 and was the first openly lesbian actress to play an openly lesbian character on TV. She experienced intense discrimination following her coming out, including the cancellation of her sitcom. This did not stop Ellen. Even though some did not agree with her sexual preference, others loved her enthusiasm and kind heart. Ellen continued to prove herself in the industry, landing her own TV show in 2003. Many associate Ellen with her selflessness, positive attitude, and her dance moves. Each day she strives to use her gifts to make the world a better place.

You will experience unfair or prejudicial treatment by others. Remember the phrase from the play *Hamlet*, where the father Polonius advises his son, Laertes, as he departs for Paris:

"This above all: to thine own self be true,
And it must follow, as the night the day,
Thou canst not then be false to any man.
Farewell, my blessing season this in thee!"

Appreciate your tenacity when you are challenged to stay the course.

Movies Depict the Heroine's Journey

The heroine's journey describes a woman's search for wholeness. The protagonist confronts her dark side and emerges stronger. This quest is a recurring theme in movies.

The 2015 comedy film *The Intern* followed seventy-year old Ben Whittaker (Robert De Niro) as he began his new internship position at a fast-growing fashion startup company. Ben worked for Jules (Anne Hathaway), the company CEO, who was skeptical of him.

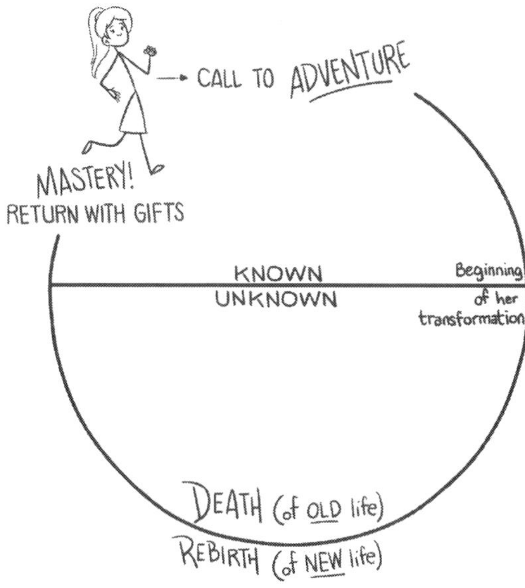

Jules' call to adventure began when she was challenged to decide between her marriage and her CEO position. She goes from the known to the unknown. She confronts challenges (the board of directors pressures her to quit, her husband has an affair). Her guide along the unknown path is Ben. He shares wisdom, support, and encouragement as she faces her internal obstacles of doubt, fear, and uncertainty. She returns with gifts and mastery—increased self-confidence and self-trust. She knows how to maintain balance with her career and family.

Identify your call to adventure and seek out guides to support you along the unknown journey to success.

This Too Shall Pass. Like a Kidney Stone, It Will Pass

Judy called me on a Friday afternoon, frantic. She had struggled to make her sales numbers at work, which meant her bonus checks had dried up. Then she got the news that her husband lost his job. Their prudent reserve fund was depleted, and she was at her wit's end.

When life throws curveballs, do this:

1. Take three deep breaths. You might notice that your breath starts shallow and fast, but becomes deeper and more regular as you relax more deeply.
2. Identify sounds. Focus on the most obvious sounds, such as birdcalls and traffic.
3. Feel your arms resting on your lap and your legs on the chair. Notice any pains, muscle tightness, or fluttering in your stomach.
4. Move. Go to the bathroom, grab a cup of coffee, take the dog for a walk, or unload the dishwasher.

I asked Judy to take three deep breaths and to move her body. I told her to walk around her office and look at her left foot, then her right foot, while repeating, "Left/right, left/right, left/right." This technique interrupted her thought loop and got her to focus.

As she calmed down, she was able to consider her options. Judy knew the challenge was real, but she and her husband had been through hard times before.

When things are bad, remember it won't always be this way.
So far, you've survived 100 percent of your worst days.

No Mouth Breathers, Please

Proper breathing technique is done through the nose, not the mouth.

A bad cold can clog your nose and force you to breathe through your mouth. Your sinus passages sting, your mouth is dry, and your throat hurts. It is a wonderful feeling when you are well enough to breathe deeply through your nose again. Keep taking deep breaths through your nose.

Watch your breathing. Notice if your chest or abdomen moves. Breathe into your abdomen, not your chest. You should see your belly rise and fall. This is your diaphragm working properly. Your diaphragm muscles pull your lungs down to allow them to expand and effectively circulate oxygen to the whole lung. Count to four on each inhalation and each exhalation. Do this for five to fifteen breaths.

Practice at stoplights, in the grocery line, before a meeting starts, and during commercials.

Attention on your breathing prevents health issues such as asthma, high blood pressure, and aches and pains.

Set a reminder to practice deep breathing through your nose.

Shallow Breathing Impacts Anxiety Sufferers

Chest pains, lightheadedness, weakness and tingling, and a rapid heartbeat are symptoms caused by a common anxiety problem—shallow breathing.

The sheets were knotted at the foot of her bed. Doreen took another quick glance at the clock: 3:42 a.m. A muscle twitched at the corner of her right eye. Her chest, still tight and painful. Her brain raced with jumbled thoughts.

Get up. At least you can prepare your presentation one more time, she thought.

All her preparations fled her mind as she frantically looked for her phone. Her chest tightened as she grabbed the corner of the dresser to steady herself. She couldn't see the phone next to her bed, where she always put it.

Shallow breathing is when you take small, short breaths. It is most commonly associated with panic attacks. It wreaks havoc on people with anxiety.

Anxiety causes shallow breathing because it activates your fight-or-flight system. It's how your brain is wired. When you sense danger, your heartbeat speeds up and you breathe faster in order to get more oxygen to fight or flee. Your body releases adrenaline and reacts as though you are in a fearful situation, even when you are not.

Notice when you are shallow breathing. Look for signs like tightness in your chest, dizziness, or a rapid heartbeat. Take very slow breaths. Breathe in, counting to five. Hold your breath for three seconds. Breathe out for six seconds. Do this five times.

Doreen sat on her yoga mat and turned on her Breathe2Relax app. Her body settled with each deep breath. Her chest released its relentless grip.

Notice the signs of shallow breathing.

Don't Let the Crabs Pull You Down

The Crab Effect describes what crabs do when they are in a pot. Individually, each one could climb out and escape. However, collectively they grab on to each other and all meet their demise.

When you are making changes in your life, other people may act like crabs and try to pull you back. This behavior is found in all segments of society.

"Don't change. You are fine the way you are. I had a friend who tried what you are doing and it turned out really bad. What's the big deal? You should be grateful." Each one of these statements is a claw that holds you back and demands that you not change.

Your success may make others uncomfortable. "If you change, what does it mean to me? Will I have to change? Will you leave me? If I'm suffering, you must suffer too."

Assemble a team of positive, supportive people around you. These are people who will help you move forward to achieve your goals. They want the best for you. Let go of the crabs that will pull you down.

Identify people who are ready and willing to cheer you on as you make the changes necessary to achieve your goals.

A Real Heroine on Her Journey

Misty Copeland became the first African American female principal ballerina of the American Ballet Theatre in 2015.

The heroine's journey is about a woman who finds the courage to save herself. Success is measured by her survival and increased self-reliance. The journey is internal and circular, repeating trials and obstacles until she changes and grows.

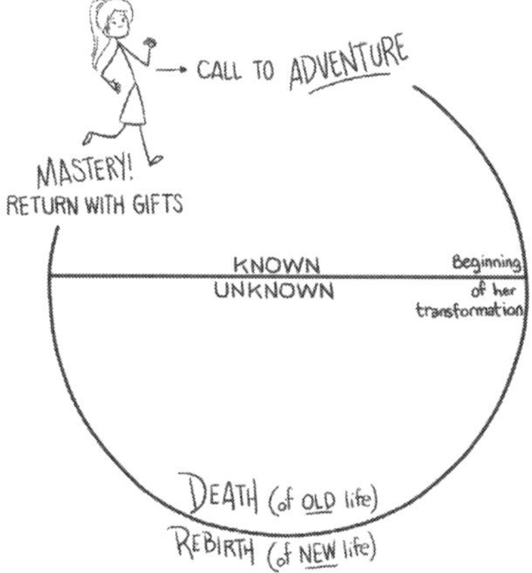

Misty's call to adventure was going into a sport where there were few African Americans. She knew she loved ballet. She did not know how the unknown path to mastery would turn out.

A 2015 documentary, *A Ballerina's Tale*, follows Misty Copeland's everyday ballet routine. The film is narrated by Misty as she describes the love she felt performing certain dances and the pain she endured through her various physical injuries. She discovered ballet when she was living in a run-down hotel room with her five siblings at the age of thirteen. Her muscular build and skin color did not match the other ballerinas. She faced constant racism. Her guides supported her to persevere. She returned with mastery as she was selected as the first African American principal ballerina of the American Ballet Theatre. She changed the face of ballet.

Misty answered her call to adventure.

Embrace the unknown and stay on your path.

It's OK to Have Needs

A tree needs air, water, and sunlight to grow and thrive. A dog needs food, water, and love. You have needs, too, that are beyond basic survival.

Coffee with Maddie always lifted Ginny's spirits. "How are you doing with the breakup?" Maddie asked.

Ginny shrugged. "It's OK. I'm good. I don't need a partner. It's more trouble than it's worth." After dating only a few months, her partner had broken up with her.

"This is the third relationship to end after a few months," said Maddie. "Do you see any similarities?"

"They all say I'm too needy."

"What are your feelings about that?"

Ginny sighed. "I'm sad and don't even know what my needs are."

"You do have needs," Maddie responded. "What are your rules about needs and needing?"

Ginny rattled off that she thought that having needs was selfish, other people's needs were more important, and it was a waste of time.

Write down the things and experiences in life that bring you the most joy. Look in your examples for needs such as acceptance, creativity, intellectual, safety, simplicity, harmony, control, independence, freedom, challenge, connection, accomplishment, or contribution.

Ginny accepted that she had needs for safety, play, and nurturing. She realized she kept unconsciously picking partners who were unable to meet these needs.

Pinpoint the limiting beliefs that block you from knowing your own needs.

Identify Your Needs

Needs are neither good nor bad. Only your judgment makes them so.

"You working late every night makes me feel unimportant. I need time with you. Don't you need this too?" Doug asked Shania.

Shania looked down as she shuffled her feet. She shoved her hands in her pockets and mumbled, "I don't know what I need." Shania's overworking fulfilled a subconscious need that she had and was not aware of. At the same time, she had other needs she had not identified.

Look for examples of things and experiences that bring you meaning, satisfaction, and joy. For example, work, relationships, or hobbies.

Ask yourself what emotions these experiences generate in you. For example, love, competence, security, control, positive emotions, being seen, being heard, validation, contentment, or excitement.

Identifying your needs will explain why you thought, felt, and acted the way that you did. It will also boost your motivation to change the way you are currently getting your needs met.

Shania journaled about a few experiences and discovered her need for connection and competence. She accepted Doug's invitation to play a round of golf and experienced her real needs getting met.

Get to know your personal needs and find meaning, satisfaction, and joy in your life.

OBSTACLES TO EFFECTIVE DECISION-MAKING–PART 1 OF 2

Fear and Fatigue

Fear and fatigue drive the train of unskillful decision-making.

Fear is the emotion caused by the belief that someone or something is dangerous, likely to cause pain. Fear drives decisions and sounds likes this: "Hurry up. You're behind. Other people already figured this out. You should know this by now."

Fatigue is a feeling of tiredness, which is distinct from weakness, and has a gradual onset. Unlike weakness, fatigue can be alleviated by periods of rest.

Fatigue in our society is actually rewarded and driven by the belief that sleep and rest are wasteful. The belief is to value only those things that are "productive and generate revenue."

What are the consequences?

- Overworking because of the constant thought and belief that you are behind and there is not enough in the world.
- Overfunctioning because "If I don't do it, nobody else will."
- Neglecting self-maintenance such as sleep, healthful eating, downtime, taking sick days.
- Not being present because you are thinking about the regrets of the past or the wreckage of your future.

If you are tired or afraid today, take time for self-care.

OBSTACLES TO EFFECTIVE DECISION-MAKING–PART 2 OF 2

Change Your Mental Framework

A mental framework is an explanation for how something works in the real world. It is the basis for your thoughts and actions. The framework is the story you tell yourself. All the stories you tell yourself are based on a bunch of hidden assumptions.

Read the following two descriptions of mental frameworks and identify which one resonates with you:

1. There is a finite amount in the world and I have to get my share now.
2. Because I believe in an abundant and friendly universe, I take time to exercise today.

These are two mental frameworks—*the story you tell yourself*—and they impact your decision-making. One will drive you relentlessly and the other will allow you to stay present and help you identify your fears about making the wrong decisions.

Here's a clue to help you identify your mental framework: when you have downtime, do you feel uncomfortable, not know what to do, or feel undeserving or selfish? This is an example of the first mental framework.

Changing your mental framework:

- Increases awareness of the thoughts and beliefs that drive your decisions
- Increases objectivity when looking at a problem
- Lowers the frequency of second-guessing your decisions
- Reduces harm to yourself and others
- Relieves pressure about making the "right" decision

Let your thoughts and actions spring from your new mental framework and see what happens.

Change the stories you tell yourself.

Resistance Is an Obstacle to Effective Decision-Making

A mental framework is an explanation for how something works in the real world. It is the basis for your thoughts and actions. It is the story you tell yourself.

We will use the following two mental frameworks to explain how resistance gets in the way of skillful decision-making:

1. There is a finite amount in the world and I have to get it now.
2. Because I believe in an abundant and friendly universe, I practice mindful success every day (get adequate sleep, exercise, eat healthfully), and I need never worry again.

These frameworks are two stories you tell yourself and they impact your decision-making, what you think of yourself, and your ease of being.

Let's say you have made a decision to choose framework #2.

When you begin practicing this new mental framework of believing in an abundant and friendly universe, you'll encounter resistance.

It sounds like this: "This is stupid. It's not for me. I've tried this and it doesn't work. What if I try it and fail? Nobody else is doing this. I'm sticking with what I already know. I may be unhappy, but at least I'm not uncertain."

This inner dialog is normal and to be expected. You are building new neural pathways in your brain. Your brain is wired to resist change, to gain pleasure and avoid pain. It sees change as a threat. It has a positive intention in avoiding change: to keep you safe. That's why all that chatter of "change back" happens.

Resistance blocks out the good reasons you are making this change.

1. Decide which mental framework are you going to choose today.
2. Notice your thoughts and reactions to practicing a mental framework of abundance.
3. When you encounter resistance, use a curiosity phrase: "Oh, isn't this interesting! I think I'm resisting using a different mental framework." This takes the judgment out of your learning.

Improve your decision-making by understanding that resistance to change is normal and to be expected. Accept that your brain blocks out the good reasons you are making changes in order to keep you "safe."

Resistance is a messenger. Listen to it.

Ask for Appreciation Feedback

Feedback is gathering information to help you move closer to your heart's desire.

Callie shrugged as she walked out of her boss's office. She gazed down and stumbled back to her chair, letting out a deep sigh. "He didn't even acknowledge that I completed the task ahead of schedule and helped win the deal."

Appreciation feedback conveys, "Thank you. I see you. I hear you. I know you've been working hard. You matter to me."

When your boss says how grateful she is to have you on the team, that's appreciation. Appreciation is fundamentally about relationship and human connection.

Being seen and feeling understood by others matters deeply. As children, these needs are right on the surface as we call across the playground, "Hey, Mom, watch this!" As adults, we never outgrow the need to hear someone say, "Awesome! Look at you!" or the need for acknowledgment that says, "Yes, I see you. I hear you. You matter to me."

Appreciation motivates us. It gives us energy to keep going. When people complain that they don't get enough feedback at work, they often mean that they wonder whether anyone notices or cares how hard they're working. They don't want advice. They want appreciation.

Ask these types of appreciation feedback questions:

- What was the one thing you liked about my approach?
- What are the key takeaways you received from me that helped you solve your problem?
- What are the three key characteristics you admire in me?

Callie decided to ask a friend for validation. She asked Dee, "What are three things you admire about me?" Doing this made her feel stupid and self-centered. Dee responded, "Do I have to limit it to three?"

Receive appreciation feedback and let it into your heart.

Record How You Spend Your Money to Gain Clarity and Confidence

"Graham is OK. He broke his leg playing baseball and had surgery. His recovery is going well." Melissa shared the details with her aunt Janice. "What's really bothering me is how I'm going to pay the medical bill of $1,850."

"Dip into the money I gave you for emergencies. That's what it's there for."

Melissa felt sick to her stomach. She paced the kitchen; her heart raced. "I spent that to pay our credit card bill." She felt her aunt's judgment and disappointment through the phone.

Vagueness and avoidance around money compounds your anxiety. Worry stops you from learning how to be responsible with it. Fear—of not knowing how to manage your money, lack of planning, and bad experiences in the past—is scary to face, but not insurmountable.

Fact: two-thirds of Americans would struggle to scrounge up $1,000 in an emergency, according to *The Associated Press*, NORC Center for Public Affairs Research.

Get clear about your spending. Write down every penny you spend and take in for thirty days. See where and how much money you spent. This is the first step toward financial literacy and saving for emergencies.

Be honest with yourself. Record what you spend every day to stop vagueness.

Send Love and Blessings

Kindness in words creates confidence. Kindness in thinking creates profoundness. Kindness in giving creates love.

—Lao Tzu

Matt clenched his hands. Through pursed lips, he yelled at Betsy, "Why did you say you're going to head up the project to our customer? You made me look stupid. What were you thinking? Do you know what I have to do to clean this up? I want you to think long and hard about how badly you screwed up this meeting."

Betsy's chest heaved up and down. Her eyes dampened and her stomach cramped. She locked the bathroom door behind her and cried. "How was I supposed to know? He never told me I couldn't say that." Shaken, she played the scene over and over.

Fear and anger trigger the body's fight-flight-freeze response. The adrenal glands flood the body with stress hormones, such as cortisol and adrenaline. One way to deal with fear and anger is to step away from the situation. Take a biology break. Nobody will stop you from going to the bathroom. This gives you time to regroup and pinpoint the exact reason you feel upset and identify options to remedy the situation.

To calm your mind, use the Loving-kindness Blessing. It changes your mindset and attitude to a positive one. It interrupts the angry and fearful thoughts.

May I be peaceful.

May I be happy.

May I be safe.

May I be free.

May I awaken to the light of my true nature.

Once you've said it for yourself, say it for the person with whom you are upset:

May you be peaceful.

May you be happy.

May you be safe.

May you be free.

May you awaken to the light of your true nature.

Betsy repeated in her mind, "May I be peaceful, may I be happy . . ." Her breathing slowed down. "May I be safe." She let out a long, deep sigh. "May I be free, may I awaken to the light of my true nature." A thought popped in her mind of her dog climbing into her lap and licking her face. A smile stretched across her face. She was able to think clearly.

Say a loving and kind statement for yourself and for others to interrupt fear and anger.

Breathe Deep and Relax

To effectively manage stress, you need to activate the body's natural relaxation response.

The relaxation response is a mentally active process that leaves the body calm and alert. This is done through focused, deep breathing. It increases the supply of oxygen to your brain and stimulates the parasympathetic nervous system. This system activates the more tranquil functions of the body to maintain long-term balance.

When you are annoyed or anxious, pause and take three deep breaths. Say and repeat the phrase, "Alert mind, calm body" to yourself. Imagine yourself smiling inwardly. It is a feeling and not obvious to anyone. This prevents the facial muscles from adopting negative expressions.

With practice, the relaxation response becomes an automatic skill used in stressful situations.

Repeat, "Alert mind, calm body" while breathing slowly.

Signs of Afterburn

Afterburn is when you do something that is good for you—a new behavior, ending a relationship that has served its purpose, or stepping out of your comfort zone in some way.

Then you feel icky and your inner critic says, "Change back. You shouldn't have done that."

The following responses are normal and to be expected:

- You may experience afterburn when taking a positive action toward your heart's desire.
- You may feel unsure how to act or feel disoriented while you are assimilating new experiences. It's like the analogy of peeling the layers of an onion: you may shed a few tears and feel off.
- You may feel worse before you feel better. This is normal.
- It feels like you want to crawl out of your skin. Keep in mind that feeling uncomfortable will not be a permanent state. Remind yourself it is temporary and will pass.

Afterburn is a sign you are changing.

Call a friend when you are experiencing afterburn and say, "I'm in afterburn. I did something good for myself and now I want to take it back." It interrupts the thought loop and eases the discomfort.

Don't Try So Hard

The Taoist phrase *Wu Wei* means non-action or non-doing.

Wu Wei means to accept and go with the flow. When you live according to Wu Wei, you don't need to "have to" anymore.

Wu Wei is about connecting with your inner strength, with what makes you happy. It's not about things. It's about experiences—with yourself, with nature, with others.

Rachel wanted to learn how to write songs. She went online and researched options. She found formal, structured classes like the Berkeley School of Music. She preferred to work one-on-one with a tutor. She found another website that matched students with instructors. After searching for someone in her area, she came up empty-handed. She continued to search, yet didn't find anyone who offered what she wanted.

Wu Wei is like a dance. You're being led and asked to follow along gracefully. Sometimes the dance is fast and sometimes it's slow. Sometimes you move backwards, sometime forwards. Sometimes you have to take a break and get a sip of water.

Wu Wei is listening and following what you hear in your heart, without needing to know what it means. You will want the answer to why before you start. Let go. Afterwards you'll learn about the why.

Rachel decided to practice Wu Wei. "I don't have to make it happen. If it's meant to, it will." During one of her daily meditation sessions, she heard, "Go online and search song writing, Sedona, Arizona." Sedona? She knew there were well-known song-writing places like Los Angeles, New York City, and Nashville. She put it in the search engine. A name came up: Sandy, a published songwriter, musician, performer, and tutor. They've been working together weekly and Rachel is well on her way to writing songs.

Don't second-guess your impulses. Trust them.

We All Need Moms

Nurturing is a way to be fed and protected, supported and encouraged. It fills your tanks.

"Do you have a 'third place'?" Julie questioned Kelly and Joy.

"What's that?" Kelly asked.

"You have your home—that's your first place. You have work or community—that's your second place. Your third place is where you go for nurturing. I go to my cousin's house for a weekend. I can be myself and let my hair down. She cooks great meals. We hang out and talk, and sleep, and watch Netflix."

Kelly turned to Joy. "Being here with you is my third place. It's quiet and safe, you make great meals, the bedroom is a sleep chamber, and I decompress."

A third place is a retreat. It's a place where you get nurtured, you are safe, you are with the right people. You can just *be*. Let your inner child out. Rejuvenate.

Your third place can be a location like a friend's home or weekend at the beach. It can be a massage, meditation, or time on the couch reading a book.

Identify what nurtures you.

Joy identified her third place. "I go to see Bev Natang. She does craniosacral massage. She spends two hours with me, and I am the most important person to her. She is completely present. She listens to me. She nurtures me like a mom. It reminds me of times when I was sick as a child. Mom would bring me soup, aspirin, and an extra blanket. She tucked me in and said, 'I'm here to take great care of you. Rest.'"

Allow "moms" in your life to deeply nurture you.

Don't Drink Poison and Wait for the Other Person to Die

Resentments held over time become habitual thought patterns that harm you.

Holding grudges and resentments indicates you have a desire to hurt the people who hurt you. It's like the boy who was sitting on a park bench squirming in pain. A woman walked up to him and asked what was wrong.

The boy answered, "I'm sitting on a bumble bee."

"Why don't you get up?" she questioned.

The boy replied, "Because I'm hurting him more than he is hurting me."

Minimize resentments by clarifying what the person meant by their comment or action. Assumptions are often made, but not checked for accuracy. Don't label something as fact in your mind until you have verified it. If you experience a perceived slight, check for understanding. Say, "I heard you say X. Did I understand this correctly?" Check to see if somebody is having an off day. Maybe they lack people skills—or they are sitting on their own bumble bee.

Stop recycling thoughts that cause psychic stress.

If She Can Do It, You Can Do It Too

Julia Ward Howe was an American author and poet. She wrote *The Battle Hymn of the Republic* after visiting Washington, DC, and meeting President Lincoln at the White House in 1861.

She wrote the original Mother's Day Proclamation in 1870, as a protest to the carnage of the American Civil War, for women who had lost their sons. It asked women of the world to join for world peace:

Arise, then, women of this day! Arise all women who have hearts, whether our baptism be that of water or of fears!

Say firmly: "We will not have great questions decided by irrelevant agencies. Our husbands shall not come to us, reeking with carnage, for caresses and applause. Our sons shall not be taken from us to unlearn all that we have been able to teach them of charity, mercy, and patience.

We women of one country will be too tender of those of another country to allow our sons to be trained to injure theirs. From the bosom of the devastated earth a voice goes up with our own. It says "Disarm, Disarm! The sword of murder is not the balance of justice."

Blood does not wipe our dishonor, nor violence indicate possession. As men have often forsaken the plow and the anvil at the summons of war, let women now leave all that may be left of home for a great and earnest day of counsel. Let them meet first, as women, to bewail and commemorate the dead. Let them then solemnly take counsel with each other as to the means whereby the great human family can live in peace, each bearing after their own time the sacred impress, not of Caesar, but of God.

In the name of womanhood and of humanity, I earnestly ask that a general congress of women without limit of nationality may be appointed and held at some place deemed most convenient and at the earliest period consistent with its objects, to promote the alliance of the different nationalities, the amicable settlement of international questions, the great and general interests of peace.

Decide one action you will take to make your world more peace-filled.

Rituals Support Focused Attention

Mental focus allows you be more productive and successful.

Sidney Crosby is a Canadian hockey player and captain of the Pittsburgh Penguins. During his first year, he set multiple records, received the Most Valuable Player award, and led his team to win the Stanley Cup.

Before each game, he performs the same ritual. He avoids walking by the other team's locker room, eats a peanut butter and jelly sandwich, prepares his sticks, and hangs out with the team. Crosby believes this system allows him to be at his best on the ice physically and mentally.

Create a ritual to enter and exit focused blocks of time. Light a candle when you start and blow it out when you stop. Control distractions and interruptions. Put an auto-responder on your email that says you are unavailable until a specific time. Silence your phone and turn off your email. Start with small blocks of time and build up.

Pay attention on purpose, nonjudgmentally, to the present moment.

Maintain control over your attention.

You Are Magnificent!

Do you believe you are magnificent—without any qualifiers? A qualifier goes like this: "I'll be magnificent when I get that bonus, lose weight, or clean out my closet."

Does it feel like bragging if you tell yourself you're magnificent? It's not, but it may feel like it is. Many of us were taught to put ourselves last and, as a consequence, we attract feelings of being unworthy and undeserving.

Are you willing to change the concept of yourself? This means to be willing to change what you believe to be true.

Here are a few ways to change the mental framework (qualifiers) about yourself:

- Give yourself an A+ today in every area of your life. Does this feel uncomfortable? It may, because you have a mental framework that you believe you have to *earn* the A+. Doing this experiment is one way of relaxing into yourself. When was the last time you gave yourself a break?
- Track your successes—all of them. I have one client who puts her successes on green sticky notes (the color of life) and pins them on a cork board. At the end of the week, she is delighted to see how magnificent she is. She moves them to a journal and starts the process over again the following week. A success can be saying no instead of yes, asking for help, speaking up, asking for a raise, or giving tough feedback.

What do you have to lose? Maybe some misery, self-loathing, and irritability! What do you have to gain? Self-assurance, confidence, and breathing room!

Act as if you believe you are magnificent.

Multitasking Lengthens Your Day

Doing more than one thing at a time slows you down and causes you to make more mistakes.

Emilia raced out of her last meeting. If the traffic gods were with her, she would make it to her son's soccer game on time. She called her mom on the way. "I know I haven't called you back. Work has been crazy and the kids have activities almost every night." She munched on popcorn as she replayed the last meeting over and over in her head.

"Emilia? Emilia? Did you hear what I said?" her mom shouted.

"You jerk, you almost hit me!" Emilia barked as she swerved to miss another car. Her popcorn toppled over and peppered the passenger floor.

Research shows that people doing two tasks simultaneously take up to 30 percent longer and make twice as many errors as those who completed the same tasks in sequence. Research also shows that when employees are interrupted by email, it takes them fifteen minutes to fully regain their train of thought.

Batch your tasks—such as email or calls—so you reduce the constant switching from one mindset to another. Decide on the best times of day to do each batch of tasks. Remove distractions such as email and phone alerts.

As she cleaned up the popcorn from her car floor, Emilia decided to put her phone on "do not disturb while driving" mode.

Single-task to get ahead.

Sometimes the Hardest Part of the Journey Is Believing You Are Worthy of the Trip

Beliefs are mental constructs and only as true as the investment you place in them. Your beliefs are malleable and formed from consciousness.

Here are ten common self-defeating beliefs to become aware of and reject:

1. Emotional perfectionism: I should always feel happy, confident, and in control of my emotions.
2. Performance perfectionism: I must never fail or make a mistake.
3. Perceived perfectionism: People will not love and accept me as a flawed and vulnerable human being.
4. Fear of disapproval or criticism: I need everybody's approval to be worthwhile.
5. Fear of rejection: If I'm not loved, then life is not worth living.
6. Fear of being alone: If I'm alone, then I'm bound to feel miserable and unfulfilled.
7. Fear of failure: My worthwhileness depends on my achievements (or my intelligence or status or attractiveness).
8. Conflict phobia: People who love each other shouldn't fight.
9. Emotophobia: I should not feel angry, anxious, inadequate, jealous, or vulnerable.
10. Entitlement: People should always be the way I expect them to be.

(Based on the work of Aaron T. Beck, MD, Father of Cognitive Therapy)

When a limiting belief comes to mind, ask yourself, "This belief is real, but is it true?"

Believe you can and you're halfway there.

Feel Comfortable in Your Own Skin

Most women are waging war on their bodies and the food they eat. You never have a moment free from fretting about it and the thought of going for a swim—and putting on a bathing suit—causes panic.

Self-judgment results from thoughts you have about yourself and the meaning you give to those thoughts. You attach judgments to the way you look, the number on the scale, and what others think of you.

Stop assigning meaning to self-judgments because once you give them weight, they weigh you down. The goal is to render negative self-judgments as neutral.

Identify the limiting beliefs you have about your body and weight. "I don't deserve to eat unless I'm thin." "Thin people are happier." "I'm weak because I can't lose weight."

Change your limiting beliefs to empowering beliefs. "Successful women take time to nourish their bodies by eating a healthy breakfast, and I'm a successful woman." "I deserve to eat healthful, nourishing food." "Moving my body feels good." "Successful women make exercise a priority, and I'm a successful woman."

Alter the quality of your beliefs so they support your sense of well-being.

FACE THE FEAR

Day 1 of 3: Fear of Losing Safety and Control

Everyone has the same three fears: losing safety and control, abandonment and disconnection, and unworthiness. Accept this part of yourself and learn to work with it.

"When are you going to put that phone down?" Jim screamed. "We are at the frigging Grand Canyon."

"Just one more text." Rose's thumbs were a blur.

"Why do I even bother going on vacation with you? You never leave work at work." He barreled through the crowd of tourists.

Fear of losing safety and control is part of your old brain, the limbic system. It is wired to trigger at the first sign of danger or insecurity, pain or discomfort. You control to feel safe, and everyone wants to feel safe.

Fear is behind the limiting belief to value only those things that are "productive and revenue-generating." It drives the constant sense of urgency: "It has to be done now and by me." Relationships with yourself and others suffer.

The first step to deal with fear is to acknowledge it. When fear comes up, invite it in. "Here it is again. I wonder how it will be this time?" Set a timer for fifteen minutes to quiet the inner critic that barks, "If you feel this fear, it will never stop."

Rose stared at her husband's back. Her eyes stung. Trembling, she knew it was time to face her fear or lose her marriage.

Cultivate intimacy—Into-Me-See—with yourself. It comes when you acknowledge and feel the uncomfortable feelings of anxiety and fear.

FACE THE FEAR

Day 2 of 3: Fear of Abandonment and Disconnection

Fear of aloneness drives unskillful behaviors like getting into relationships, having affairs, busyness, and over-responsibility.

Marci convinced herself she had time to take one more call. "It's mid-morning, so traffic will be light." On the way out of the office, she ran into Barbara, who asked for "just a second." Marci caught the last five minutes of her son's Mother's Day Celebration at preschool. Her breath caught as her eyes met her husband's glare.

"The client kept yelling at me on the phone. Then I got stuck in traffic!" Marci struggled to keep up with her husband, Ted, and son, Devon. "Devon and I are going out for lunch," Ted snapped. "Go back to work."

The first step in dealing with fear is to acknowledge it. Feeling your emotions will not hurt you, but avoiding them does.

Marci watched her husband and son drive away. Slumped over the steering wheel, ragged, grasping wails filled the car. Tears and snot covered the horn until no more tears came.

Welcome your courage to face your fear.

FACE THE FEAR

Day 3 of 3: Fear of Unworthiness

The belief in unworthiness drives you to sacrifice your health and well-being.

"Mommy, you work too much," Anna whined.

"I'm sorry, honey. Mommy needs to work really hard right now."

"That's what you always say." Anna skipped into the den to play with her sister.

Beverly's face flushed as she unpacked her daughter's backpack. Blood pooled in her stomach and a tinny taste flooded her mouth. She stared at her daughter's school picture. Her toothy grin, chocolate specks in the corner of her mouth, her hair a matted nest, because Beverly wasn't home to brush it that day. She was at work.

She overworked out of an unconscious fear of not being good enough. She constantly measured and monitored herself. "Did I do more today than yesterday?"

This fear comes out in many forms—not good enough, thin enough, smart enough. It drives you to overfunction and neglect self-maintenance activities.

The first step to deal with fear is to acknowledge it. Notice how different areas of your body feel. You don't have to figure anything out, just be aware. The more you sit with these feelings and allow them to pass through you, the more you experience true connection and the ability to accept love.

Beverly turned her phone on airplane mode and joined her daughters in the den. After putting them to bed, she snuggled under a blanket, said a prayer, and sobbed. She experienced her first good night's sleep in months.

Change how you think about work and worth.

Emotional Incontinence Has Nothing to Do with Bodily Functions

I watched a lot of cartoons growing up. One of my favorite characters was the Tasmanian Devil. He was shown as ferocious, notoriously short-tempered, and impatient. He spun like a vortex, biting through everything, while making only grunting and growling sounds.

For people, out-of-control emotional output leaves others upset and disoriented. Their emotions create toxic environments. Emotions are sticky, and they can be contagious.

To inoculate yourself from "catching" others' emotions:

1. Check to see if you are feeding into the negativity.
2. Pay attention to your feelings in different settings and when you're with different people and groups.
3. List the people or groups that bring you down, drain your energy, or make you feel off.
4. Look for clues:
    - Do you tense up every time you go to your aunt's house?
    - Do you start out your day happy and, once at work, your mood changes to sadness, anger, or frustration?
5. Distance yourself from these people as much as possible.
6. Tell the person the negative impact they have on you.
7. If you can't change the circumstances, practice self-care: adequate sleep, nutrition, exercise, and lots of self-love.

Emotions are contagious. Hang out with others who are happy, resilient, and aware. And let the whirling dervishes whirl.

The Core of Stability Is the Acceptance of Instability, of Change

Yes, living life comes with many responsibilities. Staying busy all the time can be a way of controlling, to avoid the feelings of loss, misfortune, and pain.

Warren Buffet is one of the most successful investors of all time. He is the fourth wealthiest person in the world, with a net worth of $86.3 billion. His approach to picking stocks is straightforward. He picks companies that are undervalued by the market, confirms that the company is a quality one, and is capable of generating earnings. He buys the stocks and lets go of control. He does not look at them every day or every week. He waits a few years. His company's most recent annual revenue was $223.6 billion.

If he can let go of control, so can you.

When you are overly busy, you feel like you are just keeping up, that you can't take a break or slow down. You regularly feel overwhelmed and exhausted. You may ask yourself, "What is the point of all this?" Busyness is not a badge of honor, an identity, or proof of your worthiness.

Acceptance, not busyness, brings you to a peace-filled place.

Make a decision that you want to change the distractions of busyness to experience a more meaningful life. Make space for the feelings you avoid when you are too busy. Make a list of what matters most to you—your health, family, work—and eliminate everything else for a month.

Ask yourself, "Do I want to be busy or do I want to be at peace?"

Accept what you do not have control over and enjoy your life more.

Ask the Right Questions

The Why/What If/How question model is a process that helps grow your curiosity.

Most people skip the *Why* and *What If* and go straight to *How* because you are not rewarded for questioning. Start with *why* to gain context and framing.

Ask *why*. "I wonder why _______________ is happening."

A person encounters a situation that is less than ideal and asks why. Example: "I wonder why I'm so hard on myself?"

Ask *what if*. Linger in the question. Connective inquiry is when you connect exiting ideas in unusual and interesting ways. The more creative, the better.

A person who asks why after encountering a less-than-ideal situation comes up with ideas for possible solutions.

Example: "What if I believed I had a fairy godmother who sprinkled kindness dust on me that made me love myself?"

Ask *how*. After asking why, a person who encounters a less-than ideal situation takes one of the possibilities and tries to implements it or make it real.

"I wonder *why* I am more comfortable being hard on myself than self-compassionate?"

What if I declared this month, "Be Kind to Me Month"?

How to implement Be Kind to Me Month: list ten ways to be kind to myself.

Use this curiosity statement: "Today I will be kind to myself by not worrying about anything. If I do worry, I will ask myself, 'I wonder why I'm worrying about my kids, business, body,' and be wildly curious."

A Bad Case of Stripes

David Shannon wrote the children's book *A Bad Case of Stripes*. The story is about a girl named Camilla Cream. She loves lima beans, but never eats them because the kids at her school don't like them. She worries about how to fit in, so much so that she breaks out in a bad case of rainbow stripes.

Camilla realizes she has to be true to herself and her own desires. She eats a handful of lima beans and the stripes disappear.

Adults also get a bad case of stripes. You may desire to change careers, or get out of a relationship, or sell your artwork. Vulnerability, uncertainty, fear, and discomfort come up. "What if I do this and end up worse off?" Rainbow stripes appear. You go along to get along. "It's silly to want to learn how to sing at my age." "My art isn't that good."

To be comfortable in your own skin, start small. Research singing coaches in your area. Tell a friend you want to sell your art. Look online for job opportunities. Write your heart's desires in a journal.

Question anything that causes you to change who you are just to fit in.

Improve Your Problem-Solving Skills with Mind Mapping

Mind mapping is a technique used to outline information visually. You create a diagram drawn around a single word. Then you add associated words, ideas, and concepts. Your "map" helps you make connections and see patterns. Mind maps are flexible, easy to create, and clear. They enable a free flow of ideas that help you solve problems faster and easier.

Mind mapping helps you organize information, clarify ideas, and solve problems. This makes it an ideal tool for brainstorming, thinking visually, and studying more efficiently.

Follow these steps to create your mind map:

1. Begin in the middle of the page by writing or drawing a central word or image, using three or more colors.
2. Use images, symbols, codes, and dimensions to represent other ideas.
3. Use many different sizes of words, images, and lines.
4. Use arrows to make connections between words and images.
5. Use only one key word per line.
6. Connect the lines, starting from the central image or word. Make the central lines thick, then thinner as they radiate outward.
7. Print all words.
8. Make the line length equal to the word length.
9. Develop your own style of mind mapping.

Mind mapping uses more of your brain because it adds visual patterns, color, images, and dimensions—thus stretching your ability to associate ideas. You experience:

- Better thinking and perceptual abilities
- Increased creativity and confidence
- Better notes; you'll find it easier to summarize someone else's thoughts and organize your own thoughts

- Time savings because you are noting only key words, saving more than 90 percent of the time you would spend with traditional note-taking.
- Improved memory: you will remember more easily because there is a clear association between words.

Play with mind maps. Solve a problem.

You've Got a Friend in Me

Songs touch you emotionally and can transport you to another place and time.

I feel shivers whenever I hear the song, "You've Got a Friend in Me," by Randy Newman. It's from the soundtrack for *Toy Story*, the animated film about a boy who loves his cowboy doll Woody.

It takes me back to 1998. Every morning I drove my son Stevie to preschool. We listened to the *Toy Story* soundtrack. I'd peek in my rear-view mirror and watch him sing along. Strapped in his car seat, his tiny hand clutched the toy he named Big Guy. The smell of syrup filled the car.

With one hand on the steering wheel, I'd wipe my tears. My heart ached with joy, gratitude, and vulnerability of how much I loved him.

Listen to your favorite song and allow it to take you to a special place in your heart.

Songs are more than a collection of sounds interspersed by silence. They are a regulating force on your moods. They wake you up, calm you down, and motivate you.

Embrace your uniquely human capacity to feel emotion through music.

Emotions Connect Us to Each Other

Emotional intelligence refers to a person's ability to accurately perceive emotions, comprehend information related to those emotions, and an ability to effectively manage them.

There is a global deficit in understanding and managing emotions. According to Talent Smart, the administrator of the emotional intelligence assessment (EQI 2.0), only 36 percent of the people who took the assessment were able to accurately identify their emotions as they happen. The impact of this deficit is seen in the workplace, relationships, and within yourself.

You are also wired to be socially connected. According to Matthew Lieberman, professor of psychology at UCLA, "Being social connects our brain's lifelong passion. It's been baked into our operating system for tens of millions of years." In his book, *Social*, he explains the need to interact through social media, phones, and TV. The need to becoming more socially connected is an essential part of our survival.

To improve your emotional survival and increase your biological need for connection, be aware of all your emotions—both negative and positive. Start with the five basic emotions: mad, sad, happy, anger, and fear. Identify what people, places, things, and events triggers these emotions. Keep a journal and look for patterns.

Expand your need for social connection through the acknowledgment and acceptance of your own emotions.

With more than 3,000 words for feelings in English, start with learning the foundational five.

Say "Oops" When You Make a Mistake

The only real mistake is the one from which we learn nothing.
—John Powell, author

So often we beat ourselves up when we make a mistake. A gentler approach is to say, "Oops!"

Patricia is a real estate agent. The spring season keeps her busy from the time she gets up until she goes to bed. She is a successful and caring realtor. One morning she poured coffee and sat down to catch up on her email. The blood drained from her face. A deep panic grabbed at her heart. Her hands shook. She read an email that showed the documents her client was to sign in order to sell the house didn't go through. It was supposed to be signed the night before to ratify the contract. Patricia had gone to bed the night before thinking it had been completed.

Mistakes happen. Sometimes technology gremlins eat documents or appointments mysteriously disappear from our calendars. Other times we miss the mark.

Recognize when you make a mistake and think, "I am a mistake" instead of "I made a mistake." Interrupt the first thought by saying, "Oops." It takes the judgment away and makes the mistake right-sized.

"Oops," Patricia said. "Oops, oops, oops! Now, how do I fix this?" Without judgment, Patricia was able to call the buyer agent and get the deal back on track. This technique is one of her best tools to fix the volume of mistakes that happen during the spring housing market.

Treat mistakes nonjudgmentally and with humor.

Control is a Response to Fear

Whatever you try to control has control over you and your life.

Control is an illusion that comes in many forms: meddle, monitor, fret, ruminate, advise, fix, and the sense that it's all on you.

Daniella woke up with a knot in her stomach. Her mind raced from one family member to the next. "What do they need? Are they going to be OK today? How do I help them? What if Andrew forgets to fill the gas tank? I'll go do it. I don't want him to run out on the drive to school. My husband has a big day at the office. I have to be sure he doesn't forget anything that might cause problems later. I want to make sure everyone is safe. I can prevent a lot of mishaps. Gosh, I'm exhausted."

Determine if your helping is effectively changing anything for the better. Daniella asked her husband several questions and gave him suggestions on what he needed to do before he left for work. Doing so, her husband may end up angry or annoyed at her intrusion.

Implement a No Advice Day. When you want to say, "Have you ever tried . . . ?" or "I know someone who can help you with . . ." or "Here is a book I thought might help you with . . .," stop. Replace it with, "Tell me more." "Interesting." "I know you can figure it out."

Daniella accepted the fact that she controlled her family members as a way to feel safe. She sought counseling to help her deal with her underlying fears.

You do not have to plan and control everything.

CHANGE AND TRANSITIONS

Manage Transitions to Successful Change

The key to successful change at work is to think through who will have to let go of what when the change occurs. Change involves transitions. Unless transition occurs, change will not happen.

Change is situational. It involves new processes or products, a new boss, or a new team member. It is external and focused on the outcome.

Transition is the psychological process people go through to accept the new situation. It is internal. It involves letting go of the old reality and the old identity they had before the change took place.

Transition starts with an ending. Think of starting a new job. You have to let go of your old peer group, commute, favorite lunch place, or current competency level. Even when making positive changes, transitions involve letting go and a sense of loss. For example, moving your office to a new building can be experienced as a loss.

The failure to identify and be ready for the endings and losses that accompany change is the largest single problem that organizations in transition encounter.

Follow three steps to increase successful change:

1. List exactly how employees' behaviors and attitudes will have to change.

   Consider the consolidation of two teams into one. It is not enough to say, "Work together as one team." Be clear and direct in describing how teamwork looks now, using behavioral and attitudinal examples. Define what individuals must stop and start doing.

   Let's say the change is that Monday staff meetings held in person will be virtual meetings on Friday mornings.

2. Determine who will lose something with this change.

   The group that always had virtual meetings loses nothing. The group that enjoyed their Monday face-to-face meetings is losing a type of connection that is important to them.

3. Sell the problem that is the reason for the change.

   Communicate the problem from your perspective to the group that enjoys the Monday staff meetings.

Identify what employees will have to let go of in order to make organizational change successful.

Change and Loss Go Hand in Hand

The key to successful change at work is thinking through who will have to let go of what when the change occurs.

A company decided to change its leave policy. It made sense to go from their separate sick, holiday, and annual leave policy to one paid-time-off policy. It would reduce costs and save administrative time. Jack, the Director of Operations, identified that employees accruing time off at different levels was ineffective and costly. Now he needed to figure out:

1. What specific loss was happening to everyone?

   Maybe the company was growing and the loss was about "the good old days" when employees were in one office and helping with several different functions. Or it could be the unspoken assumption that things will always be the same for those employees who have been with the company a long time. It may seem to be a threat to the company's values, vision, or mission.

2. Who is going to have to let go of what?

   He needed to dig into the specific behavior and attitude changes for everyone.

3. Expect resistance to the losses and endings employees will experience. This is normal and to be expected.

   Jack listened to his employees. He did not minimize their losses by arguing with them. He acknowledged people's feelings with statements like, "I hear you." "I'm sorry that we're having to make this policy change. It does affect everyone."

4. Deal directly with the losses openly. Do not sugarcoat it in any way.

   Jack talked about the loss despite his own personal discomfort. He was prepared for people to overreact. He realized that employees do not have much experience with openly experiencing the stages of transition.

Teach employees how walk through transitions so the next change will be easier.

As a leader, acknowledge loss openly, sympathetically, and understand and expect others to exhibit signs of grieving: anger, bargaining, anxiety, sadness, disorientation, depression, and acceptance.

Take Something Away, Give Something Back

When loss occurs in transitions at work, look for ways to compensate for them. This principle is important to plan for if change is to be successful. Remember, you are managing people's loss and leading them to the other side, to acceptance and commitment to the change.

People go through stages of grief at varying degrees. By thinking of all the ways you can "give back," you can help them move faster through these stages:

1. Shock and denial—avoidance, confusion, fear, numbness, blame
2. Anger—frustration, anxiety, irritation, embarrassment, shame
3. Depression and detachment—overwhelmed, feeling blah, lack of energy
4. Dialog and bargaining—reaching out to others, desire to tell one's story, struggle to find meaning in what has happened
5. Acceptance—exploring options, a new plan
6. Return to meaningful life—empowerment, security, self-esteem, meaning

Identify options to give back to balance the "loss" associated with the change. If people are losing responsibilities, add them to a training task force that relies on their technical expertise to move everyone through the transition. If it has to do with losing recognition, host a one-time employee recognition event that highlights their contributions. Acknowledge that their work is allowing for the next group to excel, standing on their shoulders and showing appreciation for this foundational work. Without their contributions, the company would not be in a position to grow. If people experience a sense of loss around knowledge, skills, and abilities, provide just-in-time and just-enough training for them to experience immediate learning successes.

Successful leaders plan for ways to give back to employees when they make changes that feel like a loss.

Plan for successful change by compensating for perceived losses.

Be Practical. Go Out and Play

The opposite of play is not work; it's depression.

—Brian Sutton-Smith, Play Theorist

Having unstructured time to do spontaneous, non-results-focused activities decreases stress and anxiety.

Recently I went to the Smithsonian National Museum of Natural History with my friend Elizabeth. We saw the movie *National Parks Adventure* in 3D. We went on a Thursday morning. Elizabeth and I have play dates about once a month. We plan them. We look weeks ahead and put them on the calendar. We make them happen. Sometimes we have to reschedule, but mostly we make them happen. Our approach is a combination of playing hooky from responsibilities and a field trip. It brings us feelings of being joyful, mischievous, and curious.

Play is a process that is fun and pleasurable. If the word "play" bothers you, try "unstructured time."

Why don't we make time for play or have unstructured time to explore our world, like we did when we were kids?

You may think:

- It's unproductive
- You're too busy
- It's unnecessary
- It's a distraction from your responsibilities

What are the benefits of unstructured time?

- Builds relationships
- Connects disparate ideas to generate new ones
- Integrates new information
- Re-energizes our strategic thinking
- Improves our problem-solving skills
- Releases tension, reduces stress, and promotes joy

In other words—it's practical!

Identify one activity that brings you joy and schedule a block of time to do it.

All Work and No Play Makes Jane a Dull Woman

Play is an essential source of relaxation and stimulation. It relieves stress, boosts creativity, and keeps you feeling energetic.

How to play:

1. Pick activities that excite you. Read, run, learn pickleball, binge watch a TV series.
2. Play doesn't have a particular purpose. This can be a challenge. Most of us are driven to produce results. Start small and build up. Color one page in an adult coloring book. Download an audio book and listen to it for one hour on a Saturday afternoon.
3. Dance, jump, or skip. It is a spontaneous desire to get out of gravity. Get a lemon twist and have fun while skipping.
4. Be with other people. Social play could be a Zumba class with a friend, paint night, or a baseball or hockey game.
5. Join a community activity that brings you joy—soccer, yoga, knitting, wood-working.

Play benefits the brain in several ways. Just like sleep and dreams, play or unstructured time has major biological functions and provides huge benefits:

- Generates a lot of impulses in the frontal lobe—the executive functioning part of our brain
- Helps contextual memory develop
- Establishes the basis of human trust through play signals

Successful women build unstructured time into their week to relax and be spontaneous.

Build your brain through one play activity today.

The Universe Has Your Back

Janice is a super achiever. She loves to accomplish lots of tasks and feels happy when her to-do list is complete. This drove her to ignore self-maintenance responsibilities, such as adequate sleep, healthful meals, and regular exercise. Her anxiety increased, and she was more irritable.

She asked me to help her achieve a better work/life balance. She knew how to work, but found herself at a loss for balancing it with friends, health, and family.

"What if you pretend that the Universe has your back today? What would you do differently?" I asked.

"I'd sleep in." Janice knew she was fatigued and needed more sleep. She started with small steps: sleeping in for fifteen minutes for a week and taking one nap on the weekend.

She found it uncomfortable to do this. Her habit of driving herself took time to change. This is why *start small and build up* is key to successful habit building.

Each day she repeated, "I believe the Universe has my back, so I can sleep fifteen more minutes." After two weeks, her anxiety and irritability eased up. She experienced pressure relief. Her self-trust increased, and she embraced the discomfort of change in order to have a more balanced life.

Act as if you believe the Universe has your back today.

Do You Want to Be Right or Do You Want to Be Happy?

"If everybody agreed with me, they'd all be right!"

Nadine's thoughts came quickly, one after another after another. She leaned onto the table as her words tumbled out, rapid-fire. "You know I've done event planning for twenty-five years. Your choice to take the conference to a new venue at that time of year is going to make your attendance numbers drop through the floor." Her voice got louder as she continued shooting facts at them.

The board decided to go with their choice and not Nadine's.

"Why don't they listen to me? I have twenty-five years' experience managing this annual conference. I know how to fill the hotel. I know what the attendees want. This new board won't listen to me." She racked her brain. "Maybe if I present numbers from the last three conferences, or share statistics of how bad choosing that time of year for a conference is, or say it nicer/meaner/in writing."

Her brain raced as the board continued with their meeting. She missed the nonverbal cues from them to let it go, because she was busy trying to convince them she was right. She was not happy. She didn't know another way of looking at or thinking about the situation.

At what point do you decide you've done all that you can and choose to be happy?

Change the way you look at situations from black-and-white thinking to shades of gray. A gray perspective eliminates the winner/loser, gain/loss thinking. It gives you a moment to pause.

Take these steps:

- Acknowledge to yourself that you are right.
- Understand that you judge people and situations to feel in control and as a way to feel safe. Everyone wants to feel safe.
- Identify the ways that being right keeps you safe. "They won't be able to fire me, or yell at me, or hurt me."
- Say the following phrase first in your head, then out loud: "You may be right." You are not agreeing with them. You are acknowledging gray.

- Identify three shades-of-gray options. "They may be right or there is another possibility here that I'm not seeing. I'm going to get curious and list three other options."

Nadine took three deep breaths. This settled her down. She smiled and made eye contact with each board member. She decided to be happy.

Choose happiness. It is a skill to learn and a habit to form.

Get in the Flow of Life

Eric Butterworth was a minister, radio personality, and best-selling author of sixteen books. He was a prominent leader in the Unity and New Thought movement. He focused on the divinity of all people and dedicated his life to helping people help themselves. Oprah Winfrey praised his books and Dr. Maya Angelou referred to him as her teacher.

In his book, *In the Flow of Life*, he describes a technique to get into the flow of life. Before you get out of bed in the morning, get your thoughts consciously on the right side. Affirm the following: "I am in the flow of life, and I move easily with the flow. I am radiantly and enthusiastically alive. I am free from tension, stress, and strain, and I go forward in the flow of life—unhurried and unworried."

Make the decision to approach each day from this position. When you feel stressed or anxious, repeat the affirmation. Take three deep breaths. Maintain your right consciousness. A shorter version of it is, "Fundamentally, I am in the flow of life; I am wonderful."

Live life from within.

Act in Your Best Interests, Even When It Feels Wrong or Uncomfortable

Jessica is a successful CEO. She came to me to help her gain balance between her work and family life. She loved her work and yet struggled with turning it off when she was at home. As a leader, she knew the importance of having time to think, not do. Her belief was that spending time thinking was not productive, that she was neglecting her responsibilities, and slacking off. She believed in the results-by-volume approach to work.

Another group of CEOs invited Jessica to attend an offsite meeting to think and strategize. This is what successful CEOs do. Such an invitation usually made a person feel good inside. It made her feel awful.

The demons in her head shouted, "I shouldn't do this. I have to be productive. I'm doing something wrong if I say yes."

She said yes and experienced extreme discomfort and afterburn.

Afterburn is when you do something that is good for yourself—a new behavior, when you step out of your comfort zone in some way. Then you feel icky and your inner critic says, "Change back!" "I shouldn't have done that!" Growing pains is another way to describe afterburn.

This is the primary reason people don't make positive changes in their lives—walking through the feelings of discomfort and experiencing afterburn.

Identify what comes to mind when you think about discomfort that comes with change. For example: all the bad things that can happen, how it affects others if you change, fear of the unknown.

Determine the reasons is it important to embrace discomfort. For example: growth, increased confidence, peace of mind, opportunity.

Jessica attended the offsite meeting and experienced breakthrough ideas to move her organization forward. It was worth the discomfort of taking new actions.

Making positive changes induces feelings of discomfort and a belief you are doing something wrong. Take the action anyway.

Don't stop before the miracle happens.

Curiosity and Being Present

Always say "yes" to the present moment. Surrender to what is. Say "yes" to life and see how life starts suddenly working for you, rather than against you.

—Eckhart Tolle, author, *The Power of Now*

Lia finds her thoughts lingering in the past or future, impatient with herself and her progress, wanting more, and trying to figure out how to have more control in her life. She's running so fast, she has no time or energy to see the good in front of her right now: a conversation with her son, a funny story, someone letting her into traffic.

Everyone around her seems to be doing the same thing: driving too fast, overscheduling their days, and not sleeping.

What am I running from?

The present moment.

Most of us are never fully present because we unconsciously believe the next moment must be more important than this one. Then we miss our whole life, which only happens in the now.

Have you ever thought, *If I stop, I'll never start again* or *If I stay present, I'll see something I don't like and I'll have to fix it and I'm already exhausted?*

Our minds usually come up with the most drastic scenarios. I call this "the wreckage of my future."

What if there was a different way to perceive the present moment? What if there was one tool that would allow you to "see" the present moment without judgment or fear? Would you use it?

That tool is *curiosity*. Curiosity allows you to see yourself, others, and situations as they are right now, without condemning, running away, or needing to fix anything. It keeps you in the present moment.

When you find yourself in a situation like getting cut off in traffic, a sick child, a client yelling at you, or receiving a nasty email, ask yourself:

"I wonder why (fill in the blank) is happening?" Or "Isn't this interesting!"

Why? Your mind cannot be curious and judgmental at the same time. Curiosity is a way to hit the pause button and see the present moment. It is a tool to help you "be here now."

The other night, the overhead light in my bedroom turned on at 4:00 a.m. I got curious: "Isn't that interesting?" "I wonder why that light turned on and woke me up so early?" I shared this experience with my girlfriend and she said, "Maybe it's your wake-up call."

Use curiosity today to increase your joy and satisfaction.

Combine Mindfulness with Exercise

ChiRunning is different from “regular” running in that it is about relaxation, inner kindness, and body posture. It is a conscious way of running that increases your present-moment awareness and reduces negative inner chatter.

The technique’s premise is that your thoughts are real, but not necessarily true. “I’m not a runner.” Not true. “Running is for other people.” Not true. When you are running, you are running. When you are free from these thoughts, running becomes easier.

Thoughts like *I’m so out of shape* or *I can’t do this* drain your energy and you get tired quicker. Focus your attention on the now to increase your energy and run longer.

The success stories from doing this practice are powerful. BJ went from the couch to running seven miles three or four days a week, pain free. Winnie from Indonesia went from only being able to walk for fifteen minutes to running five miles regularly. Patrick had so much back pain from running a marathon that he couldn’t raise his hand at church. Now he runs several marathons pain free.

The benefits of being in nature, running, and mindfulness are increased creativity, happiness, and clarity of thinking.

Let go of physical and mental tension with ChiRunning.

Unrealistic Expectations Stifle Having Fun

According to a poll from the National Alliance for Youth Sports, about 70 percent of children in the United States stop playing organized sports by the age of thirteen because "it's just not fun anymore."

Sports give kids the opportunity for physical activity, team building, taking risks, building resilience, and experiencing success. Yet the expectations put on kids to be the best takes the fun out of it and leads to them believing, "If I'm not the best, then I've failed."

You may have experienced this when you were young. If you weren't first chair in the band, captain of the cheerleading squad, or on the debate team, did you think, "It's OK to be second chair" or "it's not worth doing at all"?

Check to see if you have unrealistic expectations:

- Do you expect to get things right the first time?
- Are you overly critical of yourself?
- Do you set goals according to other people's expectations?
- Do you take on too much?
- Do you expect yourself to be at 100 percent all the time?

Question your expectations of yourself. Ask whether your expectations align with your values, needs, and who you are as an individual. If not, you may have them to please others.

Adjust your expectations and go have some fun.

Play for the sake of play.

Bookend to Complete Tasks Faster

Bookending is a technique to help you complete tasks. Think of bookends. They sit on two ends of a row of books, holding them up. Bookending is when you call, email, or text another person and tell them about the task you are committing to complete. Follow up with them after you completed it.

Use bookending whenever you feel stuck, need someone to support and hear you as you take action, or are nervous about taking the next step. The results are that you'll accomplish tasks that you haven't been able to on your own.

Bookending is a form of accountability. You tell someone you are going to take an action, you do the action, you tell them you did the action. You will only hold yourself accountable for goals that others know about.

Tell someone about one task you're taking to move forward today in an email, text, or phone call. Bookend once you've completed the task.

Bookending is a fast and easy way to keep moving forward.

Breathe

Deep breathing helps manage stress and anxiety.

Tesa gulped her smoothie as she scanned the highway for cops. The voice in her head droned on, *You're late again. You're running out of time. You're always late. You're not doing it right.* Her chest and head pounded. *I can make it on time.* She pulled into the parking spot with two minutes to spare. Tesa brushed her hair with her hand, pasted on a smile, and greeted her client.

She didn't take time to breathe.

Tesa has a limiting belief that drives her behavior. "If I slow down at all, I'm afraid I'll stop completely and never get going again. This is how I've been successful. It's exhausting, but at least I know it works." Tesa used anxiety as a motivator to perform.

Deep breathing reduces stress and blood pressure. It strengthens abdominal and intestinal muscles. It promotes better blood flow, releases toxins from the body, and improves sleep.

Change your limiting belief about time to an empowering one: "Time is my friend, on my side, abundant, kind, and generous, supportive of my dreams and desires. I have enough time to breathe deeply."

Start to anchor your breath practice to mealtimes. When you sit to eat, place your feet on the floor, sit up straight, and place your hands in your lap. Close your eyes. Focus on your breath, moment by moment. Count twenty breaths and recite slowly, "In one, out two, in three, out four." Open your eyes.

As Tesa practiced deep breathing, she experienced clearer thinking and less anxiety.

Take a deep breath to boost your energy level and improve your stamina.

You Know You're a Control Freak When Your Theme Song Is Frank Sinatra's "My Way"

A control freak is someone who has a habitual desire to take charge and make sure things go their way. They attempt to control aspects of another person's life or manipulate others into doing what the controlling person wants.

Complete control can never be achieved. The drive for control through criticism, judgment, and micromanaging leaves you lonely and exhausted. But at least it keeps you away from the underlying anxiety you want to avoid experiencing.

Uncertainty triggers anxiety and the need to know what's going to happen in the future. There is no guarantee that everything will be OK. Being a control freak is an attempt to eliminate uncertainty.

Identify what things fall into primary control and secondary control.

Primary control is when you assert your will on circumstances, such as what groceries you buy, what flowers you plant, or how you decorate your office.

Secondary control is when you adapt to things that cannot be controlled. Your husband gets laid off from work, your child gets cut from the basketball team, or someone hits your car.

Both play a role. Primary control is changing the world to fit yourself. Secondary control is changing yourself to fit the world.

Think about the Serenity Prayer: Grant me the serenity to accept the things I cannot change (secondary control) and the courage to change the things I can (primary control).

Sing a new song, "They did it their way."

Stop Expecting the Other Shoe to Drop

Dahlia had been struggling for a long time. Her loveless marriage of several years was ending, her children were leaving home, and she needed to go back to work.

She got her real estate license. She had a knack for connecting with people and an innate ability to run numbers in her head and negotiate effectively. She began to sell houses and felt good about her contributions. Then she met someone. This person shared an emotional and social connection with her that had been missing for years.

The one investment she got as part of the divorce had appreciated enough to pay for her rent for the entire next year.

Even with all the good things happening in her life, she worried about her future. "What's going to happen next? When is the other shoe going to drop?" she asked.

This is foreboding joy. When life is working, we are fearful it's going to end, so we don't enjoy it when it is happening. It is a defense mechanism. We think that if we worry about the future, we are safe and in control. In the process, we miss out on the joy-filled moments of our life.

To feel joy, we have to be present in the moment.

Practice easing into joy. It is the process of staying in the present moment, of experiencing the vulnerability that comes with staying present. This melts away the hardened parts of your heart that have been hurt. It replenishes your mind, body, and soul.

Dahlia was relieved to know she could learn how to enjoy the good things in her life. When she felt anxious about the future, she took three deep breaths and said, "I am where my feet are."

Allow the present moment to create your future.

Stay Connected

Your well-being depends on connection with others.

According to scientist Matthew Lieberman, the need for connection is as fundamental as the need for food or water. Data suggests that humans suffer greatly when social bonds are threatened or severed. Connection is hard-wired in your operating system.

But technological advances are leading smaller groups of communication with less interaction. People are more comfortable connecting via text, Snapchat, Instagram, and Twitter than interacting face-to-face. Not only are people OK with beginning a relationship online, they are comfortable with ending one online, too. Connection is being sucked up by screen time.

Some people trying to create businesses that revolve around togetherness. Granny's Finest is a social enterprise focused on preventing loneliness among aging adults. The idea is that a grandparent and grandchild make a knitted product together. They connect. They find purpose and meaning. They make money.

Determine how you will maintain connection with others—whether a book club, paint night, running, or tea on Sundays. Honor the neuroscience of human connection.

Come together right now, over me.

Social Media Platforms Connect You to Others

YouTube is a video-sharing website and app that allows people to share videos. Started in 2005, it has revolutionized everything from entertainment to education. It has brought people together from all over the world, helped aspiring artists get discovered, raised funds for various causes, and has given people a platform to share the truth of what is happening in their countries.

It has expanded crowdsourcing and collaboration and awareness of social issues.

Now, as the world's largest video platform, YouTube has impacted many fields. In 2006, Khan Academy offered free tutoring and turned it into what is now considered the largest nonprofit school in the world, with ten million students. President Obama's re-election campaign included thirty staff working on YouTube. The anti-bullying It Gets Better Project expanded from a single video directed to discourage LGBT teens from considering suicide. Within weeks, hundreds of It Gets Better response videos were uploaded to the project, from celebrities to cabinet secretaries.

Technology can bring you to loneliness and also bring you out of it. If you live in a small town and are transgender, technology connects you with others to gain support and guidance.

You are never alone. If something is happening to you, it has happened to someone else. There is someone who has shared that experience.

When you need help, reach out for it.
When you are called to help, respond.

Stop Underliving

Underliving is any thought or belief that leads to behaviors that block you from living the life you want.

Gina giggled as she read the flyer: "Writer's Weekend Retreat: Starting from Scratch to Success!" She read it again. She exhaled deeply as her body settled into the chair. Her thoughts drifted to a weekend filled with words, coffee, and comfy solitude.

Statements of underliving intruded:

- "It's not practical."
- "Don't get your hopes up."
- "Other things are more important. Besides, you can't make a living writing."

Underliving is a way to avoid disappointment. It also is a form of self-harm. It supports the limiting belief in your unworthiness.

There are many small ways you reinforce underliving:

- "I'm too old to take a dance class."
- "Hiking the Appalachian Trail for three weeks is an impossible dream."
- "I'm not going to buy that magazine because it's too expensive."

Take one small step today:

- Buy the magazine you haven't allowed yourself to buy
- Get books from the library on hiking the Appalachian Trail
- Sign up for a dance class at your community center

The only person in your way is you.

Gina told her best friend about her dream of spending a weekend writing. Her friend responded, "If you sign up, I will too!"

Give yourself permission to want what you want.
Take one action toward what you want. Tell someone else. Do it.

Take Your Foot Off the Accelerator

When you've had a busy week, it's hard to slow down.

Isabelle had a "hair on fire" week. Her work ebbs and flows, and this week was exceptionally busy. She ate meals in the car while driving to appointments, skipped exercise, and missed a few family dinners. The following work week was slower paced.

This made her feel uncomfortable. Her inner critic said, "You're doing something wrong. You must be lazy." Something inside her didn't feel right. "What do I do with space in my day?" she asked herself.

Busier weeks can feel "normal," and then on slower weeks we label ourselves as "bad" or "lazy." It's a challenge to reset to a normal pace when you've been firefighting.

Isabelle decided to call a friend and plan her slower week ahead of time. She acknowledged her discomfort around spending time eating healthfully, exercising, and getting home in time for dinner with her family. She committed to exercise twice during the week, and planned to sit at her desk and eat lunch. She felt silly doing this, but it worked.

When you've had a busy work week and are going into a slower week, pause. Tell yourself, "This transition from busy to slower feels uncomfortable and this is normal."

Bookend with a friend how you plan to manage your time for optimal work/life balance.

CURIOSITY

Curiosity Creates Connection

Ask questions that are more expansive and opportunistic.

A twenty-four-year-old man was looking out from the train's window. He shouted, "Dad, look! The trees are going behind us!"

His dad smiled.

A couple sitting nearby looked at the twenty-four-year-old's childish behavior with pity, as he exclaimed, "Dad, look! The clouds are running with us!"

The couple could not resist and said to the father, "Why don't you take your son to see a doctor who can help him?"

The father smiled and said, "I did and we are just coming from the hospital. My son was blind from birth and he just got his eyesight today."

Judgments are the lens through which you see the world. They are made based on your perceptions. You don't see things for what they are; you see things through the lens of your mind.

Change how you ask questions to move out of judgment and into curiosity.

Judgment: "There's something wrong with your son."

Curiosity: "I wonder why he's so joyful today?"

By judging, you unconsciously create separation and lack of acceptance of other people's beliefs.

Do not fuse with your judgments or perceive them as reality.

Questions Interrupt Budding Resentments

Questions move you out of judgment and into curiosity.

Gina sent a text: "Sorry, I can't make it to ur party"

"Really? Are you kidding me?" Rosalie huffed and dried a ceramic bowl as if she were trying to remove the glaze.

"Why is your face all red?" Jessica asked, as she opened the refrigerator and grabbed a beer. "Hey, you're not supposed to do any work. This is your birthday party. I'll do the dishes later."

"She did it again. Gina cancelled at the last minute. She always does this." Rosalie threw the dishrag on the counter and stormed out of the kitchen.

Interrupt judgments with the Why/What If/How question technique.

You encounter a situation that is less than ideal and ask *why*. "I wonder why Gina didn't come to my party?"

Ask *what if*. Be creative and outrageous with your ideas.

- "What if Gina ran away?"
- "What if she ran away and joined the circus?"
- "What if she got arrested and is sitting in jail?"

Instead of being mad at Gina, you are now curious and maybe even a little empathetic.

Ask *how*.

"How do I find out the truth of why she didn't come? I can call her, text her, or stop by her home."

Rosalie exhaled deeply. "I know Gina loves me. I'll call her after the party." She allowed the experience to just be.

Any time you find yourself in a less-than-ideal situation, ask yourself, "I wonder why this is happening?"

Face Your Fear

I have lots of fears. I fear rejection, abandonment, and failure. When I answered the questions below, I discovered my greatest fear is that if I express my creativity, people will laugh at me. Silly, perhaps, yet it felt real, deep, and painful. This fear has blocked my creativity, authenticity, and speaking my truth for years. I chose the "safe" route to avoid facing the possibility of being laughed at. My choices were subconscious.

The questions below help to bring your fears to your awareness, which enables you to do something about it. My answers follow.

Q: What are the words that best describe what I am experiencing when I think about my fear?

A: Shame, less than, want to hide, I'm being stupid.

Q: What does this fear prevent me from doing and/or having?

A: It stifles my creativity, my ability to share my ideas through words and images that help people transform. I feel very small. It inhibits my success and lowers my confidence. It stops me from reaching one million women.

Q: If I gave myself permission to achieve these desires, what would I be?

A: I would be a wildly creative and successful woman, easily able to express my ideas visually, verbally, and in writing, in a way that others can easily understand and apply to their lives. They experience amazing transformations and miracles every day.

The fear got smaller once I wrote it out. I told a few friends and it lost more power over me. I have an easier time creating programs and products. I enjoy creating and my shame is gone.

Bring your fear to the surface, share it with a friend, and experience freedom.

You Cannot Walk Forward by Looking Backward

New ideas are nourishment for the brain. In order to make space for them, you have to let go of old thoughts that no longer serve you.

Stacy grimaced. Her stomach lurched, and her throat tightened. "I hate this part of the job. I feel guilty not giving an end-of-year bonus to the operations director. He just meets the minimum requirements. Sometimes he talks down to his employees, and he has several unexcused absences. I need to tell him why he isn't getting one, but I feel bad about it," she explained to her board chair, Jared.

"Stacy, you said the same thing about giving constructive feedback to your CFO. This pattern of feeling guilty when you do the right thing is getting in your way."

Like Stacy, decide on one thought that no longer benefits you. Make the decision to say no to it. Your subconscious mind knows the word NO as a law of elimination. Mentally picture yourself as no longer having the problem for several minutes. Change your focus to something that is interesting, creative, and pleasing to you. If you begin thinking of the problem, stop. Shift your attention back to the fact that it no longer exists in your world.

Stacy created a different mental picture. She imagined herself free from guilt as she talked to her operations director with empathy and authority. Each time she worried about doing it, she imagined her body relaxed, the right words flowing easily from her mouth, and peace of mind, knowing it was the right decision for everyone and that her guilt was no longer a problem. She acted as if she believed this until she did.

Identify habitual thought patterns to release.

Work with Difficult Feelings

We all encounter rough patches and unwanted experiences. In response to them, we may feel angry, jealous, or fearful.

We are not taught to sit with difficult emotions. We are taught to push them away through busyness, food, social media, and other people. The result is that they get stuck inside the body and come out in unskillful ways. You scream at your kids for giggling or spend extra hours at work and come home exhausted, and numb out with TV and food.

We all want to change how we feel sometimes. Instead, make space for all your emotions. Invite them in for tea. Accept them as they are. Ask them what they are here to teach you. Decide to stay present for all your feelings. Find a quiet space where you will not be disturbed. Set a timer for ten minutes and say, "OK fear, anger, grief, come on in. Give me your best shot."

Emotions are meant to be experienced, not ignored.

Every moment is useful, no matter what is happening. Feel all your feelings. It is as important as breathing, sleeping, and eating.

People Are Naturally Creative, Resourceful, and Whole

When you believe this statement, you are better able to stay in your own sandbox and allow others the dignity of making their own choices.

How easy it is for you to stay in your own sandbox?

Do you find it difficult to stop picking up other people's responsibilities? For example, do you tell your partner, "You should take better care of yourself, change jobs, be happy?" Do you do for others what they should be doing for themselves?

This is being mentally in someone else's business. Focusing on others is a great distraction because then you don't have to look at yourself, your choices, responsibilities, or stay in the present moment. You have an overdeveloped sense of responsibility. There is a constant sense of urgency: "It has to be done now and by me." When you stop, you regain the energy, time, and power you have been giving away.

Reframe how you look at people. Believe that all people are naturally creative, resourceful, and whole. When you do this, you make different choices.

List the people you feel resentful toward and the reason for your resentment. "I'm angry that Mary expects me to always clean up her reports." "I wish my husband would make dinner sometimes."

This shows you where you are being overly responsible and not believing that people are naturally creative, resourceful, and whole.

Start small. Set aside time to tell Mary that you will no longer clean up her reports. Clearly define your expectations and consequences. Give her a few test runs, then let her go. Ask your husband to pick one night when he makes dinner. The kids can do their own laundry, your employees can accept the authority and accountability of their tasks, your husband can make his own flight arrangements for work. Why? Because they are naturally creative, resourceful, and whole.

The next time you feel anxious or stressed, ask yourself, "Whose business am I in?" This question brings you back to yourself and to the present moment.

People are naturally creative, resourceful, and whole. When I believe this, I am more balanced and self-responsible.

Create an Empowering Belief about Your Worthiness

Take the road less traveled and believe in your own worthiness.

When I share that most people believe they are unworthy, they don't understand what I mean. I ask, "When was the last time you gave yourself downtime, slept in, saw a matinee, or did something because you wanted to, not because it would produce a result?"

All of them stare at their feet and mumble. "It's too uncomfortable. If I take my foot off the gas pedal, I'm going to crash!"

Then I tell them that most people believe the following: *Because I believe in scarcity and unworthiness, I value only those tasks that are "productive and revenue-generating."*

This leads to:

Overworking

- Constantly believing and feeling you are behind
- No buffer zone—time between appointments, time to transition from work to personal time
- Confusing busyness with productivity

Overfunctioning

- Doing for others what they can do for themselves
- Overdeveloped sense of responsibility
- Constant sense of urgency: "It has to be done now and by me."

Neglecting Self-Maintenance Actions

- Sleep
- Healthy eating
- Regular exercise
- Downtime
- Sick time
- Play time
- Journaling

Not Being Present

- Fixated on the regrets of the past or the wreckage of the future
- Doing the same behaviors expecting different results
- Believing the next moment is more important than this moment

Then they get it and agree.

Notice your thoughts and reactions to these empowering beliefs about worthiness:

"I have inherent worth and value just as I am. No prerequisites, no qualifiers." "People who believe in their inherent worth and value have a lightness and playfulness about them. They recognize all of their desires, the work ones and the ones that fill their soul, and they comfortably ask for what they want. I have inherent worth and value."

Create your own empowering belief about your worthiness.

Focus Your Attention to Achieve the Results You Want

Focus can be a challenge, and there's a good reason why. Scientists discovered that the brain receives 400 billion bits of information each second. Our brain then condenses the 400 billion bits of information down to 2,000 bits. What we choose to focus on is only one-half of one-millionth of one percent of what's out there.

Are you focusing on the right bits of information? Or do you check Facebook, email, and spend your energy on other distractors?

Attention is a limited resource. Your brain uses a lot of glucose and other metabolic resources every time you focus on higher-level tasks, like problem solving and decision-making. Don't waste your energy on distractions.

To accomplish what's important, block a short amount of time to work on a specific task. The brain can only focus on a limited amount of information for a limited amount of time.

Put a sign on your door or cubicle that you are not to be disturbed until a specific time. You want to explain this to your colleagues ahead of time, so there's no confusion or conflicts about your new habit.

Turn off all buzzing things (phone, computer, etc.).

Set a timer. When the timer goes off, go outside and walk for five minutes. Your brain needs a breather.

Start small: focus on one task for fifteen minutes. Turn off email, social media, phone, and any other distractions. Close your door if you have one. Do this once a day for five days. Increase it to thirty minutes the next week. Before you know it, you will accomplish the tasks that get you the results you want.

Focus your attention on what's important and ignore the rest.

Get to Know All Your Emotions

Sometimes I lie awake at night, and I ask, "Where have I gone wrong?"
Then a voice says to me, "This is going to take more than one night."

— Charlie Brown

To function effectively in the world takes commitment to develop the physical, emotional, spiritual, and mental aspects of yourself. If one is underdeveloped, it causes disharmony with the others.

Emotional development is the one area that gets neglected more than the others. This is because, unlike mental thoughts, emotions touch you deeply. They include pleasure and pain, happiness and sadness, and several in between. Our brains are wired to avoid pain and gain pleasure, so it makes sense that we neglect emotional development and those feelings that hurt—grief, disappointment, anger, fear.

You can't pick and choose which emotions to feel or numb. If you stop feeling sadness, you also miss out on happiness. Make space for your all your emotions. Invite them in. Set a timer for fifteen minutes and say to them, "OK ___________ (emotion name), come on in. You are welcome here. I want to know what you have to teach me." Notice the emotions you experience and where you feel them in your body.

Allow your emotions to teach you their vastness and trust they will remain in balance with the other areas of your life.

Dealing with Disappointment

Everyone has a special dream: starting your own business, having children, climbing Mount Everest. Mine was to sail around the Galapagos Islands and enjoy the amazing animals, plants, and volcanic islands.

I was talking with my friend, Elizabeth, in the beginning of July. My boys were away at camp and she asked me, "What do you want to do while the kids are away?" I responded, "I want to go to the Galapagos Islands."

Elizabeth has heard me talk about them and watch shows about them, and she knows how much I've wanted to go. She suggested I check to see if there were any last-minute deals. Reluctantly, I started looking. I say reluctantly because I couldn't bear the disappointment if I couldn't afford it or it somehow didn't work out. I hate feeling disappointed, especially when it's my lifelong dream.

I looked. I found a great deal. I took it. I would leave in two weeks, flying first from DC to Miami, then on to Ecuador. Another flight, six hundred miles west over the Pacific Ocean, and I would finally realize my dream.

The flight from DC to Miami was uneventful. I boarded the plane to Ecuador, the cabin door closed, the engines roared, and we were ready to take off. Then the captain came on the speaker: "Everyone deplane. We are delaying our flight due to a volcanic eruption in Ecuador. We will try again tomorrow at 6:00 am. Be back at the airport at 4:00 am. We are not removing your bags from the plane. Have a nice day."

We all want to avoid feeling disappointed, whether it's when the person who says they want to marry you changes their mind, or the promotion you worked for months to get is given to someone else, or the dream car you bought gets a dent on the first day.

When feeling disappointment:

1. Call a friend. Express what's inside you and get it out. It's uncomfortable to be so vulnerable, but getting it out means it doesn't stay inside you and come back for processing later, at a worse time, and mess up the next situation.

2. Talk back to your inner critic. When the inner critic speaks up and says, "See, you got too big for your britches and the universe showed you! You're so stupid! What were you thinking? Stop being selfish," reply, "I know you are disappointed and I will do everything possible to correct this. I hear you are scared, and I will handle this situation. You can go play now." It's cheesy, but it works.

3. Find acceptance. This is hard to do. You want to hide, blame others, and be afraid. Instead, practice acceptance. You don't have to like the situation, the feelings, and the uncertainty. Acceptance is a choice. Just like working out to build muscles is a choice, learning to accept that disappointing events happen throughout life is a choice too.

How did it turn out? I went to the gate, put on my headphones, and listened to 70s rock-n-roll music as loud as I could tolerate. Everyone around me was frantic. The plane took off, and I realized my dream.

Treat yourself compassionately when you are disappointed.
It helps you move through it faster.

You Can Never Prepare Yourself for Betrayal

Being betrayed at work or in personal relationships is one of the hardest experiences to process. Many times we wonder, "How didn't I see it coming? I should have known this!" Blaming ourselves for someone's behavior only makes our recovery process take longer. Betrayal shatters your assumptions, has many motives, and leaves you shell-shocked.

Janet hired Mary, a woman new to the insurance business. She spent tons of time and energy teaching her the business. Mary was a quick learner, excited every day to learn more, and was successful at growing her clientele list. They formed a close working relationship and enjoyed sharing their love of country music by going to an occasional concert together.

Without warning, Mary submitted her resignation, effective immediately, giving no explanation other than "it's a personal situation," and departed.

Janet was left feeling dazed and confused. She questioned whether she did something to offend Mary. Because there was no clear reason for the abrupt departure, Janet started making up stories of how she should have seen it coming or prevented it from happening.

Six months later, Janet found out that Mary had gone to a competitor.

Mary had signed a one-year noncompete agreement with Janet. Digging a little further, Janet discovered Mary had been sharing confidential information with the competitor while still at Janet's company. Janet felt like she'd been kicked in the stomach. She began doubting all of her hiring decisions, client relationships, and especially herself. She felt horrible.

Dealing with betrayal and coming to terms with the hurt inflicted on you by people you love and trust is a huge thing.

Practice self-compassion and self-kindness:

- When self-doubt comes up, say, "I will not turn this on myself. I'm going for a vigorous walk instead."
- Acknowledge that betrayal is nothing you can prepare yourself for.
- Ask for and accept help. Tell one trustworthy person what happened.

Allow yourself time and space to process betrayal.

Curiosity Is Good for Your Brain

Research has shown that curiosity increases your ability to learn and retain information.

When you are curious, the limbic system of the brain illuminates. This is the part of your brain that influences your emotional health and helps you form and retain memories.

Curiosity also increases your tolerance of anxiety and uncertainty. If you are uncomfortable in social situations, curiosity will improve your experience. Think of three topics you are curious about, such as birds, black holes, or national parks. Instead of asking what a person at the party does, ask, "I was thinking about our national park system and wonder what is your favorite one." "What is an app you discovered that makes your life better or more fun?"

The brain can't ignore questions. Help it light up like a Christmas tree.

Use curiosity to keep your brain active and healthy.

Successful Leaders Take Vacations

Christy could barely keep her eyes open. She drove home from work and scarcely noticed if the lights were green, yellow, or red. Her stomach growled, yet she was too tired to stop for food. She left the office late again, feeling sad she would not see her kids before their bedtime.

She still needed to go to the dry cleaners, bank, and pharmacy. The flight for their family vacation left the next morning and there were piles of laundry to wash for packing. At the same time, her mind raced back to work, wondering if she left anything unfinished or in limbo.

A vacation may seem like it's not worth the hassle of the time to prepare. Change your approach and you can enter and exit vacations with less grind, stress, and strain.

When you schedule your vacation, add one buffer day before and one buffer day after your vacation. These are days out of the office that give you time to run errands, pack, and open mail when you return home.

Delegate 25 percent more than you think you can. Determine who monitors your emails, voicemails, and social media accounts. You will be less likely to monitor work activity if someone else is.

Change your voicemail. This manages the callers' expectations and gives them directions of what to do while you are unavailable.

Christy applied the buffer time to her next family vacation. She experienced less anxiety, barely yelled at her kids or husband, and didn't collapse in bed for several hours when she arrived at their destination.

If the average length of most Americans' vacations is only four days (Glassdoor Employee Satisfaction Survey), then what gets in the way of you adding two more days to experience a smoother wrap-up and reentry experience?

Give yourself permission to schedule buffer days before and after your vacation to actually enjoy your time away.

Take a Well Day

Don't let your "never-to-be-finished" to-do list keep you from living life.

Recently I saw a commercial advertising the beach town of Ocean City, Maryland. It depicts people wearing t-shirts that read, "VACATION DAY." One woman says, "I (vacation day) was used to assemble bunk beds." A man says, "I (vacation day) was used to wait for the cable guy." A couple says, "We (vacation days) were used to reorganize the garage." A lifeguard yells, "Come on people! They are called vacation days for a reason. Put yours to better use at Ocean City, Maryland."

It's good to have a prudent reserve of paid-time-off days for when life happens. You get sick. Your child breaks a bone. The hot-water heater dies.

There are other times when your body, mind, and spirit need a Well Day. This is when you focus on yourself and do what you need and want. You take time to fill your tanks. Read a book cover to cover, take a half-day hike, go to a matinee, binge watch a TV show.

Start with two hours. Answer this question: "What do I want to do if I had two hours to myself?" Do not list "shoulds": "I should do the laundry, pay bills, clean the kitchen." Do one thing on your list. Tune up and ride your bike for thirty minutes. Sit outside and read. Take yourself out to lunch.

Expect resistance to this. Society has a strong belief in scarcity, and values only those things that are productive and revenue-generating. The belief is you have to sacrifice your health and well-being to survive and succeed.

Beliefs can be changed. Start with one gallon of soul fuel. Cars don't run on empty tanks. Neither do you.

Accept that you will always have an unfinished to-do list.

Take a Break from Your Troubles

Forcing solutions doesn't solve a problem faster. Even Jell-O needs to be left alone to form.

Imagine if you were inside a house that was on fire. What would you do? Leave the house as fast as possible. Leaving a burning building is moving toward a solution. Dwelling on sickness, fear, and limitation is staying stuck in the problem.

Interrupt your thoughts with the Animal Alphabet exercise. Think of the name of an animal for each letter in the alphabet—antelope, badger, cat, dog, elephant. By the time you get to the letter Z, you will have given your brain a rest from the problem. Now go for a walk. Call a friend. Watch a funny video.

It's OK to put your troubles aside. In fact, by doing so, you will feel more energized and focused.

Chillax to the max.

Curiosity Found Nemo

Curiosity opens you to possibilities and solutions.

Finding Nemo is a Pixar animated film about a clownfish named Marlin who sets out on a journey to bring his son Nemo home. Along the way, he meets an absent-minded fish named Dory. Her positive attitude often conflicts with Marlin's pessimism, but her curiosity leads the way to finding Nemo.

The definition of curiosity is when you are eager to learn something new. The definition of questioning is inquiring. The way you get curious is by questioning.

Questions are a catalyst of change. Your brain is programmed to be hooked by questions. You can't ignore them. Questions cause your mind to shift a little from autopilot. Think about driving your car home from work. Your brain is usually on autopilot, and you can't remember your drive. Questions are like taking a different route home.

Practice curiosity by asking the question, "I wonder why?"

- When you're driving:

"I wonder why that person cut me off?"

- When you are in line in the grocery store:

"I wonder why I'm in the line that is moving the slowest?"

- When you are in a boring meeting:

"I wonder why this meeting is so boring?"

- When you are washing dishes:

"I wonder why no one is helping me with the dishes?"

Curiosity helps you solve problems and increases your confidence. It reduces stress in the moment because you are not judging the situation as good or bad.

Stop and question to move forward with a clearer sense of direction and purpose.

What Does Your Bumper Sticker Say?

A single slogan directs your attention to what's important in your life.

My accounting director is a bright, talented, and enthusiastic colleague. She loves her job, numbers, and the stories numbers tell. She loves the numbers so much that she loses sight of the results she needs to produce. She spends hours fine-tuning the general ledger, journal entries, and projections, and is late turning in the financial data I need to make decisions.

Employees have several distractions: meetings, social media, phones, email. When under pressure, they choose the tasks they like the most or feel confident doing. Their choice may not be the tasks that are most important, and so they spend time inefficiently.

To help my employee stay focused and prioritize, I developed a bumper sticker for her: *Accurate, Timely, Financial Data*. Every time she got distracted, I asked, "What's your bumper sticker?" She answered, "Accurate, timely, financial data." I reminded her that 80 percent is good enough and that I needed the data. Done is better than perfect.

Develop a bumper sticker for each team member. It helps them stay focused and prioritize tasks, especially when shiny objects appear.

Create a slogan that describes your priority and focus.
Share it with your colleagues.

Breathe Deeply for Pain Relief

Deep breathing reverses your body's natural reaction to stressful conditions. It releases endorphins, which improves feelings of well-being and provides pain relief.

Visualization is a tool that helps deal with stress in a healthier way and can reduce pain.

Imagine you are seated comfortably on the beach. Your toes push into the warm sand. Take a slow, deep breath. Feel how grounded you are in the warm sand. Let go of any pain, tension, or fear in your body and watch it drain into the sand and be carried out to sea. With each deep breath, flush your fears and worries out to the ocean. Allow the sun's energy to fill your body, starting at the top of your head and spreading down your neck, spine, arms, legs, and feet. Your skins glows with healing light. Your body is repaired and revitalized.

Visualize pain leaving your body.

F.O.C.U.S.: Focus One Course Until Successful

Use the parking lot method to stay focused on one task. The parking lot is a place to write down thoughts, actions, or other tasks that arise when you are committed to complete a current task.

Marcia is an executive at an insurance company. She was ready to change jobs and made time to discover her "what's next." When she sat down to research job opportunities, she thought of doing her taxes, sending an email to a client, fixing a snack, or filing her papers, and felt guilty for not exercising. All these distractions kept her from doing the task at hand: look for another job.

She bought a small notebook and jotted down tasks and reminders as they came up. She felt relief, knowing these were written down. She was able to focus on looking online at job postings, undistracted.

Buy 3x5 cards, a small notebook, or sticky notes to capture tasks or feelings that come up during your focused-attention time. This is your parking lot. Set a time to return to the list. This tells your subconscious mind to let it go until that appointed time.

Life is like a camera: focus on what's important and you'll capture it perfectly.

See Things Differently

To change ourselves effectively, we first had to change our perspective.

—Stephen R. Covey, *The 7 Habits of Highly Effective People: Powerful Lessons in Personal Change*

Perception is the ability to see, hear, or become aware of something through your senses. It's how we interpret what's going on outside ourselves. An example of perception is seeing a glass as half empty or half full. Both are correct. All people do not "see" the same thing when looking at a visual image.

Every day we interact with others. We choose to perceive relationships as good or bad, easy or hard, convenient or inconvenient. Carl Jung, a Swiss psychiatrist and psychotherapist, said, "Everything that irritates us about others can lead us to an understanding of ourselves."

The next time your spouse or friend does something annoying, say to yourself, "I do that too. I leave dirty dishes in the sink. I forget to take out the trash. I speak disparagingly about others." This phrase, "I do that too," changes your perception of the person and situation and allows you to respond more skillfully.

Choose to see things differently. It will shift the situation in a positive direction.

WORTHINESS

Somebody Doesn't Live Here Anymore

Recognize the rules you put around reality. You created them. And you can change them.

"Somebody needs to walk the dog." "Somebody needs to buy a new rug." Like a magnet, women are drawn to answer the call to do the work "somebody" is asked to do.

Women try not to disturb other people's lives. We've trained others that we'll take care of everything.

I have a desire to travel and have my business be flexible and mobile. I put constraints on how mobile it can be and how much I can travel based on rules I created: where I live, who will take care of my dog, how will my sons do without me around full time. I say that all these others things need to be met first, then I can meet my own needs.

Identify what is it that you want to do. List the reasons you can't.

My Can't List:

- The family adopted a dog. We can't give him up again.
- I need to maintain residency in my state for in-state tuition.
- I've moved twice already. I can't move again and disturb my adult sons, who spend most of their time away at college.

Then list all the ways you can.

My Can List:

- Ask my former husband to take the dog.
- Have my adult son maintain residency in the state.
- Sublet my home.

I realized that my constraints were fixed only in my mind.

Choose to do what is yours to do. For you is not against others.

Don't be somebody anymore.

A Swing and a Miss Is Better Than Watching an Opportunity Go By

In the game of baseball, accumulating constant singles wins the game. A single is a hit that allows the batter to get to first base.

Grand slams have the WOW factor. I love to watch Bryce Harper, right fielder for the Washington Nationals, step up to the plate. The anticipation of him hitting a home run or grand slam is exciting and highly likely. He is one in a million. All pitches have the potential to be a home run, but getting one is a different story. People succeed by constantly hitting singles.

To hit a single is to take one step toward your goal. Call five prospects. Ask for a raise. Volunteer for the customer service improvement committee. Commit to taking the step with another person. Follow up once you completed it.

It is the single steps you take that move you to where you want to be. Grand slams do happen, but most of the time, you get to home plate one base at a time.

Swing at singles. They win the game.

Control Freak and Perfectionist Are Synonyms

Done is better than perfect.

Things that are not perfect cause control freaks stress. Your kids put the dishes in the dishwasher incorrectly. You redo it. Your husband does the laundry and doesn't fold it. You rewash, dry, and fold the clothes. Your employee submits an acceptable report that you redo to make it "better." Intervening keeps you from learning that you can wait out your stress.

The next time you have the urge to redo something to make it "better," wait ten minutes. Expect to experience discomfort. This is normal.

Build your distress tolerance. This is your perceived capacity to withstand negative emotional states and the behavioral act of withstanding distressing internal states.

When your friend leaves her drinking glass on the table for thirty seconds, tolerate the discomfort of not putting it in the dishwasher.

Do something—sit there.

Tie a New Habit to an Existing One

Beth's high school reunion was a few months away. "I know how to get into shape," she told her husband, Doug. Beth was a cross-country runner in high school and had enjoyed a lean figure for years.

But when she hit forty, her body began to shift. Work and family demands made it difficult for her to be consistent and stick to an exercise routine and healthy eating habits. Determined, Beth told Doug every night before bed, "I'm going to run in the morning."

Each morning her feet crackled as she headed to the bathroom. Her neck ached from sleeping on it wrong. She fed the dog and took him for his morning walk. She yanked him forward. "Hurry up! I have to get my run in." The dog winced, his ears pinned tight to his head. She yanked on his leash again. "Hurry up, you stupid dog." On her return she slammed the front door and continued to yell at the dog. "You made me miss my run."

When you want to start a new habit, take one *small* step and anchor it to a current specific habit.

1. Start small and build up. The biggest mistake people make is not going small enough.
    a. Put your running shoes out the night before.
2. Anchor your new behavior to a regular habit.
    a. Identify a habit you do regularly. For example, every morning you turn on the coffee pot.
    b. Once you identify your anchor habit, tie your new behavior to it. Push the ON button on your coffee pot and put your running shoes on. Do this for five days.
3. Add additional small steps every few days.
    a. After you hit the ON button of the coffee pot, put your shoes on and walk around the block.

Beth identified an anchor habit of turning on the TV when she woke up. She anchored her new habit by placing her running shoes next to the TV the night before and putting them on after turning on the TV. After a week, she started running.

Start one new behavior and anchor it to something you already do regularly.

Expect Obstacles

As you learn new behaviors, you will experience both internal and external obstacles. Prepare for them.

Internal obstacles include your inner critic, limiting beliefs, self-doubt, lack of confidence, and relying on past experiences.

Examples of Internal Obstacles:

- "I don't have enough time to do this work. If I take my foot off the accelerator, my life will fall apart."
- "Doing ________ seems frivolous to me. It isn't productive."
- "I'm going to fail again. I hate feeling uncomfortable and what my inner critic tells me is true. I'd rather be unhappy than uncertain."

External obstacles include things like your child getting sick or your car breaking down.

Examples of External Obstacles:

- "I had time set aside to do this work and I got an urgent call from a client."
- "I was leaving work on time in order to get home and spend time with my family. Then my boss grabbed me as I was walking out and asked to talk with me about something important."

Beth was determined to get in shape for her high school reunion. Her internal obstacle was to rely on past experience: "I've always been able to get in shape quickly in the past. It should work again, even though I'm ten years older and have different demands on my time." Her inner critic barked, "You should look better than you do now. How could you let yourself go?"

Beth's external obstacle was the dog that took longer to do his business, making her miss her run.

Steps to Overcome Obstacles:

1. Select a goal you want to achieve.
2. Identify and write down your internal and external obstacles to this goal.
3. Notice your thoughts and feelings about the obstacles. Write them down.
4. Select actions to take when you encounter obstacles. Complete the following sentence:

"When I experience ________________ (internal or external obstacle), I am going to take three deep breaths, call a friend, listen to music for five minutes, and identify four things for which I am grateful."

Beth expected her inner critic to speak up. When it did, she responded, "I hear you and I promise I will exercise regularly." She acted as if she was new to running and set newcomer goals. She got up ten minutes earlier to allow the dog time to explore on their walk.

Greet your obstacles like a friend: "I've been expecting you and have a plan for us to work together."

Make Your Talents Built to Sell

John Warrillow wrote the book *Built to Sell: Creating a Business that Can Thrive Without You.* He developed a systematic approach to help business owners build more valuable companies that are designed to thrive without the owner. Most entrepreneurs are the primary salesperson of their business. Clients only want to work with them. This dependency slows growth and they end up chained to the business.

The author tells a story of a business owner who wanted to sell and, through this story, teaches readers how to focus on what they are good at and create a repeatable process that can be made into a product.

It works not only for business owners who want to sell. It's for individuals who want to take something they are good at and make it a repeatable and teachable "product" and make money outside their day job.

Abby knew she had a talent for organizing. Running a house with three children and a husband, while working a part-time job, taught her how to focus on structure and routines to keep her home, finances, and mind in order. Her friends regularly asked her to teach them. She started to help others and realized she wanted to grow this service into something beyond herself.

1. Focus on one thing you do really well. Even a service business can be "productized" by creating a standard service that is the focus of the business.
2. Put a process in place, from sales to production, for this one thing you do really well.
3. Say no to work outside the scope of your business. A narrow focus is what helps you excel.

Abby took detailed notes of every step, task, and checklist to capture her process of organizing homes. She hired an assistant to test out the steps and refined them. She hired two more assistants and taught her "product" approach that was not dependent upon her doing the work.

Identify one talent you are really good at. Develop it into a repeatable process. Document it. Teach it to others.

Conduct Happiness Interviews

Nancy Drew is a fictional character in *The Nancy Drew Mystery* book series. She is an amateur teenage detective. Eighty million copies of the books have been sold and it's been translated into forty-five languages.

Nancy is a beloved heroine: bold, brave, and independent. She spends her time solving mysteries, assisted by her best friends, cousins Bess Marvin and George Fayne. No mystery is too baffling for her to solve. A few titles are: *The Secret of the Old Clock, The Mystery at Lilac Inn, The Clue in the Diary*, and *The Quest of the Missing Map.*

Nancy's success at solving mysteries can be attributed to her curiosity. She asks questions without any preconceptions. It allows her to see more possibilities. In order to handle the constant conditions of the new, the unfamiliar and the unknown, she maintains a sense of wonder and willingness to try new things.

Use curiosity to conduct happiness interviews. The purpose is to solve the mystery of how to love yourself. Choose the happiest person you know and ask them what they do to be compassionate with themselves versus judging themselves. The person you ask will be delighted. Apply the approaches they use. Watch your heart expand.

Nancy Drew's tenacity helped her solve mysteries for nearly a century. It's your turn to solve the mystery and wonder of you.

Use curiosity to unlock the mystery of inner compassion.

Perspective Is Not What You See, But the Way You See It

Jenny paced as she chewed her fingernail. The phone call had left her confused and anxious. Another agent had been rude to her. She wanted Jenny out of the house she was showing clients at 4:00 p.m. Jenny locked the door and put the key in the lockbox at 4:00 pm. She stood on the porch with her clients, and at 4:10 the homeowners pulled up. She and her clients quickly left.

The realtor called. "I'm disappointed you didn't follow my instructions to be out of the house at 4:00 p.m." She proceeded to yell at Jenny for several minutes.

Jenny was taken aback. "This woman was so nice during the open house and walk-through. She was a completely different person on the phone. Why did this happen? What is wrong with her?"

Perspective is the ability to look objectively at a situation from an unbiased, neutral standpoint. When you know how to gain perspective, you know how to change the meaning of a circumstance. Your new perspective changes the meaning of the event, which changes the feelings you have in response and what actions you take.

When something happens, ask yourself: "What perspective would help right now?"

Jenny took a quick walk around the office. She drank a glass of water. Then she asked herself, "What perspective would help me right now?"

The other agent had multiple escalating offers and was dealing with older clients who were struggling with the sale of their lifetime home. "I imagine the agent was really stressed and concerned about recommending the right offer to take."

This perspective shifted the meaning and Jenny's response. She texted the agent and asked how she could support her during this stressful time.

When you have a challenging situation, ask yourself, "What perspective would help right now?"

No More Hiding

Our deepest fear is not that we are inadequate. Our deepest fear is that we are powerful beyond measure.

—Marianne Williamson

I'm the youngest of eight children. There was constant motion and noise with ten people under one roof. Whenever people fought, I hid. My favorite spot was behind an armchair in the living room.

I loved my hiding place. It was safe. I imagined I was on a playground, where I climbed the monkey bars, swung as high as my legs would pump on the swing, and dug in the sand pit. It was my coping mechanism and it worked.

As an adult, I continue to hide. I don't share for fear of getting hurt. I have a beautiful armor of confidence that hides my vulnerability. "Let me help you. I'm here for you first. I'm focused on what you need." These are examples of how I hide. I don't know how to receive the same type of support for myself. My childhood coping mechanism is hampering me.

How do I know I'm hiding? Because my dear friends tell me. They gently coax me to come out from behind the armchair. I'm willing to learn how to stop hiding because I crave connection and belonging.

Here are the steps to come out of your hiding place:

1. Notice when and how you hide. Ask, "Am I keeping it together or caretaking the needs of others to the exclusion of mine? When they ask me how I am, do I answer, F.I.N.E.?" This acronym stands for Frantic, Insecure, Neurotic, and Egotistical.

2. Acknowledge your discomfort when sharing. This is normal and to be expected.

3. Identify the payoff you get from hiding. There are four.

    a. I don't have to change.

    b. I don't have to learn a new behavior.

    c. I don't have to take personally accountability.

    d. I don't have to make a choice.

4. Start small. Share one thing you normally wouldn't. For example: "I think I made a mistake in taking on this client." It may feel big in your head until you say it out loud.

Doing these four steps with friends enabled me to connect, to belong, and to see that they don't leave when I share who I am. I experience an endless series of magical miracles!

Identify one hiding behavior. Tell a friend that you are ready to stop and be seen.

Fixed or Growth Mindset

In *Mindset: The New Psychology of Success*, Carol S. Dweck, PhD shares her extensive research showing that the view you adopt of yourself profoundly affects the way you lead your life. She found a simple belief about yourself that guides and permeates nearly all parts of your life. This belief limits your potential or enables your success.

It's *mindset*—how you think about your talents and abilities, where they came from and whether they can change.

There are two kinds of mindset: fixed and growth.

People with a *fixed mindset* think their intelligence and talents are simple fixed traits, and that talent alone creates success—without effort.

People with a *growth mindset* believe their abilities and talents can be developed through hard work, good strategies, and input from others.

It's not just our talents and abilities that bring us success—but whether we approach them with a fixed mindset or growth mindset.

She cites an example: Enron. In 2001, the company went under. Why? Malcolm Gladwell wrote that it was their mindset that did them in. Their "talent mindset" created a culture that worshiped talent, thereby forcing its employees to look and act extraordinarily talented. Basically, it forced them into a fixed mindset. People with a fixed mindset do not admit and correct their deficiencies.

When companies esteem employees for their innate talent, they face grave difficulty when their image is threatened. They will not take the remedial course. They will not stand up to investors and the public and admit that they were wrong.

It's been documented by Jim Collins, who wrote *Good to Great*, that one important factor distinguishes successful leaders in thriving companies: a growth mindset.

These are leaders who are not constantly trying to prove they're better than others. Instead, they are trying to improve, they're able to look squarely at their own mistakes and deficiencies, and ask what skills they and the company will need in the future.

If you embrace challenges, persist in the face of obstacles, see effort as a path to mastery, and learn from criticism, you have a growth mindset.

Get That Energy Out of Your Body

I discovered I have a lot of energy inside me that needs to be expressed. What kind? I can use labels such as anger, grief, resentment, and regret. I prefer to lump them all together and call them *energy*.

What happens when I don't express my energy? I overeat, overwork, focus on what other people should or should not do, and compare myself to others. I experience a general irritability. Life feels like it has to be endured.

Recently I went to the batting cages and hit sixty-two balls. Correction: I swung at sixty-two and hit fifty-six.

How to express energy:

- Hit softballs or tennis balls
- Take a boxing class
- Pull weeds
- Beat up pillows
- Jump rope

What happens when I do express my energy? I focus back on myself and the present moment. I make better choices. My body feels lighter. I sleep better. I am gentler with myself and others. People and things don't bother me as much.

Check your irritability level. It may be time for an expression session.

Get Unstuck

Josh Waitzkin is an eight-time National Chess Champion. He won his first title at the age of nine. He was the subject of the book and movie, *Searching for Bobby Fisher*. Josh published his first book, *Josh Waitzken's Attacking Chess*, at the age of eighteen. He is now a martial arts champion and holds twenty-one national championship titles.

His success is due to the learning techniques that bring together his mind and body. In his book, *The Art of Learning*, he details his methods to master performance.

One of his techniques is called End Game. He focused on the final two moves that would win a chess match. Focus kept his mind less distracted. He did not cram too much information in his head. He learned to do less incredibly well.

If you were writing an essay, you may experience writer's block. Instead of focusing on all the information you need, get clear on the end of the story. Focus on one particular part to reduce distraction and clogging your brain with too many facts.

Apply this to work projects, when you want to clean out closets or drawers, or plan a vacation.

When you're stuck and don't know what to do, start with your end game.

We All Fall Short

Daniela knew she should slow down. There were speed traps on the way to her ex-husband's house. *I can't be late again.* His chastising voice rattled in her head.

Jason and Trey threw their backpacks in the trunk and climbed in her car. Jason slammed his door.

"What's that about?" Daniela hissed.

Jason was a sophomore in high school and struggled with schoolwork. "Since when are you and Dad allowed to force a tutor on me? It's my life and I don't need one."

"Don't you tell me what I can and can't do. Sometimes you are the most ungrateful brat. You don't know how lucky you are!"

Jason snapped. "Real lucky. You and Dad have screwed up my life and now you want me to be grateful?"

As Daniela and Jason screamed at each other, Trey cowered in the back seat. "Is anybody hungry?" he squeaked.

Trey's voice broke her angry trance. At the stoplight, her head flopped and tears fell in her lap. "This is the last thing I wanted to have happen," she cried. The stress of the divorce affected everyone.

Self-forgiveness is essential for emotional health and peace of mind. When you've made a mistake, take a deep breath and forgive yourself.

Daniela pulled into the Panera parking lot. "Please forgive me, Jason. Let's discuss this over dinner. We'll figure it out together."

Place both hands on your heart and say, "I deeply and completely forgive myself for ______________ (yelling at my child)" and move on.

Gratitude Keeps You in the Present Moment

There is a Buddhist parable about a monk who is walking the mountains when he is confronted by a fierce tiger. The tiger chases him to the edge of a cliff. Below the cliff is the sea. The monk chooses to lower himself over the cliff on a thick vine. As he hangs on the vine, he sees a plant with leaves and one bright red strawberry. He picks it and eats it, savoring the sweetness.

When you are being chased by tigers in your mind—how you wish life was different, that other people and circumstances would change so you could be happy—stop. Look at past experiences where you were about to be eaten by situations and were saved. When you worry about what today will bring, accept that things are the way they are, and enjoy the sweet moments—playing with your dog, a conversation with your child or husband, a nice note from a friend, a good night's sleep.

Gratitude in the moment gets you out of just surviving another day and gives you the perspective you need to be present and fully alive.

Practice gratitude and enjoy the miracle of being here, now.

Make Rejection a Good Thing

When you hear NO, do you feel sick to your stomach? Deflated? Ready to quit? One of the hardest things to deal with is a flat refusal, which is perhaps why cold calling is one of the most disliked activities. It's easy to take a rejection of a sales call as a rejection of you personally. It seems as if people don't like you in some way, or that you have failed somehow.

If, however, you can turn a refusal into an interesting and valuable experience, then your job can become much more interesting and even fun.

Stop making YES your success metric. Make NO your new success metric. This technique takes the dread out of hearing NO. You'll have a sense of excitement when you hear NO. Every NO brings you closer to a YES.

- Each week or month, count your NOs and try to get 25, 50, or 100 people to say NO—to setting an appointment or buying your product or service.
- Add one more NO if they are not even willing to have you call them back.
- Count how many NOs you go through to get to a YES.

You will get better at dealing with the NOs. The more you practice, the tougher it becomes to get those 25, 50, and 100 NOs. You will find more YESs sneaking in.

Make the number of "NOs" your success metric when cold calling.

CHANGE THE STORIES YOU TELL YOURSELF–PART 1 OF 5

Identify an Adversity

The benefits of resilience go beyond just helping you feel good. Studies have shown that boosting your resilience increases your resistance to stress and even prevents stress to some degree. It is a quality that helps you act in appropriate and productive ways, quickly bouncing back from adversity. Resiliency is the ability to face setbacks, failures, crises, and pain—both emotional and physical—with confidence and courage. You can develop resilience by managing your thoughts, behaviors, and actions.

The way you explain events to yourself (your explanatory style) determines how helpless you can become, or how energized, when you encounter everyday setbacks. Explanatory style is the manner in which you habitually explain to yourself why events happen.

Dr. Martin Seligman wrote *Learned Optimism: How to Change Your Mind and Your Life*. He has found success in teaching a form of learned optimism to people using the ABCD approach. "ABC" refers to how you react negatively to success or adversity, while "D" refers to how you can rethink the pessimistic reaction into an optimistic one.

The following story is from his book:

Two University of Pennsylvania MBA graduates, Mark and Bill, were laid off by their Wall Street companies eighteen months ago. Both went into a tailspin: they were sad, listless, indecisive, and anxious about the future. For Mark, the mood was transient. After two weeks, he told himself, "It's not you; it's the economy going through a bad patch. I'm good at what I do, and there will be a market for my skills." He updated his resumé and sent it to a dozen New York firms, all of which rejected him. He then tried six companies in his Ohio hometown and eventually landed a position. Bill, by contrast, spiraled into hopelessness. "I got fired because I can't perform under pressure," he thought. "I'm not cut out for finance. The economy will take years to recover." Even as the market improved, he didn't look for another job; he ended up moving back in with his parents.

Use the ABCD Model to improve your resiliency.

A (Adversity)

Adversity is the event that happens. Adversity sets off your beliefs, your expectations, and your interpretation of why things went wrong.

Recall an adverse event or setback you experienced recently. This could be spilling coffee on your shirt, getting stuck in traffic, a large bill, or inattention from your significant other. Record your description of what happened, not your evaluation of it. Be objective in your description.

Example: "I had a fight with my significant other because I forgot to go to the grocery store." Do not record, "He was unfair."

Identify a recent setback and apply the ABCD model to bounce back faster from adversity.

CHANGE THE STORIES YOU TELL YOURSELF–PART 2 OF 5

Record Your Beliefs and Consequences

The first step to improve your resilience with the ABCD model is to identify an adversity. In the previous story, Mark and Bill were laid off by their Wall Street companies.

The second step is to identify your belief about the adversity.

B (Beliefs)

Your beliefs are how you interpret the adversity. Record your beliefs, not your feelings.

Bill's beliefs were, "I'm not cut out for finance," "I got fired because I can't perform under pressure," and "The economy will take years to recover." "I feel sad" is a feeling.

Mark's beliefs were, "It's not me; it's the economy going through a bad patch. I'm good at what I do, and there will be a market for my skills."

Next, identify the consequences of your beliefs.

C (Consequences)

Consequences are the feelings and actions that result from your beliefs.

Record your feelings and as many actions as you were aware of. Did you feel sad, anxious, guilty, or joyful? Did you feel like you could do anything about it? Did you go back to bed, or have no energy? These are all actions.

Even as the market improved, Bill didn't look for another job. He ended up moving back in with his parents. He felt hopeless.

Mark updated his resumé and sent it to a dozen New York firms, all of which rejected him. He then tried six companies in his Ohio hometown and eventually landed a position.

Record two or three examples of feelings and actions and look for the link between your beliefs and the consequences.

CHANGE THE STORIES YOU TELL YOURSELF–PART 3 OF 5

Dispute Your Limiting Beliefs

D (Dispute)

When you have a negative belief, find evidence to argue against it. Question whether your beliefs are the only explanation.

Ask these four questions:

1. "What are the **alternatives**?" There are usually multiple causes, so why latch on to the worst one? Focus on the changeable, the specific, and the non-personal causes.

2. "What is the **evidence** for my beliefs?" Show that it is factually incorrect.

3. "What are the real **implications** of my believing this way, and do they make it worth holding on to my beliefs?" The negative belief you hold about yourself may be correct, so ask yourself about the implications and how likely are those (usually awful) implications.

4. "How **useful** are my beliefs?" "Do I or others get any benefits from holding on to them, or would we benefit more if we held other beliefs?" For example, some people get upset because life isn't fair. The belief that life should be fair may cause more grief than it's worth. What good does it do you to dwell on this?

Listen closely for your beliefs, observe the consequences, and dispute your limiting beliefs. Don't search adversity out. Wait until it happens, then tune into your internal dialog. If you change the habitual beliefs that follow adversity, your reaction to adversity will change as well.

Change the destructive things you say to yourself when you experience setbacks using the ABCD model.

CHANGE THE STORIES YOU TELL YOURSELF–PART 4 OF 5

Putting It All Together

Willa slammed the dryer door and dumped the dry but wrinkled clothes on the floor. The bang sent the dog scampering under the kitchen table. Her kids decided it was a good time to go outside and play.

She applied the ABCD model to change her response to adversity.

Adversity (the event that happens): "I got into a fight with my husband, Darren, because he didn't take the clean laundry out of the dryer like he said he would. Now the clothes are all wrinkled and I have to wash and dry them again."

Beliefs (how that adversity is interpreted): "He's so disrespectful of my things and my time. I can't believe he just lets my clean clothes get wrinkled. I always have to do everything around here. He doesn't care about me."

Consequences (the feelings and actions that result from the beliefs): "We got into a big fight. He was angry because he thought I was blowing it out of proportion. I was mad because I felt he didn't respect me."

Dispute (When you have a negative belief, you find evidence to argue it. What are the real implications of the belief? What are the alternatives? Is the belief even useful for you?): "Darren does respect me. He regularly helps clean the house and do laundry. He didn't intentionally try to upset me. I was triggered by this because my mom used to make me do everything around the house."

Willa changed the story she was telling herself. She and Darren talked and realized that they were both tired from working long hours. They cleared their calendar for Friday night and went to the movies and dinner.

Choose to look at adversity dispassionately.

CHANGE THE STORIES YOU TELL YOURSELF–PART 5 OF 5

Putting the ABCD Model into Practice

Stephanie checked herself in the mirror again. Her legs fidgeted as she smoothed her hair. “Crap!” she said as she dropped the back of one of her earrings. Instead of looking for it, she chose her biggest hoop earrings. “Why not. I’ve gone this far. Might as well go big tonight,” she said to the image in the mirror. Stephanie was hosting a dinner party and wanted to make a good impression on her guests, one in particular. It didn’t go as she’d hoped.

She applied the ABCD model to change her response to adversity.

Adversity (the event that happens): “I threw a dinner party for a group of friends, and the person I was trying to impress barely touched his food.”

Beliefs (how that adversity is interpreted): “The food tastes awful. I am such a lousy cook. I might as well forget getting to know him any better. I’m lucky he didn’t get up and leave in the middle of the dinner.”

Consequences (the feelings and actions that result from the beliefs): “I felt really disappointed and angry with myself. I was so embarrassed about my cooking that I wanted to avoid him for the rest of the night. Obviously, things weren’t going as I had hoped.”

Dispute (when you have a negative belief, find evidence to argue it. What are the real implications of the belief? What are the alternatives? Is the belief even useful for you?): “This is ridiculous. I know the food doesn’t taste awful (evidence). He may have not eaten very much, but everyone else did (evidence).”

“There could be a hundred reasons why he didn’t eat much (alternatives). He could be on a diet, not feeling well, or have a small appetite (alternatives).”

“He told some funny stories and seemed to be relaxed (evidence).”

“He even offered to help me with the dishes (evidence). He wouldn’t have done that if he was repulsed by me (alternative).”

Stephanie was able to change the story she was telling herself. Her mood lightened as she disputed her negative beliefs. She thought about the good things that happened during the evening. “I’m going to host another party again.”

Dispute your negative beliefs and bounce back faster from adversity.

Forgiveness Leads to Freedom

Forgiveness is the vehicle for correcting our misperceptions and for letting go of fear, condemning judgments, and grievances. Forgiveness releases us from all thoughts that seem to separate us from ourselves and from others.

Forgiveness is the process of changing thoughts and beliefs about people, places, and things.

"He's doing it to me again!" Celia paced and waved her arms as she talked. "He's inconsiderate and selfish. He says he supports me in my new job and then 'forgets' he agreed to pick up the kids from school. Now the kids are mad at me. I'm not letting him off the hook for this one."

Maybe he is doing it to Celia on purpose. Maybe not. Celia's perception of it makes it so.

Ask yourself, "Do I want to be right or do I want to be happy?"

"I want to be right, darn it!" Celia cried.

The price for being right is high. You lose sleep, overeat, or overfunction. You drive aggressively and experience strained relationships.

Ask yourself:

1. "What story do I tell myself about this person, place, or institution?"
2. "What is the payoff for holding on to it?"
3. "Is there another way of seeing the situation?"
4. "Do I want to be right or happy?"

We all judge, control, and blame others to feel safe. Forgiving ourselves and our attachments to our opinions and judgments frees us to see and think differently, from a detached place of curiosity and openness. Forgiveness lowers stress, pain, and blood pressure. It also gives you space to be human.

Practice forgiveness as the vehicle for correcting your misperceptions and for letting go of fear, condemning judgments, and grievances.

Reframe the Way You Look at Situations

Reframing is the process of changing the way you see a situation and finding alternative ways to view it. This process reduces stress and increases access to your frontal lobe, the executive functioning part of your brain.

At the airport after a tiring business trip, Leila's return flight was delayed. She went to the airport shop, bought a book, a coffee, and a small packet containing five cookies. The airport was crowded, and she found a seat in the lounge next to a stranger. After a few minutes' reading, she became absorbed in her book. She took a cookie from the packet and began to drink her coffee. To her great surprise, the stranger in the next seat calmly took one of the cookies and ate it. Stunned, she couldn't bring herself to say anything, nor even to look at the stranger. Nervously, she continued reading. After a few minutes, she slowly picked up and ate the third cookie. Incredibly, the stranger took the fourth cookie and ate it, then, to the woman's amazement, he picked up the packet and offered her the last one.

This being too much to tolerate, Leila angrily picked up her belongings, gave the stranger a nasty look, and marched off to the boarding gate, where her flight was now ready. Flustered and enraged, she reached inside her bag for her boarding ticket, and found her unopened packet of cookies.

Reframing is a habit of explaining negative events to yourself; it is self-talk after an experience.

Ask yourself, "Do I want to be right or happy?"

Pause and Question

Someone who pauses to question can fully engage, act boldly, and seize opportunities.

Most people are busy doing. Stop to ask why you are *doing*.

Let's say you are climbing a mountain. Stop and ask yourself why you are climbing the mountain. It could be to reach the top, plant a flag, or spend time with your friends.

If you stop and ask questions, you may learn you're hiking the wrong mountain, or that you don't like to hike. Asking questions leads to other questions.

- What is waiting for me at the top?
- What am I going to do once I get there?
- Am I enjoying the climb itself?
- Should I slow down or speed up?
- What am I leaving behind?

This metaphor applies in all areas of your life: health, work, and relationships.

Spend time with a question instead of trying to answer it right away. You give your brain a chance to come up with fresh insights and possibilities that can lead to breakthroughs.

Master the art and skill of questioning.

Journal to Discover What Your Inner Critic Wants You to Know

Writing helps clarify what your inner critic is saying to you:

- "I can't believe you said that!"
- "How come you're always late?"
- "Don't wear that outfit. It makes you look fat."

Your inner critic speaks from a place of positive intention, which may be to keep you employed, healthy, or feeling like you belong. When you write down what your inner critic is saying, you can determine its positive intentions for you.

Answer these questions:

1. Identify the situation that may have triggered the inner critic.

   You get called into a staff meeting. You don't want to be there. They are celebrating somebody's birthday. You eat a piece of cake. You didn't want to eat the cake. Your inner critic starts in on you.

2. Identify your feelings about the situation.

   "I'm angry. I don't want to be here. I was dragged in. I'm really angry."

3. Identify what you are afraid of.

   "I'm afraid I'm going to turn my report in late and I don't want to submit it late."

4. What if that did happen? What are the consequences?

   "My boss is going to yell at me. I don't want my boss to yell at me."

Keep writing to identify your vulnerable feelings about the situation. This is what the inner critic is protecting you from feeling. Journaling helps you sort through complex sets of emotions and experiences.

Spend five minutes a day journaling to identify your inner critic's positive intentions for you.

Forgive for Your Own Sake

Norman Cousins was an American political journalist, author, professor, and world peace advocate. He wrote, "Life is an adventure in forgiveness."

By the time you are an adult, you have suitcases full of experiences of abuse, rejection, neglect, betrayal, and humiliation. Without forgiveness, you pack your suitcases full of these memories and drag them behind you. They slow you down and keep you looking backwards.

Begin the process of forgiveness. Ask yourself what you want: love, connection, harmony, success, fulfillment, friends, security? To make space for these, let go of the stories of the past. Empty your suitcases.

The first step is to become willing. Only you can initiate the movement toward forgiveness that leads to your wholeness.

Be willing to let go of the anger and guilt toward others and yourself.

For Me Is Not Against You

Trust yourself and your intuition that leads you on your path. If you are on someone else's, take the next off ramp.

Manon blurted, "I was approached by an insurance broker to join his new firm."

"Tell me more."

Manon straightened up and leaned forward. She went into the details.

"This new job has 80 percent of what you love to do. How much does your current job have?" her friends asked.

"Thirty percent." She leaned back in her chair and looked down. "If I take it, my boss will be mad at me. She's done so much for me. Nobody would have given me the opportunities she did."

"So you should stay on her path?"

"No."

"What's getting in the way of you saying yes to this?"

"Me. I don't want to disappoint her."

When you identify your heart's desire, you may run into internal obstacles like guilt, defensiveness, or resignation. These keep you from going after what you want.

Fear of how others will respond to your choices is normal and to be expected. Think about the conversation you need to have with the people your choice impacts. Practice clear and direct phrases. Expect discomfort before, during, and after your meeting.

Manon journaled on the statement, "*for* me is not *against* you." It helped reduce her anxiety about resigning. She chose the following phrases and practiced them: "You may be right." "Yes, and . . ." "That doesn't work for me."

Speak your truth to yourself first.

F.E.A.R. Is False Evidence Appearing Real

Beverly signed up for a program that would help her earn a life-coaching certification. Her excitement and motivation quickly turned to procrastination and fear.

She asked a friend to hold her accountable for completing and turning in her first assignment. She set a deadline and, if she missed it, she had to give $50 to a political party she did not support. A jumpstart like this would get her unstuck. She turned it in by the deadline.

She received evaluation feedback from the instructor. She started to read it, but felt terribly uncomfortable. She had an adrenaline rush, her heart beat fast, and she began to sweat. She closed the document after reading a few sentences. She doubted herself. "This is too hard. I don't understand how to do it. Why did I sign up for this?" Fear stopped her from taking action, thinking clearly, and finding solutions.

A week later, she took a deep breath, opened the document, and read it from beginning to end. At the end of the document, the evaluator said, "This is good. A-."

She tortured herself for a week thinking she couldn't do the work. Fear told her not to look at the document.

Look for evidence that your fear is justified. Nine times out of ten, you'll come up empty-handed.

The Key to Happiness Is Reflection and Gratitude

Every day, dwell on one thing that makes you grateful.

Hailey Bartholomew had what seemed to be a perfect life. Loving husband, two sweet daughters, a home with a garden in Brisbane, Australia. Yet she was restless, tired, and irritable. She wrote in her journal, "I have everything, but find my life uninteresting and I can't enjoy a thing."

She sought support and advice from a local nun and learned to focus on the little things that made her feel grateful. Determined to change her outlook and attitude, she grabbed her Polaroid camera and decided to take a picture each day for a year of something that made her feel grateful. The first thing she noticed was her husband. Before doing this project, she had labeled him as unromantic. She discovered things she had missed before. One night after dinner there were two pieces of pie left for dessert. One was a bit mushy. The other had a crispy topping and crust and was twice as big. He gave her the biggest and best piece of pie on her plate. She realized every day he was choosing her. At the end of the project, he told her, "I feel like I'm enough for you now."

Hailey's 365 gratitude project spread through Flkr and Facebook. People started doing their own gratitude projects. She created a website, 365grateful.com, to inspire others and discover more about the power of gratitude.

Gratitude helps you look at the world with fresh eyes.

Interrupt your habitual thinking patterns with gratitude.

Shaming Is Not a Management Style

Shame-based management kills productivity and people's spirits.

Shame is used as an attempt to control others. It can work in the short term. Employees produce out of fear, not inspiration. In the process, they lose confidence and self-trust. This leads to more mistakes and loss of focus.

Shame comes in many forms: sarcasm, name-calling, expressing disgust, eye-rolling, teasing, and phrases, such as:

- "What were you thinking?"
- "You could never do what they do."
- "Why don't you act like the other women in your department?"

Instead of shame-based management, use open-ended questions:

- "Tell me more about the problem."
- "What were your assumptions when you started this project?"
- "Can you help me understand that a little better?"
- "What challenges does that process create?"
- "What changed since we last talked?"

Leaders create an environment in which employees can thrive and succeed. What you say and how you say it is the difference between success and failure.

Teach others to "do" better, not "be" better.

Don't Let Guilt Harden into Shame

She inhaled the aroma of the bag and immediately felt herself walking through the markets of Florence. A red Dolce and Gabbana Sicily handbag, made out of dauphine leather with leopard print lining. It retailed for $1,895 and was on sale for $1,100. Damaris bought it, not worried about the no-return policy. Still dreaming as she drove home, Damaris saw herself carefully selecting the right items to put in her new bag.

"Are you kidding? We have $9,000 in credit card debt already. We don't know how much our health insurance is going to increase and you went out bought a $1,100 purse. What were you thinking?" Ben shouted.

Damaris slumped in her chair. Her face flushed and her hands were cold and clammy. "I'm sorry," she whispered.

Guilt and shame are feelings.

Guilt pertains to an action: "I made a mistake." It is helpful in that it shows you when you have violated your own values.

Shame pertains to a person: "I am a mistake." Shame is destructive because it leads to the belief that you are unworthy of love and belonging.

Self-forgiveness moves you out of guilt and into healing. Put both hands on your heart and say, "I deeply and completely forgive myself for ________ (buying a purse that I can't afford at this time)."

Ben held Damaris as she cried. Through sniffles, she explained, "I was overtaken by the beauty of it. Please forgive me."

"I love you, Damaris," Ben comforted her.

Feel your feelings, then take corrective actions when you miss the mark.

Your Inner Critic Has a Positive Intention for You

In the movie *The Wizard of Oz*, Dorothy discovers the Great Wizard is a bumbling man behind a curtain, projecting anger, fear, and intimidation in order to protect himself. Dorothy's dog Toto pulls back the curtain to reveal this man pulling levers and pushing buttons. "Pay no attention to the man behind the curtain," he bellows.

The Wizard built an emerald palace and used smokescreens and scary images to keep people away from him. This is like your inner critic, who speaks in a loud, angry voice.

Your inner critic speaks from a place of positive intention. For example, it may say, "You're not going to eat that piece of cake, are you?" The positive intention is to keep you healthy. Or the inner critic says, "Don't take time to relax, sleep, or eat. It's not productive."

Talk with your inner critic. Recognize and allow it to speak up. Try these statements:

"I hear you and I promise __________ (I will take care of you, make more money, stop stuffing my feelings with food, sleep more)."

"Thank you for speaking up. I hear you and I promise I am taking care of it."

The example of answering eating the cake can be, "I hear you and I know you want me to take care of myself and I promise you I am exercising and eating healthy on a regular basis. It's OK for me to have this one piece."

Dorothy talks with the Wizard. At first she yells at him, "You're a bad man!" Oftentimes we do the same thing to our inner critic. He tells her, "I'm a very good man. I'm just a bad wizard."

Discover what positive intention your inner critic has for you today.

Practice Compassionate Accountability with Others

Helping others using compassion and accountability offers the opportunity to be consistent, to learn and grow, get more done, and build stronger relationships.

Compassionate accountability is the strong foundation and supportive structure that empowers people to do their best and own the success in their lives. It has several benefits:

- Openness to one's own and others' feelings, needs and wants, validating emotions without commiserating or discounting
- Increases resourcefulness around problem solving; individuals explore possibilities without taking over responsibility for the solution
- Persistence around commitment, goals, and boundaries without threats, ultimatums, or implicit expectations

Most people are never taught how to allow others to own their accountability, let alone how to do it compassionately. The consequences are significant.

Compassion without accountability:

- Leads to dependence and no sense of ownership
- Believes listening, consensus, and empathy are sufficient motivators of behavior
- Avoids asking directly for things
- Views confronting negative behavior as uncaring and mean
- Results in poor follow-through and low confidence that goals will be accomplished

Accountability without compassion:

- Believes rules, consequences, and expectations are sufficient motivators of behavior
- Views empathy as a sign of weakness
- Avoids listening
- Comes across as harsh and unforgiving
- Diminishes the individual's understanding of what has occurred and provides no sense of dignity when mistakes are made

When meeting with a colleague, explain the task, deadline, authority, and accountability.

When they get stuck, ask a compassionate accountability question: "What are you going to do about it, and how can I help?" It keeps the responsibility with them, provides the support and dignity to brainstorm, and is a way you can support without taking over.

Compassionate accountability honors our humanity, while allowing us to grow without internal or external criticism. Practice compassionate accountability with one person this week.

Copycat Deep Breathing

In groups, people tend to mimic each other's breathing patterns. This explains the reason you pick up on other people's tensions.

He stormed into the conference room and threw his folder on the table. The other members leaned back in their seats. The stale smell of coffee drifted upwards as Bill poured himself a cup.

Still standing, he chided the group. "How did you miss the deadline again?" He crossed the room. Messing with his hair, he blurted, "Anyone?" His eyes darted back and forth from person to person. He continued to pace.

Each member reacted differently—one fidgeted, another tapped their pen, bit their nails. All of them synced with Bill's breathing—short and shallow.

Shallow breathing is a symptom of stress. Deep breathing is one of the best ways to lower stress in the body. It sends a message to your brain to calm down and relax. When you find yourself in a stressful situation, notice your breath. Start with an inhale and count to four. Hold your breath for four. Exhale for four. Check to see if your belly expands on the inhale.

One member inhaled deeply, held his breath, and exhaled slowly. As he continued, others joined him. Finally, Bill sat down and exhaled.

Ask, "How deep is my breath?"

Just Say No

Sometimes the problem of declining a request is not having the phrases that help you say no. The next time someone asks you to do something you are not interested in, try one of these phrases:

- I need to get back to you on that.
- Thanks, but that doesn't work for me.
- Here's what will work for me.
- I appreciate your asking, but I can't.
- I know this is important, but I can't.
- That isn't doable for me right now.
- Oh, I wish I could.
- I can help you find a solution.

Be clear and direct when you say no. It is an effective and compassionate form of communication.

Curiosity Lets You Imagine the World from Inside the Heads of Other People

Brian Grazer did extensive research for his #1 *New York Times* bestselling book, *A Curious Mind—The Secret to a Bigger Life*. He found the following takeaways about curiosity:

- It is the key to understanding people's personalities and motivations.
- It is a vital storytelling tool—and storytelling is the best way to engage and persuade other people, in your work life and your personal life.
- It is a fantastic source of courage.
- It is the best, most underused management tool—a great way to create engagement in your fellow workers, but also a great way to transmit values and priorities.
- It is the spark for creativity and innovation, the best long-term investment you can make.
- It is the best way to stay connected to those who are most important to you.

Practice emotional curiosity. Pay attention to what people say, how they say it, their body language, and how they respond to your questions. Identify their emotional tones. This approach allows you a glimpse into their point of view, while interrupting yours.

Use curiosity to expand your perspective.

Fail Fast

I Love Lucy is an iconic American TV show that tells the story of Lucy, her husband Ricky, and their friends Ethel and Fred Mertz. These four often find themselves stuck in unimaginable situations that illustrate many struggles of an American household.

One of the most famous *I Love Lucy* scenes is in the episode titled "Job Switching." Lucy and Ethel get jobs at a chocolate factory to prove to their husbands that they are capable of doing what men do. With a very strict boss, they are put to work at a conveyor belt to wrap the chocolates as they pass by. As the conveyor belt goes faster and faster, Lucy and Ethel are left with so many unwrapped chocolates that they stuff them into their mouths, aprons, and throw them on the floor. Eventually the boss finds out and they are fired.

When you get in over your head, surrender. It's OK to fail. Walk away as fast as possible. Forgive yourself and move one.

Lucy and Ethel confess their failure to Ricky and Fred, who in return express their love and gratitude and give them a five-pound box of chocolates.

Say, "My bad" and move on.

Look for Evidence of What You Are Doing Right

Write down your successes, all of them, on sticky notes. Over time, you will see the changes you are making and will be able to own them.

There is a phenomenon I find associated with high-achieving, successful people. It's called *imposter syndrome*. It is a collection of feelings of inadequacy that persist in the face of information that indicates that the opposite is true. It leads to self-doubt.

> "I feel like a fake."
>
> "They are going to find out I don't really belong here."
>
> "They made a mistake in hiring me."
>
> "My success is just really luck."
>
> "My achievement is no big deal."

Success sticky notes provide evidence over time that disputes imposter syndrome beliefs that discount your success, attribute it to luck, or make you feel like a fake.

Select one brightly colored sticky pad. Write down your successes each day and post them on a wall, corkboard, or your bathroom mirror. At the end of the week you have evidence of what you are doing right.

Take the notes and place them in a notebook. Start the process again. At the end of the month, you will see how your inner dialog is changing. Imagine what a year's worth of success sticky notes will do for you!

Acknowledge your achievements.

Stop Comparing Your Insides to Other People's Outsides

Comparison is the thief of joy.
—Theodore Roosevelt

I was sitting at my computer and turned on Facebook to check my business page. I felt sick to my stomach. My hands were sweating and I craved popcorn. I was reading other people's posts. Beverly was on vacation in the Caribbean and looked fabulous in a bathing suit. Mary hosted a dinner for twelve and everyone was laughing. I felt heavy and sad.

I journaled so I could figure out why these posts were bothering me so much that I couldn't look at them. I realized that because I was in the middle of my divorce, seeing others carrying on with their lives and looking happy and content felt painful. They were happy and had it all together. Life for them was great.

I was comparing my insides to other people's outsides.

When you go through difficult times, whether it's a divorce, the loss of a loved one, or when you feel stuck, give yourself a break. In my case, it was limiting time on Facebook.

I decided to do the minimum Facebook work necessary for my business and focused my time on self-compassion instead of self-comparison.

When you are stuck, place your hands on your heart (H.O.H.) and say, "I deeply and completely love and accept myself as I am." Do it even if you think it's silly and won't work. It will.

Use Top-of-Mind Phrases to Keep You Focused on Your Priorities

Just Do It. *Got Milk?* *Be All You Can Be.* *Because You're Worth It.*
—Nike, California Milk Board, U.S. Army, L'Oreal

A top-of-mind phrase is one that reminds you of something you want to focus on and achieve.

Jeff wanted to focus on advancing his sales pipeline. His typical day was filled with meetings, conference calls, and a barrage of emails. By the end of the day, he had spent little time advancing the pipeline. Frustrated and concerned, he thought, *What if I don't hit my targets? Will I keep my job?*

A sticky note, a password phrase on your phone or laptop, or an alarm on your phone are ideal ways to keep a key word or phrase top-of-mind.

- Change your computer or phone password to your key word or phrase.
- Set an alarm on your phone to go off three times a day as an auditory cue to remind you to focus on your goal.
- Download an app that allows you to prominently feature a word or phrase every time you unlock your phone.
- Change the location and wording of your top-of-mind phrase. Your brain stops "seeing" your word or phrase after a week.

Jeff wrote the word ADVANCE on two sticky notes. He placed one on his bathroom mirror and another on the dashboard of his car. Every morning he read the note on the mirror. This helped him focus on the top three actions he would take during the day to advance his sales pipeline.

One word or phrase kept top-of-mind can help you focus on your priorities and reduce the number of times you are OBE (overtaken by events).

Use sticky notes, passwords, and alarms as top-of-mind tools to stay focused on your priorities.

No, You Shouldn't Already Know This

The need to know exactly how to proceed in all areas of your life causes worry and anxiety. It negatively impacts your health, self-esteem, and relationships. "I should know this" is a belief that needs to be changed.

Kristen recently joined a writer's group. She dreamed of getting her historical fiction novel written and published. At the first meeting, she listened to the others share their successes, critique pieces of work, and commit to actions to take. As the meeting went along, she felt heavy, like she had molasses in her veins. Her faced reddened, and she nibbled her nails to the point of pain. Her belief that she should know how to write a novel was stopping her from writing.

No belief is neutral. Your beliefs dictate each decision you make and drive your behavior.

Change your beliefs about what you think you should know. Try the following belief statements for one day:

- "Wonderful surprises happen when I ask for and accept help."
- "I'm really good at sales, connecting with people, and learning new skills. Successful people embrace the discomfort that goes along with learning new skills, such as spending time learning how to write a storyline, and I'm a successful person."
- "Lifelong learners are open to new ideas, learning new and different ways of making their lives easier, and I'm a lifelong learner."

Kristen changed her limiting belief to an empowering one. "Successful writers are open-minded, curious, and love learning their trade, and I'm a successful writer."

Act as if you believe it's not only OK to not know how to do something, it's beneficial that you don't.

People Are Busy

When someone does not respond to you, remind yourself that people are busy or overwhelmed.

Detach from thinking that you did or did not do something. Doubts may creep in. "Am I not important to you? Are you ignoring this text? Is there something I should know?" Stop these thoughts.

- Don't assume someone has the same response-time protocol that you do.
- Determine if your response-time expectation is realistic and achievable. When in doubt, ask your clients, friends, coworkers, and partner.
- Communicate with others what you do expect. "Kids, you need to respond to my texts within five minutes."
- Don't resent others who return your text, email, or phone call at a time that is convenient for them.

Expectations are resentments waiting to happen.

Learn to accept instead of expect.

EMBRACE UNCERTAINTY–PART 1 OF 2

Uncertainty Is Inevitable

Absolute certainty is not something I strive for anymore. I've learned the hard way that destiny usually looks upon our most strident convictions with amusement, or perhaps even pity.

—Elizabeth Gilbert, author, *Eat, Pray, Love*

I didn't expect to have an anxiety attack two weeks after I left my job of twenty years. It happened in a low-end discount store in the middle of a workday in Rehoboth Beach, Delaware. I had taken time off to change gears from being the president and CEO of a 200-person company to owner of my own business. It was an exciting time. I knew starting my business was the right thing for me to do. I had the skills, experience, and drive to make it work. Then I had the anxiety attack walking through the store. There were no people in business suits; no one was on their cell phones making important business deals. The chatter in my head started. "What did I just do?"

My heart was racing. I wanted to crawl out of my skin. How can an idea seem so right and yet strike terror in my heart? Scary thoughts came fast and furious. "Can I make this work? Will anyone hire me? What was I thinking!" I froze. I could feel myself getting smaller and smaller. I tried to obsessively think of other things to control the panic. I wished I had a guarantee that it would work out. A risk-free guarantee that I knew for sure I had made the right decision. I wanted a certain outcome—success.

We are wired for certainty and want to avoid uncertainty. This is why change can be hard. We prefer things we know over risking the uncertainty of new, innovative ideas and solutions. But change involves uncertainty.

Deep breathing outside the store helped bring my anxiety in check. Then I went for a walk and talked to myself about the facts and reasons for my decision to start my own business. "Is this happening in all areas of my life?" No. "Is it permanent? Personal? Pervasive?" No. Finally, I asked myself if I could live with the worst outcome: failure. I gained perspective on my situation and learned it would be the first of many experiences where I embraced uncertainty.

Respond to uncertainty with three deep breaths.

EMBRACE UNCERTAINTY–PART 2 OF 2

Managing Uncertainty

We live in an uncertain world, and we do things to reduce our sense of uncertainty—micromanage, become controlling and nit-picky, disengage, eat more, drink more, blame others, or force solutions. While these behaviors temporarily release us from our fear of the unknown, they also reduce our ability to be our most productive and effective selves.

Take these steps to minimize damaging behavior when the need for certainty strikes:

- Identify your behaviors when you are stressed by uncertainty. Do you hide, micromanage, yell, control, or go to the refrigerator?
- Accept that everyone resists change and craves certainty.
- Get back into your body.
    - Controlled breathing reduces anxiety. Take a deep breath, in through the nose, hold for five seconds, and exhale through the mouth for five seconds. Repeat seven times.
    - Walking brings you back to the present moment. Feel each foot as it hits the ground.
    - Listen to music or call a friend and share your concerns.

Uncertainty is both uncomfortable and inevitable. While we don't have a choice about its existence, we do have a choice about how we manage it.

It's OK Not to Know What You Need

I sighed, trying to exhale the feelings away. My heart sank into my stomach as I watched my son Patrick walk away from the car.

Stuck to my car seat, tears budded in the corner of my eyes. His first day of college flooded me with joy and sadness. He was starting a new chapter in his life. So was I. Whether I was ready or not, I was now officially an empty nester. I had no clue what I needed or how to get my needs met.

When you feel lost, take a deep breath. Allow your emotions to come up.

On my long drive home, I cried and laughed, remembering all the ways my beautiful son had touched my heart. Rubbing my ear as a toddler, creating imaginary games with his friends, his first school dance, writing a note when I was down and doubting myself: "I believe in you, Mom."

I called a friend who had launched two kids of her own. "Help me. I don't know what I need and my heart hurts."

Ask others to share how they walk through times of transitions.

VULNERABILITY

Successful Leaders Embrace Vulnerability

Leaders use vulnerability to show how to overcome adversity.

In 1985, Steve Jobs was fired by Apple's board of directors, the company he had founded. Twenty years later, he gave the commencement speech to the graduating class of Stanford University. He admitted that his fear of death drove his decisions in life and helped him overcome his fear of failure. "Remembering that I'll be dead soon is the most important tool I've ever encountered to help me make the big choices in life. Because almost everything—all external expectations, all pride, all fear of embarrassment or failure—these things just all go away in the face of death, leaving only what is truly important," he shared. He passed away on October 5, 2011.

Leaders show how to overcome adversity through their stories of failure, fear, and doubt. They inspire you to take action, to shift the way you think. Share your foibles to inspire others. People want to know your struggles and how you overcame them.

Be the one who inspires, who shows others the way:
"If she can do it, I can do it too."

Set Your Intention, Pay Attention, and Release Attachments

Intention is your inner relationship with yourself, lived each day, independent of reaching a goal or destination.

Attention is concentration on a single object or thought.

Attachments are opinions and judgments. They are a way of energizing separation and based on fear, scarcity, and the need for security. Seeking security is like approaching a mirage. It keeps disappearing as you get closer to it. The search for security is an illusion. Looking for security and certainty is an attachment to the known. The known is your past. And the past is a prison.

Intention, combined with detachment, leads to life-centered, present-moment awareness. And when action is performed in present-moment awareness, it is most effective. Your intent is for the future, but your attention is in the present.

Write down your intention of how you want to BE each day: loving, free, open, self-compassionate, content, curious, powerful, alert, open, fresh, spontaneous, innocent, fearless, replenished, loving, open, curious, free, powerful, playful, focused, intentional, joyful, relaxed, confident, and patient.

Place your attention on this moment.

Let go of your attachments to outcomes.

Embrace the wisdom of uncertainty and choose the unfamiliar.

Give, Give, Give . . . Kill!

Stop putting others' needs ahead of your own.

Kasia accepted a job relocation to another state. Once she located the grocery store, dry cleaners, and pharmacy, she decided to determine her next level of needs. She wrote a personal vision: settle into the new home and make it comfy, organized, and safe; explore the neighborhood; make new friends; garden; bike.

Almost immediately, she came up with several reasons why she couldn't take steps toward her vision. "I'll do those things when my work to-do list is caught up. I'll explore the neighborhood after I take calls from my friends and my mom. They need me, and I want to support them."

When she started to make time to go for a walk in the neighborhood, her inner critic jumped in with fear: "What if you're not available for others? You don't want to regret not being there for them. They depend on you. Think of how you'll feel if you aren't there and they die before you get back to them."

Her pattern of putting others' needs first was well ingrained. This left her depleted and resentful.

Expect resistance when you take time to get your needs met. Develop an encouraging phrase that supports your new behaviors. "Successful women take time to meet their own needs, and I'm a successful woman." "I deserve this time to go for a bike ride." "When I meet my needs, I am better able to meet others' needs."

Kasia started with a fifteen-minute walk in the morning. Doing it first thing in the morning reduced the likelihood that she would be overtaken by events and not meet her own needs.

Learn to balance taking care of yourself and helping others.

This Isn't Happening to You–It's Happening for You

Your perspective determines your world view.

David Lee, a professional storyteller, told this story about perspective.

He went for a power walk on a hot September day. There were a lot of wooly bear caterpillars on the road. He didn't want to step on them, but yet he did want to get a cardio workout. He decided to take off his shirt and use it as a broom, sweeping them aside as he walked.

He wondered about the wooly bears' perspective of this experience: one moment sunning yourself on the road, the next moment being whooshed into the bushes. It's a metaphor for life. You go through change, challenges, and uncertainty. You lose your job, get sick, or your business tanks. It's frightening and traumatic. From a higher perspective (David's), it was a gift. Yet it is hard to have the higher perspective when you are the one getting swept into the bushes.

The next time you face difficulties, practice perspective. Perspective is looking at your situation from the 100,000-foot level.

- Pause. Take three deep breaths. Notice your surroundings.
- Zoom out. Once you have centered yourself, imagine you are looking through a camera lens from 10,000 feet. You are someone observing your situation. Zoom your lens farther out to take in more of what's happening around you.
- Reframe. Ask, "What perspective would help right now?"
- Reflect on a crisis in your life that happened in the past, when you felt like the wooly bear, consumed in the trauma and fear. Now, looking back with a broader perspective, identify the hidden gift, door opening, and opportunity.

Strengthen your perspective muscle.

Accountability Partners Help You Move Forward Faster

Sitting at her breakfast table drinking her morning coffee and trying to wake up, Brittany opened her laptop and started reading work emails. The first couple were fine, the usual questions and requests. Then, boom. There it was, that same old micromanaging email from her boss that she seemed to get every other week. Exasperated, she let out a heavy sigh. "Why does senior management keep making decisions that prevent me from doing my job?"

Sick to her stomach, she skipped breakfast. While driving to work, she thought, "I should look for another job. I know I have the skills an employer values. Ugh. Where do I start?"

She stopped for another coffee and a bagel and called her friend Gail for support.

Gail offered to be her accountability partner. She asked, "What is one step you can take toward finding a new job today?"

Brittany sighed. "I can update my resume."

"Great. Text me once you've completed it."

Accountability partners help you move forward when you feel stuck, need someone to support and hear you as you take action, or are nervous about taking the next step. You accomplish tasks that you haven't been able to on your own.

Tell your accountability partner one action you will take, do the action, then tell them when you completed it.

After dinner, Brittany sat at her computer. She took a deep breath, felt her stomach flip-flopping, and drafted her resume. It was rough, but complete. She felt relieved that she was finally taking action. She texted Gail and said, "I'm on the way to my next job—resume drafted!"

You will only hold yourself accountable for goals that others know about.

Q.T.I.P.–Quit Taking It Personally

Taking things personally is a habit, not a moral weakness, shortcoming, or spiritual lapse.

When you take things personally, you give certain individuals more power over you than they deserve. You allow others to question what you feel and believe, and this increases self-doubt.

Tatiana was in a mastermind group for coaches. They met each week to help each other grow in their professions. When it was her turn, she asked, "I need help with my next training module. I have too many exercises and not enough examples."

Dorinda started. "What behaviors are they doing now and what behaviors do you want them to do in the future?"

Whatever answer Tatiana gave, Dorinda responded with, "Don't change the question" and repeated her question.

When Tatiana's turn was over, she looked down at her lap. She could feel her cheeks and neck flushing and hear a whooshing sound in her head. After the session, she went home and slept for two hours.

When this happens, create some separation between the other person's words and yourself.

Answer these two questions:

1. What is my reaction to what they said? This is about *your* needs.
2. What are the other person's words? This is an expression of *their* needs.

Your answers can help you be more present and able to navigate the situation.

Tatiana wrote, "I need encouragement as I push out of my comfort zone and ask for help. What I heard was, 'You're stupid.'" Continuing, she identified Dorinda's need for clarity and brevity.

Create some distance between you and your reaction to what others say about you to gain perspective.

What to Do When Your Emotions Jump Out of You Like Beetlejuice

In the comedy movie *Beetlejuice*, Alec Baldwin and Geena Davis die in a freak car accident and end up stuck in their old house as ghosts for the next fifty years. A family of obnoxious yuppies move in and, as hard as they try to scare them away, nothing works. They hire Beetlejuice, played by Michael Keaton, to get the job done. He is a veteran, yellow-haired, snaggle-toothed, wretched spirit scare master.

Alec Baldwin asks, "What are your qualifications?"

Beetlejuice's response starts out calmly, then he escalates to the point of screaming. "I attended Julliard, I'm a graduate of the Harvard Business School, I travel quite extensively, I lived through the black plague and I had a pretty good time, not to mention you're talking to a dead guy. Now what do you think? Do you think I'm qualified?" Then he scares the couple by having snakes jump out of his face and torso.

Sometimes your emotions jump out of you like this, too.

When in an emotional moment, ask yourself these three questions before saying anything:

1. Does this need to be said?
2. Does this need to be said by me?
3. Does this need to be said by me now?

Pause when in an emotional moment, ask yourself three questions, and manage your emotions.

What Keeps You Stuck?

Marissa's marriage had been falling apart for over ten years. But for many reasons, she believed she couldn't leave. "I don't know how to be on my own. Nobody else will want me. I'm exaggerating how bad it is. I'm not *that* lonely." She continued to live in misery rather than risk change.

Eventually she asked herself, "If I hold on to these beliefs, what payoffs do I get?"

- I don't have to change
- I don't have to learn new behaviors
- I don't have to take personally accountability
- I don't have to make a choice

These excuses masked the real issues: she felt unworthy of a loving relationship and was afraid to learn new behaviors.

Once she identified her payoffs, she was able to ask her best friend for help. She started by saying, "I'm not happy in my marriage." This just about sent her over the edge with fear, shame, and discomfort. Her friend hugged her, told her she loved her, and promised to hold her hand as she traveled this path. Marissa felt a ray of light shining on her soul that lessened her isolation. It was the beginning of her feeling worthy of a loving relationship.

When you identify the payoffs you get for staying stuck, you can make different choices and move forward. Ask yourself, "If I choose to let go of this story, thought, or belief, what do I have to change?"

Identify your payoffs for staying stuck.

Win Before You Begin

Successful people:

- Step out of their comfort zone
- Ask for and accept help
- Make lots of mistakes
- Keep going
- Eliminate distractions and excuses
- Exercise their greatest power—choice

They also put *fail measures* in place.

What are fail measures?

Successful people anticipate the ways they may fail and put systems in place prior to taking an action. This reduces their probability of failing.

Mary looked away from the chair and desk at the end of the hallway. She passed it every time she went to her bedroom. On top of the desk were a new pen and blank pad of paper. Her stomach clenched. *Why bother. Get rid of it*, she said to herself. Mary dreamed of being an author. She had set up her writing space months earlier. Every time she sat to write, she distracted herself with chores.

For each new habit or new behavior, you need to decide, "How am I going to keep this going?"

1. Decide *when* you are going to do this (for example, Monday through Friday).
2. Decide *where* you're going to do this (for example, every time you sit down to have lunch).
3. Start small and build up. The number one mistake people make is not going small enough.
4. Get an accountability partner—contact them and commit to the tasks you will complete for the next week.

Mary joined a writer's club. She identified mornings as the best time of day to write. She committed to another club member that she will write on Saturdays from 8:00 – 9:30 a.m.

Create your success plan before your start a project, learn a new skill, or change a habit.

Make That Decision and Increase Your Happiness

Neuroscience researcher Alex Korb has studied the brain for over fifteen years and is the author of *The Upward Spiral: Using Neuroscience to Reverse the Course of Depression, One Small Change at a Time.* In his research, he discovered how you can create an upward spiral of happiness in your life: Make that decision.

Brain science shows that making decisions reduces worry and anxiety and increases your problem-solving skills.

"Making decisions includes creating intentions and setting goals—all three are part of the same neural circuitry and engage the prefrontal cortex in a positive way, reducing worry and anxiety. Making decisions also helps overcome striatum activity, which usually pulls you toward negative impulses and routines. Finally, making decisions changes your perception of the world— finding solutions to your problems and calming the limbic system. "

When you make decisions, apply the 80 percent rule.

This is the "good enough" decision. Making the perfect or "right" decision is stressful, while making a good-enough decision makes your brain feel in control, which reduces stress.

Apply the 80 percent rule and make that good-enough decision.

Dump Your Fear of Success

Akeelah and the Bee is an American film about an African American girl who makes it to the Scripps National Spelling Bee against all odds. Akeelah Anderson struggles with confidence and fear, yet her determination and perseverance helps her win the contest.

In the following scene, her spelling coach, Dr. Larabee, asks Akeelah to read out loud a quotation.

Akeelah: [*quoting Marianne Williamson*]: "Our deepest fear is not that we are inadequate. Our deepest fear is that we are powerful beyond measure. We ask ourselves, who am I to be brilliant, gorgeous, talented, and fabulous? Actually, who are you not to be? We were born to make manifest the glory of God that is within us. And as we let our own light shine, we unconsciously give other people permission to do the same."

Dr. Larabee: "Does that mean anything to you?"

Akeelah: "I don't know."

Dr. Larabee: "It's written in plain English. What does it mean?"

Akeelah: "That I'm not supposed to be afraid?"

Dr. Larabee: "Afraid of what?"

Akeelah: "Afraid of . . . me?"

Maximize your potential. Embrace the unknown and ambiguous. Accept yourself with all your flaws. Practice gratitude. Get out of your own way.

Give yourself permission to be powerful beyond measure.

Stop Cherishing Your Burdens

Samantha took a much-needed break, booked a room at an AirBnB, and spent a few days at the beach. The summer season had just ended, so it was less crowded and the weather was still warm and sunny.

The salty breeze greeted her as the warm sand blended with her feet. She savored the smell of suntan lotion. The sun melted away her tension as she dove into her book. Sweet freedom.

After a long day of soaking up the sun, she went back to her room and snuggled under the covers for a delicious nap. Just as she was about to doze off, she heard another group of guests coming in next door. The host gave them a tour of their room, kitchen, and outside. She could hear him point to his beach chairs. "Please, feel free to use these."

They better not take the beach chair I brought, she thought. She sat up to better hear the location of their footsteps. *Do I go out there and make sure they don't use my chair? Or do I let it go and sleep?* She slept. When she awoke she looked outside and the guests had taken her beach chair. *How dare they? That's my ten-year-old beach chair.* She stomped over to the host's shed to borrow a bike—with permission, of course, because *she* follows the rules.

Ask yourself: What thought, story, or belief do you cling to that is like that old, rickety beach chair? Do you still need it in order to be happy?

Samantha pounded the pedals as she cursed. Then it hit her. She stopped riding and beamed. Her teeth shone bright as she let out a laugh, not caring what others around her thought. *How ridiculous of me to cling to an old beach chair while my hosts generously offered their high-end bike for me to use.*

Welcome to being human.

Forgive yourself for clinging to thoughts and beliefs that no longer serve you.

Action Moves You Forward

Stephanie sang out loud on the car ride home from work. At stoplights, she bounced in her seat to the beat of the music. Once at home, she told her husband, "I found the job announcement of my dreams. I'm going to do whatever it takes to get it."

After dinner, she sat down at her computer to start reviewing the application. She noticed a pile of laundry. "I'll just throw one load in." She settled back into her chair. "Focus. Remember the excitement you felt earlier." She stared, mind blank, feeling stuck. "I need to clean the kitchen."

Stephanie was unhappy at her company. She was in her sixth month of looking for a new job. "What am I avoiding?" she asked herself. Within a short time of answering the questions below, she realized she had concerns about her competence. "What if I don't have the skills they want? What if I can't do the job?"

Complete the following steps to help you get unstuck:

1. Identify the uncomfortable moments that cause even the slightest knot in your stomach: attending a social function, traveling alone, asking for help, applying for a new job.
2. List all the ways not taking action is negatively affecting you.
3. List all the positive outcomes you would experience when you take the action you avoid.
4. Plan your response before you face the discomfort. Most people are reactive to their discomforts. Successful people are proactive.
5. Rehearse your response. Put yourself in that moment and go over it several times. Share your response with a friend. This holds you accountable for taking action.

Stephanie listed the possible positive outcomes. "I am happier sharing my talents with a company that appreciates them. I lose weight because I'm not eating over my job. My husband and I get along better."

She shared her planned response with a friend. "The next time I get stuck when looking for a job, I'm going to read my positive statements out loud. Then I will call you and commit to one small action step." She took action and applied for the job.

Plan how to respond to uncomfortable situations before you are in them.

Resenting Others Is a Sign That It's Time to Take a Break

"I'm busy. You should be too!"

When people get too busy, they become irritable with others. These "others" do annoying things like go to yoga class or stop for lunch. "How can they take time for exercise? Can't they see how busy I am?"

It's the battle cry of the stressed and exhausted.

The pressure to be all things to all people is overwhelming. The feelings of guilt that you are constantly letting someone down drives you to do more and leads to a busy snit.

In the movie *Bad Moms*, Mila Kunis plays an overworked, exhausted, and underappreciated mom pushed beyond her limits. She juggles a part-time job and two kids without help from her husband. She does all the grocery shopping, makes lunches, drives the kids to their practices and games, and volunteers for the PTA.

Fed up, she discovers two other stressed-out mothers who want to get away from their daily routines and responsibilities. They drunkenly raid a grocery store, rip open cereal boxes, and terrorize a guard. They are drunk, happy, and together.

Being busy is seen as a badge of honor in our society, yet we pay a price for it. So do our kids, spouses, and friends.

Don't allow your tanks to get to empty. Fill them up with breaks, healthy food, and adequate sleep.

By the end of the movie, each mother had discovered what matters most to them—family and friendship. They ditched unrealistic expectations about what they could and should accomplish in a day.

Busy snits are a sign that you are doing too much.
Make a different choice.

FORGIVENESS

Your Body Is Telling You to Forgive

Listen to your body. It will tell you when it's time let go and forgive yourself and others.

Look for the following signals:

- You get headaches because you keep replaying the scene in your head.
- Your sleep is interrupted because you dream about the person or situation.
- You feel distant from others because you are thinking about your pain.
- You overeat or overwork because are not present for yourself.
- Your chest tightens every time you retell the story.

Place both hands on your heart. Imagine the person or yourself. Say out loud or silently, "__________ (name), may you be happy and healthy. May you be free from suffering and delusion. May you have ease of being."

Learning to forgive is a process. No two individuals experience it the same way. It may go against your natural instinct for self-preservation. However, the benefits are limitless—reduced conflict, healthier relationships, and improved health.

Listen to your very wise body.

Balance Striving with Allowing

These two approaches—striving and allowing—complement each other and increase your success.

To *strive* is to devote serious energy and effort. We strive for excellence. We strive to do better. This is the "can-do" attitude of owning problems and developing solutions. You work toward a clear goal.

To *allow* is to make space—for feelings to come up, to take chances, to relax and take your foot of the accelerator. It is a time for exploration, to let go of outcomes and attachments, to let yourself off the hook.

For example, confidence is a success trait for which we strive. You use it to speak up and to take on challenges. If you take confidence beyond striving, you start to force solutions, controlling people and outcomes. To allow is to be confident you've done everything you can for today and *allow* the process to unfold. Tomorrow you can strive for confidence again, knowing that you will also *allow* space for exploration and other possibilities.

Strive for perfection, then *allow* the results to perfectly unfold.

Strive for excellence, then *allow* the excellence to emerge.

Strive for your goals and *allow* your intention to be to live joyfully each day, independent of reaching the goal.

Striving and allowing are the yin and yang of success.

Identify one task that you will strive to achieve and allow the results to unfold.

Pets Have PhDs in Gratitude and Are Skilled Teachers

Some people talk to animals. Not many listen, though. That's the problem.
—A.A. Milne

Cats vs. Dogs, Marley and Me, The Secret Life of Pets, and *Because of Winn Dixie* are all movies that show the beautiful gift you receive from pets: gratitude. They are grateful for being fed, cuddled, and walked. They are grateful every time you come home, and act as if you've been away for years. They don't keep score and hold past mistakes against you. They don't care how you look.

Pets are veritable optimists. Follow their lead. Be grateful when you have food to eat. Make time to play. Walk outdoors and notice what you appreciate about your neighborhood. Nap. Spend five minutes and write a gratitude list. It increases your long-term well-being by more than 10 percent.

Induce the relaxation response through the emotions of appreciation and gratitude.

CHECK FOR UNDERSTANDING

It's Not What Is Taught, It's What Is Caught

"You're a director! You should already know this!" Barbara shouted to nobody in her office. Throwing the report in the trash, she continued, "I can't believe I have to tell you how to do your job."

At every level, check for understanding to reduce mistakes and delays. Consider the saying, "It is not what is taught, it's what is caught." Employees have their own filters through which they run information. What you say may be heard very differently from what you're trying to convey.

Check for understanding. Once you give someone a task, ask, "Tell me how you understand what I just said. What do I expect you to do/produce/complete?"

If they state the outcome incorrectly, repeat your directions again and state, "Tell me how you understand what I just said. What do I expect you to do/produce/complete?"

You may think this is silly and experience frustration during the process. This is normal and to be expected. The goal is to reduce misunderstandings, which lead to delayed results.

Barbara took three deep breaths. She took a brisk ten-minute walk outside. She returned clear-headed, with a willingness to help her director understand the task at hand.

Check for understanding with each task you delegate.

Reframe the Way You Look at Situations

Do not accept unearned guilt.

Misplaced guilt is when you feel guilty for taking an action that is in your best interest.

Examples of situations that may cause misplaced guilt:

- You go into work late, having spent an hour at your child's school.
- You take an afternoon away from work to collect your thoughts, plan, and organize an upcoming project.
- You have been helping out a friend through a tough time. You've given a lot of your time supporting her. You hit your limit and say no to more requests for assistance.
- You look for another job.

Determine if you have misplaced guilt. Ask:

- "Did I do something wrong or harmful?"
- "Could I reasonably have known that a problem would ensue?"
- "Is it my responsibility to fix the problem?"
- "Is it really guilt that I am feeling?"

Clarify the guilt, the situation, and your beliefs about your role in it. Nine times out of ten, you will see you are not guilty.

For you is not against others.

A Know-It-All Is Someone Who Simply Stopped Learning

The Big Bang Theory is an American sitcom TV show. It's the story of a group of geeky and introverted friends—two physicists, an engineer, and an astrophysicist. A beautiful waitress/aspiring actress joins the group and makes for great comedy.

One character is Sheldon Cooper, a physicist and insufferable genius. He has severely limited practical life skills, yet irritates others because he acts like an expert on all topics. His behavior includes dominating conversations, offering unwanted advice, being argumentative, and engaging in pointless debates. His superiority comes across as rude and cold. He hates when others know more than he does.

He may be an exaggerated version of those you deal with at work and the world. Let the know-it-alls in your life teach you something. What they say is about them, not you. Let their behavior remind you of the value of humility, the quality of not thinking you are better than other people.

Stay teachable.

Goals and Intentions Go Hand in Hand

Use goals and intentions to keep you focused on what you want, while you stay in the present moment.

Imagine setting the goal of hiking to the bottom of the Grand Canyon so that you can look up at the vast, blue sky. It's one of your bucket list items. Before you begin the hike, you set your intention to be present to the sights along the trail, noticing each plant and rock, and enjoying the company of your hiking friends. You reach the bottom and are excited to look up at the vista you've been imagining for years. A thick fog unexpectedly rolls in and you can't see the blue sky. You did not achieve your goal. But you did achieve your intention to enjoy the hike, the views, and your friends.

What if you had only focused on your goal? How would you feel when you reached the bottom?

Goals help you get things done and are focused on the future.

Intentions are how you want to be in the moment, separate from whether you achieve your goal or not. They support you in achieving present-moment awareness.

1. Set both a goal (external achievement) and an intention (how you want to be along the way).
2. Follow this intention-setting format: "My intention is to be curious, joyful, compassionate, and flexible."
3. State your goal and intention each morning: "Today my goal is to make three cold calls and my intention is to be wildly curious during each one."

Understand the difference between goals and intentions. Use both to experience more present-moment awareness.

Set goals and intentions together to enjoy both the journey and the destination.

Your Needs, According to Maslow

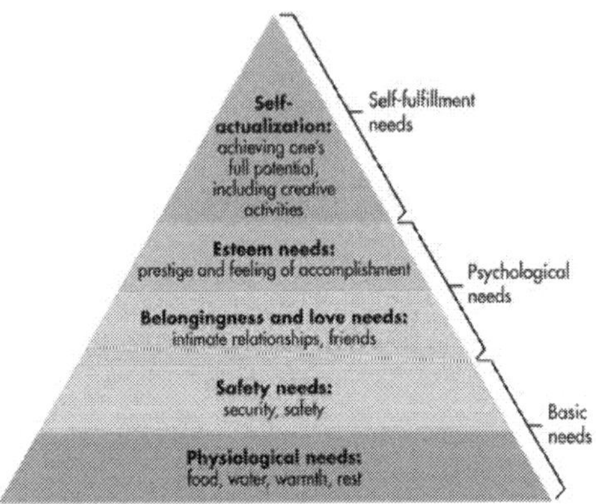

Abraham Maslow was an American psychologist who created the hierarchy of needs pyramid. It is a theory of psychological health built on fulfilling innate human needs. The satisfaction of needs is not an all-or-none model. You do not need to satisfy a need 100 percent before the next need emerges.

The pinnacle is self-actualization. It occurs when you maximize your potential, doing the best you are capable of doing. Maslow identified in his book, *Motivation and Personality*, twelve characteristics of a self-actualized person:

1. They embrace the unknown and the ambiguous.
2. They accept themselves, together with all their flaws.
3. They prioritize and enjoy the journey, not just the destination.
4. While they are inherently unconventional, they do not seek to shock or disturb.
5. They are motivated by growth, not by the satisfaction of needs.
6. They have purpose.
7. They are not troubled by the small things.
8. They are grateful.
9. They share deep relationships with a few, but also feel identification and affection toward the entire human race.
10. They are humble.
11. They resist enculturation.
12. They are not perfect.

Determine what you need now. It will differ according to your circumstances and can be multi-motivated. The order of needs is flexible based on your external circumstances and individual needs.

Identify and meet your desire to grow.

Life Is Like a Roller Coaster: It Has Its Ups and Downs, and It's Your Choice to Scream or Enjoy the Ride

A memorable scene about life comes from the movie *Parenthood.* Steve Martin and Mary Steenburgen are husband and wife and talking about having another child. Martin is frustrated, wants to control life, and wants guarantees. Steenburgen counters with, "Life is messy." Martin replies, "I hate messy!"

Her grandmother joins the conversation and shares a story.

"You know, when I was young, Grandpa took me on a roller coaster. Up, down, up, down. Oh, what a ride. I always wanted to go again. It was just interesting to me that a ride could make me so frightened, so scared, so sick, so excited . . . and so thrilled all together. Some didn't like it. They went on the merry-go-round. That just goes around. Nothing. I like the roller coaster. You get more out of it."

Life is how you perceive it. Sometimes things happen that you have no control over. You always have control over your responses. Whether you're climbing the hill of frustrations, challenges, or uncertainties, or gliding down on your successes, joys, and happiness, choose to view everything from a place of love, not fear.

Train your mind to see the good in everything.

Release the Butterflies in Your Stomach

When a sense of foreboding comes up, pause. Name your thoughts and feelings. This helps you change how you respond to an event you are dreading.

Sam was facilitating a series of strategy meetings for a client. As she made final room preparations, she had a tinny taste in her mouth. She heard voices of the attendees outside the room, and her stomach lurched. Her thoughts raced. *Did I get everything done? Is the equipment working? Did I prepare enough? I just want to get through this meeting. I want to get it over with!*

Sam thought the head honcho didn't like her style and approach to facilitating the meeting. She was giving him free reign in her head and giving away her power, which led to her dreading the session.

To stop feelings of dread about a meeting or event:

1. Notice your thoughts and feelings when you have to go to a meeting or event you dread. It could be uneasiness, a tightness in your throat, or feeling restless.
2. Spend five minutes journaling about the thoughts and feelings you noticed. In Sam's case, she wrote, "I'm afraid of screwing up the meeting and then they won't hire me again."
3. Say the following loving-kindness statement for the person(s) attending the meeting: "May you be happy and healthy, may you be free of suffering and delusion, may you have ease of being." This calms your nervous system, like releasing a pressure valve.

Sam paused and said the loving-kindness statement for the attendees. She thoroughly enjoyed facilitating the meeting. When she saw the head honcho, they shook hands and she felt happy to see him and do the best possible facilitation work for him . . . and she did!

In less than ten minutes, you can move from dreading to enjoying your next meeting or event.

Identify your physical signs of apprehension and unease.

Don't Be the Bottleneck

When you are part of a growing business, team, or family, you have to let go of total control.

The success behaviors that got you to where you are as an individual are the very ones you need to surrender in order to move to the next level of growth at work and in your family life. As an individual, work begins and ends with you. As a manager of others, a spouse, or a parent, you need to relinquish control to the right people or risk being a bottleneck. This is when you become the person who causes the work process to slow down or stop.

With increased self-awareness, you can improve how you work and collaborate.

Clarify expectations. Determine what is expected of you and of others.

Communicate ten times more than you think you need to.

Check out your control issues. Ask yourself if you get a sense of well-being when you feel in control. It is actually the illusion of control that gives you a sense of well-being. You control to feel safe, and everyone wants to feel safe. You cannot control what happens outside of you, but you can control how you respond to it. When you shift from external control to internal control, you get better results.

Accept the fact that you do not have control over the external world, that you need other people to help you grow, and when you stop responding to everyone and everything, you regain the control you can effectively exert.

PRESENT-MOMENT AWARENESS

Be Here Now

I never think of the future. It comes soon enough.

—Albert Einstein

You find yourself walking the dog and having a conversation in your head with someone who is not present. You're in a team meeting and thinking about a bill that is due next week. You're with your kids, thinking about an incident that occurred at work.

Society has taught us to believe that the next moment is more important than this one. This is not true. The present moment creates the future.

A quick way to get back in the present moment is to ask yourself, "Am I in engagement, enjoyment, or acceptance right now?"

If you answer no, you are not present.

Locate your feet. Take three deep breaths. Shake your head as if you are saying no and yes. Make circles with your arms.

Ask the question again. "Am I in engagement, enjoyment, or acceptance right now?"

Being in the present moment improves your social skills and creativity, increases your appreciation of your world, and reduces stress, worry, and overthinking.

This moment creates your future. Are you in it?

Fill Your Tanks

Constantly giving leaves you exhausted and your tanks empty. It leads to resentments and neglecting your needs.

Maya collapsed into Dana's chair. "I don't know what else to do or say or try," she exclaimed. "Why won't my clients listen to me? I missed my daughter's softball game to show them another 'dream house' and now they want to start the search over . . . again."

Dana pushed a bowl of chocolates across her desk.

"I give and give and give. You know what? Now I'm going to take," Maya barked as she grabbed the bowl. "I'm going home. And turning off my phone. And ordering in food. And don't get me started on my family." Her finger pointed at Dana. "They never help."

This phenomenon is known as Give, Give, Give . . . KILL! It's when you don't balance giving and receiving out of a limiting belief that receiving is selfish. It leads to unskillful behaviors like overeating, overworking, and not meeting your own needs. Giving without receiving creates imbalance.

List options that make you feel glad to be alive. These are simple joys you can make happen every day. They are nurturing treats. Options cannot be dependent on another person doing something.

Maya took several deep breaths. She wrote a list of fifteen ways she could get her needs met: "Turn off my phone during dinner. Take a walk after lunch. Schedule a date night with my partner. Go to bed at 8:00 p.m. with my new book."

Stop confusing receiving with taking.

RISK

Think Less, Act More

I left my corporate job after twenty years and immediately read Tim Ferriss's book, *The 4-Hour Workweek: Escape 9-5, Live Anywhere, and Join the New Rich.* He posted a contest to participate with him in a two-day live webcast at Creative Live, a company that brings inspiring experts together with the masses. His live webcast, called *The 4-Hour Life—The Best of Body, Business and Mind,* was based on his books—*The Four-Hour Workweek, The Four-Hour Chef,* and *The Four-Hour Body.*

To be considered for six available slots on the webcast, you had to post a sixty-second YouTube video of your three goals for the next year.

I knew I had to do it within twenty-four hours or I would chicken out. I didn't know anything about videotaping, YouTube, or Twitter—all required. I asked my teenage son for help. "Would you videotape me, upload it to YouTube, set up a Twitter account, and promise not to laugh at me?" Then I cried. I felt like I was twelve years old having a sibling tease me. Old messages came rushing forward.

He said yes. I wrote my script, got on my outfit, and recorded my video. My son posted it. I didn't hear from Tim, so I assumed I wasn't selected.

Four days before the webcast, I got a call on my land line. I never answer that phone because I only receive marketing calls on it. The message machine went off and I heard, "Hi, this is Creative Live and we're looking for Moira Lethbridge." I leaped out of my chair and answered it. They had tried to reach me via Twitter, but I hadn't responded because I had no clue how to use Twitter.

I was selected! There were so many entries that Tim doubled the participants from six to twelve. I immediately booked my flight to the Creative Live Studio. I was the oldest person selected, at age 47.

It was a turning point in my life. I was seen as me. No armor. No pretending. I listened to that still, small voice that said, "Do it now!" I thought less and acted more.

- When an idea comes up, get curious and follow it.
- Think less and act more.
- Set a short time limit for doing it.
- Ask someone to hold you accountable for completing it.

Life's a crapshoot. You have to take chances.

Let Three People Off the Hook—the First One Is You

Rock 'Em Sock 'Em Robots is a game from the 1970s where kids maneuvered two boxers to slug it out until one of their heads is knocked off. Kids push the head back in place and continue to duke it out.

We start each day throwing a left, then a right at ourselves. We knock our own blocks off and think we are the winner.

Choose to let yourself off the hook for:

- Not getting enough sleep
- Forgetting to return a phone call
- Getting angry at your child or spouse
- Saying mean things to yourself

We don't give ourselves a break because we are afraid if we slow down and practice inner-compassion, we will stop working and lose our edge. Yes, you will lose your edge—*your bleeding edge,* caused by knocking your block off.

When you give yourself a break, you create space, which reduces self-judgment and increases clarity.

Focus on building a habit of giving yourself a break. This allows you to spend your energy more productively.

There Are No Idle Thoughts

Watch your thoughts; they become words.
Watch your words; they become your actions.
Watch your actions; they become your habits.
Watch your habits; they become your character.
Watch your character; it becomes your destiny.

—Frank Outlaw

This quote has been used in newspapers, movies, and by others for many years. Although there are many variations of the quote and often it is associated with other writers, it still remains powerful through its words. Meryl Streep recited the quote when playing English Prime Minister Margaret Thatcher in the 2011 film *The Iron Lady*. It is believed that Buddha was similarly quoted nearly 2500 years ago.

The thought manifests as the word,
The word manifests as the deed,
The deed develops into habit,
And the habit hardens into character.
So watch the thought and its way with care,
And let it spring from love
Born out of concern for all beings.

—Buddha

You have 50,000 thoughts a day. Look at your thoughts as things on a conveyor belt. If there is one you don't like, put it back. Pick another one. Change your life.

Follow those who lived by these words: Albert Einstein, Henry David Thoreau, Henry Ford, Napoleon Hill, and Winston Churchill.

You've Got a Friend

Shaking, I slumped against the cold door in the frozen food isle at Whole Foods. Tears stung my eyes as I fumbled for a crumpled Kleenex in my purse. I called my friend Elizabeth.

"Hey, Moira. How are you? Moira? Are you there?"

"I don't know what to buy." Tears drenched my face. An intense pressure covered my chest. "I don't know what I want. I don't know when to eat. I'm so confused. I miss Patrick."

"I hear you. Having Patrick gone is a huge transition for you."

I had dropped my youngest son at college the previous month. I missed him and the structure of making him a meal every night. I had to learn to cook for one.

Change happens. Some are big, like sending your child off to college. Some are small, like switching dry cleaners. Some you can anticipate, while others you cannot. Change is situational. It involves new processes or routines, a new boss or team member. It is external and focused on the outcome.

Change also involves transitions. Transition is the psychological process you go through to come to terms with the new situation. It is internal. It depends on letting go of the old reality and the old identity you had before the change took place.

The key to successful change is to think through what you will have to let go of when the change occurs.

When change happens in your life:

- Identify what you have to let go of
- Allow space for feelings that come with letting go

I wrote a list of what I had to let go of: shopping and cooking for Patrick, scheduling my time around his comings and goings, and daily conversations over meals. I made the decision to make more space for feeling the loss. I also realized how grateful I felt for having a friend to listen. Elizabeth held my hand in the frozen food isle of Whole Foods.

Friends help with transitions.

Ask the Universe to bring you a friend like Elizabeth. She will ;)

Laughing Attracts Joy

Laughing is the best form of therapy. It triggers the release of endorphins, the body's natural feel-good chemicals.

Erma Bombeck was an American humorist, syndicated columnist, and best-selling author. Her bi-weekly column was read by thirty million readers. She wrote more than fifteen books with titles like *Family—The Ties That Bind . . . and Gag*, and *If Life Is a Bowl of Cherries, What Am I Doing in the Pits?*

Her humor chronicled the ordinary life of a Midwestern suburban housewife.

Here are quotes from her column and books that made me laugh out loud. I hope they do the same for you.

"My idea of housework is to sweep the room with a glance."

"Cats invented self-esteem."

"When my kids become wild and unruly, I use a nice, safe playpen. When they're finished, I climb out."

Wake up with laughter. Go to bed with smiles.

Don't Wait

In 2009, Bronnie Ware wrote an article entitled "The Top Five Regrets Before Dying." She shared her patients' regrets in their last weeks of life.

Patients stated they wished they had the courage to live their own life, not what others expected of them. They wished they hadn't worked so hard and had the courage to express their emotions. They regretted not spending time with their friends and allowing themselves to be happier.

In 2012, Bronnie turned this essay into a book, *The Top Five Regrets of Dying*.

Start today. Wherever you are on your journey is your starting point. Call a friend. Tell your partner what you appreciate about them. Meditate. Stay in the present moment. Screw guilt.

Live every day as if it's your last. Embrace each experience as if it's your first.

Have Curiosity Conversations

Brian Grazer is a Hollywood TV and movie producer. He was nominated for Academy Awards for his films *Splash, Apollo 13, A Beautiful Mind*, and *Frost/Nixon*. He won an Oscar for best picture for *A Beautiful Mind*.

He is a #1 *New York Times* bestselling author of the book *A Curious Mind—The Secret to a Bigger Life*. The book describes the curiosity conversations that have inspired him to create award-winning TV shows and movies. He's conversed with spies, scientists, politicians, royalty, US presidents, Nobel laureates, and artists. Each story offers a lesson in the power of curiosity to change your life.

His conversations are very relaxed and open-ended to allow new ideas, connections, and fresh perspectives to surface. He calls curiosity the secret fuel to his success.

Follow these three steps to have your own curious conversations.

1. Be present and listen. Give the other person your full attention. Turn off all buzzy gadgets.
2. Choose how to listen. Actively listen to their perspectives, needs, and thoughts without trying to find a place to jump in.
3. Ask open questions: "Tell me more." "What was it like?" "What happened next?"

Curious conversations enhance your life, connecting you with others and ideas.

Nurture your sense of wonder. Stay curious.

Thoughts Are Things

Thoughts can take you closer or further away from your goals.

What do migraines have to do with thoughts?

For the past four years, I have had migraine headaches every time I had my period. Every month I tracked when I got my period, how many prescription migraine pills I took, and how long the migraines lasted. I tried everything to get rid of them: progesterone cream, going on and off birth control pills, changing my diet. Nothing worked, except taking medication. I never went anywhere without my migraine pills.

I've done tons of work around changing my thoughts and beliefs. In fact, all my coaching programs are based on the miracles that happen when you do this. One of the methods I use to change my thoughts and beliefs is the law of attraction. Simply stated: *I attract into my life what I think about.*

I had been thinking fearful thoughts every month. *I hope my migraines aren't that painful this month. I'm worried I'll get one at work. What if I miss something important because of them?*

One day I realized I could try changing my thoughts about the migraines. What did I have to lose? I had medicine if this experiment didn't work.

I began practicing changing my thoughts through visualization. At the beginning of my period, as I felt the migraine starting, I imagined snowflakes falling on each nerve in my brain. They were cold and sparkling, and each nerve welcomed in the healing, calming salve. I pictured my brain as a snow globe with tons of glistening, dancing snowflakes. I Googled images of snowflakes to enhance my visualization. I spent twenty minutes imagining how cold and refreshing the snow felt on my eyes and forehead.

What were the results?

I have used this visualization exercise for over a year. My migraines go away within twenty minutes of doing it. I haven't taken my migraine medicine for months, and I don't feel panicked if I don't have them in my purse.

Who else knew thoughts are things? Albert Einstein, Henry David Thoreau, Henry Ford, Napoleon Hill, Buddha, Winston Churchill, and Charles Fillmore.

In fact, Einstein said, "Everything (thoughts) is energy and that's all there is to it. Match the frequency of the reality you want and you cannot help but get that reality. It can be no other way. This is not philosophy. This is physics."

There are many ways to change your thoughts. The willingness to try a new approach is the key to success.

Thoughts are things. Visualize the ideal outcome you desire.

Questions Beat Answers

Our brains are programmed to be hooked by questions. We can't ignore them. Questions enable people to think and act in the face of uncertainty. They help organize our thinking around what we don't know.

Netflix video rentals started when the founder, Reed Hastings, got fed up with outrageous late fees when he returned his movies rented from a Blockbuster store. He asked the following questions:

- "Why should I have to pay these fees?"
- "How am I going to explain these charges to my wife?"
- "What if a video-rental business were run like a health club?"

Other businesses that started by asking questions include Foursquare, Airbnb, and Pandora Internet Radio.

John Seely Brown, the self-described Chief of Confusion and a former scientist at Xerox Corporation and the Palo Alto Research Center (PARC), helps people ask the right questions. In this time of rapid change, questioners can thrive. He states, "If you are comfortable questioning, experimenting, and connecting things—then change is something that becomes an adventure. And if you can see it as an adventure, then you're off and running!"

Think of a situation in your life that you want to change. Like Reed Hastings, ask ten questions about your situation and write down your answers. You may just discover the next Airbnb.

Surprise! You Owe $450

Emotional triggers can make it hard to be clear in a given situation.

Celia received an "unexpected" invoice from a vendor for $450. Her head ached and her body shook. She shoved the bill in a drawer and went to bed. While lying under the covers, her thoughts raced: *Pay it and forget about it. Hurry up and fix it fast.* She threw the covers off and ran downstairs to retrieve the bill.

Emotional triggers are people or events that set off intense emotional reactions within us. Triggers happen in an instant. You become acutely sensitive to situations that may not have bothered you had you been emotionally balanced.

Triggers produce feelings of guilt, shame, insecurity, jealousy, anger, resentment, or withdrawal.

After being triggered, give yourself about twenty minutes before you take action. This is the amount of time it takes for the trigger to subside. Deep breathing helps your trigger lessen faster.

Once the trigger has passed:

1. Identify what happened before you were triggered. Write it down.
2. Identify where you felt the trigger in your body.
3. Describe your feelings while triggered.
4. Have someone safe to talk it through to connect to the reason for the trigger.
5. Decide on the next action to take.

Celia applied these steps to the unexpected bill:

Step 1. "I was relaxing after work, going through my mail. I received a bill for expenses I thought I had already paid for, so it surprised me."

Step 2. "My chest felt tight and I was shallow breathing."

Step 3. "I'm afraid I'll lose my job."

Step 4. "I called my friend Tammy and cried. She helped me see that I was holding on to a limiting belief that I have to make a certain amount of money now or I won't be able to stay in my house and that others won't love me."

Step 5. "The action I took was to look at the previous invoice and compare services. I did incur these additional expenses. I thought I had already paid for them from a previous invoice. I was being vague about the agreement. I had an unspoken agreement that allowed them to do work without clarifying the cost."

Identify one area in your life where you are not clear: money, relationships, or work. Take one action to gain clarity.

You Don't Have to Do It All Yourself

Recognize your needs and know there is a different way to get them met.

Mei struggled with finding time to exercise and meditate, two things that were important to her. Her kids needed her until they got on the bus at 7:30 a.m. She scheduled work meetings to begin at 8:30 a.m. This conflict made her frantic. "Oh my gosh. I have to get to work." She rushed out the door. No time for prayer and meditation.

Know that you will havc competing needs. List them:

- Need #1—time for yourself
- Need #2— time with your kids/pets/partner
- Need #3— time for work

Choose to meet one need at a time. Realize and accept the reality that there are trade-offs. Acceptance will stop you from asking, "How can I make it all work?" and start asking, "Which need do I want to meet right now?"

Look for ways to change how you get your needs met.

Mei chose to be present for her kids in the morning. She told her colleagues she would no longer look at emails before 7:30 a.m.

Mei was thrilled with her "aha" moment. "I schedule meetings at 8:30 a.m., when I can just as easily schedule them to start later." She moved her Thursday finance meeting to begin at 10:00 a.m. She delegated running the Tuesday staff meeting to her operations director. This allowed her to take care of her kids until 7:30 a.m., go to yoga class at 8:00 a.m., and get to work by 10:00 a.m. twice a week.

After two weeks, Mei reflected on the changes she made. "I'm a lot happier now that I'm not doing it all. The trade-offs are worth it."

Stop doing it all yourself, so you can do the things that support your vitality.

The Golden Rule

Don't judge others, as you would have them not judge you.

Support others and listen to what they feel they need. Help them hear their inner voice. Honor their right to choose differently from you and support them in that. This is the golden rule.

The decision to be a working mom or a stay-at-home mom is filled with opportunities to apply the Golden Rule. Both jobs are demanding. Both have their down sides. Both are riddled with self- and other-judgments.

Stay-at-home mom: "I'm not a good role model for my daughter because I'm not 'working.'"

Working mom: "Why do you need a few hours off from taking care of your kids?"

Stay-at-home mom: "She's so driven. She should just quit her job and take care of her kids."

Working mom: "I feel terrible missing my son's band concert because I have to work."

One type of work is not more worthy than other type of work.

Stop judging yourself and others.

Do unto others as you would have them do to you.

Don't Let Discomfort Stop You

The primary reason people don't make positive changes is because of the intensity of discomfort that goes along with making changes. Discomfort arises when you are getting closer to the things you really want.

Have you ever wanted to take an action to move you forward and the feeling of discomfort stops you? Do you feel bad or angry, then turn these feelings on yourself and overwork, drink too much, or get lost in busyness? Do you wish you could respond, "I feel uncomfortable, but I'm doing it anyway?"

My client Donna was in my group coaching program. After the program, the group continued to support each other. She sent out an email: "I've been in a slump. I'm stuck and feeling off." The group immediately responded, sending her positive feedback and encouragement.

Her response to them was, "This is exactly what I needed—you hearing me. As silly and small as it sounds, reaching out to the group was a huge step for me."

The intensity of feelings of discomfort is incredible. It feels like getting into a ring with an 800-pound gorilla: fear, shame, guilt, skin crawling, sweating, shallow breathing, and an intense desire to control.

Embracing the discomfort is where the gold is! It brings engagement and change.

Embrace discomfort and hit pay dirt. It's not about the size of the act you are walking through. It is about the courage of taking the action in spite of the discomfort.

Want What You Want

Suspend judgment and write down everything you want. Act as if there are no constraints of time or money. Do you want a great relationship, more money, or a vacation?

Notice your thoughts and reactions to the statement, "It's OK to want what I want." You may hear:

- "I don't want to be disappointed if it doesn't work out."
- "It's stupid to want this."
- "I should already know this."
- "It's a waste of time."

Notice if your teeth are clenched, you are shallow breathing, your brain is racing, your shoulders are by your ears, or your chest is tight. This helps you connect your thoughts to the reactions in your body.

It's time to stop thinking you should be someone other than who you are, wanting something other than what you really want, and doing something other than what you want to be doing.

Claim your space on this beautiful planet.

Stop Worrying as a Way to Control

Mary and her husband won a trip to Key West. She struggled with the decision to go. Her son Alan, twenty-two, was living at home, attending a local college. Mary obsessed about him. "What if he never finishes college? Or ends up homeless? Or worse . . . living with us?" She worried about Alan to give herself a sense of control and safety. "If only I could control his choices or say the right thing to motivate him, then he would be OK."

Mary decided to go on the trip. She called me from Key West. "It's paradise here. Our room is a palace, the beach is spectacular, the food is delicious, but I feel uncomfortable."

Worrying is a normal human emotion, so don't beat yourself up for feeling it. Identify if you are worrying about something you can't change. Use the phrase, "People are naturally creative, resourceful, and whole."

In Mary's example, she applied this phrase to her son. She journaled about it and her anxiety lessened. She was able to let her worry go and enjoy her vacation.

Use the phrase, "People are naturally creative, resourceful, and whole" to interrupt your worry loop.

Put Your Inner Critic in a Container

The inner critic is the internal voice that says, "You're late! You sounded stupid. Don't eat that chocolate. There you go again, forgetting to take out the trash."

Your inner critic is speaking up from a place of positive intention. In the example "You're late," the inner critic wants you to keep your job, and you've been late before and your boss has yelled at you because of it.

There are times when you talk to the inner critic, saying, "I hear you and I promise I'll get more sleep, leave fifteen minutes earlier, or go for a walk."

There are other times when you need to put your inner critic on pause, so you can accomplish what's in front of you.

Tanya had an important presentation to give to senior staff. She had been preparing for two weeks and today was the big day. Minutes before giving the presentation, her inner critic started yelling, "What if you forget? You didn't do enough work on the outline. I think the audience is going to find out you don't really know what you are talking about."

The container is a visual image of any kind of container, like Fort Knox or the *I Dream of Jeannie* bottle, where you place your inner critic for a period of time. Imagine a container of any size, shape, and color. Visualize yourself opening it, asking the inner critic to wait inside, closing and locking it, and stating you will come back later to address its concern.

This action allows you to focus on what you need to do next. You can always come back to the inner critic or problem. Or let it sit for a day or two!

It helps you put problems on pause so you can focus on what's at hand.

Tanya knew it wasn't the right time to chat with her inner critic. She visualized a large, blue safe that had green and yellow pillows inside. She put her inner critic on top of the pillows and said, "I'll come back to you after I've finished this presentation." She shut and locked the safe door and was able to give her presentation without interrupting thoughts.

There are right times to dialogue with your inner critic or solve a problem. When you have something important to get done, use the container to hold your problems until the right time.

Put your inner critic in a container whenever you need to focus on the task at hand.

Receive Kindness

Kindness has been found by researchers to be the most important predictor of satisfaction and stability in a marriage. Several colleges, including Harvard, are now emphasizing kindness on their admissions applications.

People perform kind acts. Identify this cooperative nature in your everyday life.

- The flight attendant who sees you crying and brings you a bottle of water and tissues.
- The colleague who goes the extra mile to locate you because you have an urgent call.
- The movers who stop asking which pieces of furniture to move and wait for you to finish crying because you are getting divorced.
- The pharmacist who takes extra time to help you figure out why your new health insurance coverage denied payment for your prescription.

Acknowledge, accept, and embrace that you deserve kindness.

Be kind to yourself as a way to build your kindness-to-others muscle.

Forgiveness Is Love Healed

Forgiveness is not about forgetting. It's about remembering.

Think about a scar you have on your body. It doesn't hurt anymore, but it's still there. You remember where you were when it happened.

When you allow your wounds to heal and forgiveness to happen, you free yourself. This is why forgiveness is for you. You forgive for your own sake. The illusion that by not forgiving you won't get hurt again is just that—an illusion. It keeps you in prison.

Ask for peace in your heart for one minute each day for a week.

Forgiveness means you can no longer blame someone else for the course your life takes.

Start the process of healing emotional wounds.

FOCUS

When Distracted, Chunk It Down

Projects can overwhelm and stop progress. Chunk them down into bite-sized steps.

"I've got 137 unread emails. I'll take a quick peek at Facebook and then tackle them." Maria convinced herself that five minutes on the Internet would not derail her from the task at hand. Another peek at Instagram and her unread emails swelled.

Big projects require focus, attention, and the elimination of distractions.

Break a big project into smaller, achievable tasks. Focus on one task at a time.

1. Describe the end state first.
2. List the component parts and the order to complete them.
3. Determine the amount of effort required.
4. Focus on one task at a time.

In Maria's case, her end state was: "I am on top of my emails."

Her component parts, in order, with the amount of time needed for each:

- Ask for help from my assistant—two hours.
- Unsubscribe from unneeded emails—two hours.
- Set up auto-filing rules for emails that can be read later—one hour.
- Set up auto-responders to manage recipient's expectations when I will respond—thirty minutes.
- Determine three time blocks during the day to read and respond to emails—thirty minutes.

Start with a quick-win component; one that you can complete and build momentum for the next component.

Maria checked her email at 9:00 a.m. and 3:00 p.m. Her systems reduced the number of unread emails and the overwhelm that kept her immobilized.

Keep your eyes on the next step—not the summit.

Grief Helps Process Failure, Disappointment, and Betrayal

Grief is not a disorder, a disease, or a sign of weakness.
It is an emotional, physical, and spiritual necessity.

—Earl A. Grollman, rabbi and author

Grief is your friend. It helps build your resilience muscle, recover faster, and learn not to turn negative experiences on yourself.

You may go through the stages of grief:

1. Shock and denial—avoidance, confusion, fear, numbness, blame
2. Anger—frustration, anxiety, irritation, embarrassment, shame
3. Depression and detachment—overwhelmed, lack of energy
4. Dialog and bargaining—reaching out to others, desire to tell one's story, struggle to find meaning in what has happened
5. Acceptance—exploring options, a new plan
6. Return to meaningful life—empowerment, self-esteem, meaning

Going through these stages is normal and to be expected. It may be linear, but usually it's a messy, back-and-forth process.

When dealing with grief:

Give yourself the gift of time. Healing is not a one-time event. Allow space for those moments when you feel like you have molasses in your veins.

- Learn from your experience.
- Practice self-compassion.

Recovering takes time. It's a process that cannot be rushed, stuffed, or minimized if you want to learn and heal from it.

Ditch Misplaced Guilt

Owning your own mistakes is a sign of emotional strength. Owning other people's mistakes or pain is an indicator of misplaced guilt.

Misplaced guilt is when you accept blame for an event that is out of your control.

- A friend gets in a car accident and does not have a car for a month. You do what you can to help out and feel guilty when you can't do more.
- A colleague's child is constantly sick, which makes them tired, anxious, and depressed. You feel guilty when you go home and take care of your own family.
- You have planned a girls' weekend away and another friend is dealing with the grief of her parent's passing. You feel guilty having fun.

It is common for women to experience misplaced guilt when engaging in self-care. Misplaced guilt destroys positive emotions.

Pause and ask, "What harm did I do to this person?" "Did I knowingly do harm to others?" You feel guilty when you have done something wrong. If you answered no to these questions and still feel guilt, you are experiencing misplaced guilt.

Manage your feelings of guilt. Identify the underlying reasons for guilt.

Exercise your choice between Teflon and Velcro.

If She Can Do It, You Can Do It Too

Perseverance is the ability to keep going in the face of adversity.

Danica Roem is a journalist and the first openly transgender woman to be elected into the Virginia House of Delegates and in a state legislature anywhere in America. She ran against and beat Bob Marshall, who had held this seat for the past twenty-five years.

She ran as a thirty-three-year-old stepmom determined to fix traffic problems on Route 28. Her opponent made her gender identity a campaign issue, with campaign flyers that repeatedly referred to Roem with male pronouns, and a header that read: "Danica Roem, born male, has made a campaign issue out of transitioning to female."

After winning her seat, she stated, "Discrimination will backfire in your face. Stop doing it and start focusing on infrastructure."

Accept that adversity is an inevitable part of life. Prepare yourself mentally to confront challenges head on. Build a support team around you that encourages you to keep going. Look for the learning opportunities in every challenge.

Danica dedicated her victory speech to "every person who's ever been singled out, who's ever been stigmatized, who's ever been the misfit, who's ever been the kid in the corner." She continued on as a lawmaker determined to fix traffic, teacher pay, and expand Medicaid.

Resolve to expect, accept, and address adversity when it shows up.

Pause to Discover What You Need

Carrie slammed her laptop shut, stood up, and through taught cheeks said, "This meeting is over. When the two of you can agree to act civilly toward each other, we will regroup. Until then, grow up!"

She raced to her office. Shaking all over, she felt as if she had stepped into a freezer. Her boss came in and explained how her numbers for the previous month were very disappointing. "What are you going to do about this?"

"Call maintenance and ask them to turn the heat up," she thought.

Her day continued to fall apart. Her husband Jack called. "Honey, our plans for tonight have changed a bit and now I need to meet you at the high school for Deidra's recital instead of riding together."

Her cheeks reddened. "I can't hear this right now! My whole day is a hot mess. I'll call you later." Her daughter was a high school senior and Carrie wanted to be at every dance recital, knowing they were the last of this chapter.

She saw her reaction as a red flag. She spent two minutes taking deep breaths and recited, "Breathe in one, breathe out two, breathe in three, breathe out four." She asked herself, "What do I need?" In that quiet pause, she heard, "Carrie, you are exhausted. Stay home tonight."

When you're in a similar situation, do this:

- If you are H.A.L.T. (hungry, angry, lonely, tired), pause and ask, "What do I need in this moment?" It may be a hug, nap, food, space, or someone to listen to you.
- Take three deep breaths. Stretch. Listen to that still, small voice inside you.
- Write down what you hear without judgment. Act on it.

Carrie told her husband and daughter that she was exhausted and going home. She heard their disappointment. She stuck with her decision, even though she felt guilty and selfish. She went home and put on her pajamas and snuggled under a blanket. Her husband texted, "There's a glitch with the high school lighting system. They canceled the recital. We are on our way home."

Pause and give your attention to the present moment. Ask, "What do I need?"

You Are Not Your Thoughts

I waged a war on food for decades. My earliest memory of feeling bad about eating was at thirteen. By age sixteen I had a full-blown, whacked-out, distorted view of my body. I thought I was fat, but I wasn't. I'd look at pictures of me and gasp at my fat thighs. They weren't. That same year my brother died of a cerebral hemorrhage. My first thought was, *He died because I have fat thighs.* I knew the thought was crazy, but there it was.

After his death, I started dieting, binging, and purging. I turned to food for comfort, punishment, love, and to relieve boredom. The obsessive thinking was relentless and the number on the scale told me whether I was good or bad. My thoughts told me, *People will leave you if you get fat.*

By the time I reached college, I was miserable and desperate for a way off the battlefield. The binging and dieting stopped working and I was getting fat. I was a cheerleader and quit the team because of it. Thank goodness for the gift of desperation. I asked for help and dealt with my eating disorder, learned how to eat "normally," and lost weight.

My aha moment came when one day I heard myself say, "You can't eat a banana. There's too many carbs in it and it'll make you fat." I realized that one banana didn't make me fat. But my thoughts about it made me fat and miserable.

Your thoughts are yours, but they do not describe you. You may think or feel you *are* anxious, but you are *experiencing* the symptoms of anxiety.

The mind adds its own negative narrative to everyday events. You accept this as truth. Notice your thoughts, but do not identify or attach yourself to them.

Not every thought you think is true and not every thought you think is you.

SELF

DECIDE

OCT 14

Your Life Is Not a Coincidence—It Is a Reflection of You

The Mountain Story

(Author Unknown)

A son and his father were walking in the mountains.

Suddenly, the son falls, hurts himself, and screams, "AAAhhhhhhh!!!"

To his surprise, he hears a voice repeating, somewhere in the mountain, "AAAhhhhhhh!!!"

Curious, he yells, "Who are you?"

He receives the answer, "Who are you?"

Angered at the response, he screams, "Coward!"

He receives the answer, "Coward!"

He looks to his father and asks, "What's going on?"

The father smiles and says, "My son, pay attention."

And then he screams to the mountain, "I admire you!"

The voice answers, "I admire you!"

Again the man screams, "You are a champion!"

The voice answers, "You are a champion!"

The boy is surprised, but does not understand.

Then the father explains, "People call this echo, but really this is life.

It gives you back everything you say or do.

Our life is simply a reflection of our actions."

Decide what you want in your life—more love, more laughter, more joy? Give more love, laugh more, and find joy in small things today.

Check Your H.A.L.T.S.S.S.

You are more likely to have an emotional trigger when you are in H.A.L.T.S.S.S.:

- **H**ungry
- **A**ngry
- **L**onely
- **T**ired
- **S**tressed
- **S**ick
- **S**cared

Recently I was offered help by a vendor with my business at a reduced rate because she believes in the work I am doing. Her expertise—as a copy editor—is an area I struggle with, so her assistance would be very valuable. My trigger went off. I wanted to cry, hide, and felt "icky."

The first thing I did was ask myself, "Am I in H.A.L.T.S.S.S.?"

I realized I was super tired. I had been working late every night to finish a deliverable and had not taken time off from work in over two weeks. I journaled for ten minutes. I could see that this was old stuff. I became overly self-sufficient at a young age and identified my triggers as having to earn the air I breathe and not deserving of receiving help. This is why I work too much.

I practiced Hands-On-Heart (H.O.H.) by placing my hands on my heart and saying, "I deeply and completely love and accept myself as I am, even if I don't believe I deserve help in my business."

I was able to receive the help and appreciate and accept the respect and admiration from this person. I was aware that this trigger is old and applied the steps above to reduce my reaction time, increase my resilience, and embrace and enjoy the gifts I am receiving!

Identifying when you are in H.A.L.T.S.S.S. increases your self-awareness to pause and take care of your needs.

When you feel restless, anxious, or off, check to see if you are H.A.L.T.S.S.S.

Good Bosses Are Self-Aware

In the movie *The Devil Wears Prada*, Meryl Streep plays a ruthless and merciless boss named Miranda Priestly. She constantly terrorizes and insults her employees. "Details of your incompetence do not interest me."

When leaders are self-aware, they are effective, focused, and attuned to those around them. They control their minds and emotions, so they can help guide those around them in developing their own self-knowledge and success. They are successful in life and business because they are emotionally intelligent.

There are four characteristics of emotional intelligence:

1. Good at understanding your own emotions (self-awareness)
2. Good at managing your emotions (self-management)
3. Empathetic to the emotional drives of other people (social awareness)
4. Good at handling other people's emotions (social skills)

To increase your emotional intelligence, practice these steps for one week:

1. Notice your emotional reactions to events throughout the day.
2. Capture what you notice; there are several apps available to track your emotions.
3. Notice what is happening in your body. Is your jaw tight, are your hands clenched, is your stomach in a knot?

After one week, look at your data. Identify your emotional patterns. Do you get angry every time a certain colleague asks for help? Do you react to your boss's unavailability? Do you shut down when your colleagues don't include you for lunch?

Awareness is the first step to increase emotional intelligence. Practice makes permanent.

Identify one emotional reaction response to change.

Reduce Tensions with Others

Tensions at work and at home are challenging. Family gatherings and work meetings are ripe for "opportunities for growth." Choose how you want to respond. Take action to change the way conflict affects you and possibly those around you.

Identify what you can control: yourself and your response.

When you have a disagreement with someone, try the following steps.

1. Find common ground.

Show that you heard the other person's point of view.

- Listen for the emotion being expressed
- Empathize with them, even if you don't agree with them
- "It sounds like you are angry with ____________ (me, politicians, causes) because ________ (I wasn't very attentive during our last discussion, politicians are all crooks, global warming is hurting your business)

Look for similarities.

- "We are both human beings."
- "We both drive blue cars."
- "We both like gravy."
- "We are both watching football."

2. Identify points you both agree on.

- Having a profitable business supports the family and community.
- Getting a good night's sleep is beneficial.
- Dogs are wonderful.

3. Use phrases.

- "Isn't that interesting."
- "You may be right."

- "I hear you."
- "That doesn't work for me."

4. Set a goal and intention.

- **Goal**: "I'm going to find ten similarities with this person."
- **Intention**: "My intention is to be open minded, curious, and happy."

5. Assume "good person in bad circumstances."

We have lots of conscious and unconscious assumptions about others. These influence our interactions with them. Instead of thinking,

- *"There they go again"* try
- "I wonder what could be going on with them?"
- "What might they be feeling or fearing?"

Come up with two possible reasons for the behavior you've observed. Maybe they didn't sleep last night, or their boss gave them a written warning, or they received an unexpected bill they can't pay.

Follow these steps and make it easier to be in control of yourself and your emotions.

Successful People Spend Ten Hours a Week Just Thinking

Often he who does too much does too little.

—Italian Proverb

Warren Buffet, an American businessman, investor, and philanthropist, is the second richest person in America. He spends 80 percent of his time reading and thinking. His wide-open schedule is against the norm of constant busyness, yet critical thinking time is essential in a VUCA (Volatile, Uncertain, Complex, Ambiguous) world.

There are many ways to spend time thinking:

- Run, meditate, cook, garden, journal, or walk the dog.
- Block time on your calendar. Pick your highest energy time and a specific day of the week. Spend two hours with no set agenda. See what comes up. Do this for four consecutive weeks. You will develop a habit and results that will show you the value of thinking time.

Expect resistance to doing this. It is normal and to be expected. Start small and build up. Before you know it, you'll spend ten hours a week just thinking.

Leave Your Good Girl Out of the Workplace

Mary tastes stomach acids in the back of her throat. She hears muffled sounds instead of words coming from her client. Her hands are clenched and lips are pursed. She feels her cheeks flushing.

How can he keep demanding more and more from me? she wonders. *I've given him way more than he's paid for, and yet he keeps demanding more.* Mary has allowed her good girl to run the show.

The good girl gives and gives and gives to the point of exhaustion. She believes that being clear and direct in her communication is not nice. "If I set boundaries, I will lose the deal." "If I say what I mean, I am mean." She has no frame of reference of how to speak clearly and directly in the workplace. She uses good girl skills where they don't belong.

Use clear and direct communication at work.

It may feel like the world will come to an end when you are clear and direct. It doesn't. Not being clear and direct keeps you stuck and ineffective. When you are clear and direct, you allow others the dignity of making their own choices based on what is good for them and not at the expense of yourself. Being clear and direct empowers others.

Use the following phrases to practice clear and direct communication:

- "That doesn't work for me."
- "You may be right."
- "Let me think about what you've said, and I'll get back to you by the end of the day."

Say what you mean, mean what you say, but don't say it mean.

Change Your Thoughts to Match What You Want

For as he thinks within himself, so he is.

Proverbs 23:7

Our thoughts are energy and they have an impact on everything.

Don Miguel Ruiz, author of *The Four Agreements,* stated, "Everything we do in life is based on the agreements we have made with ourselves, with other people, with society, and with God. But the most important agreements are the ones we make with ourselves. In these agreements, we tell ourselves who we are, how to behave, what is possible, what is impossible." His first agreement is the most important: *Be impeccable in your word.*

If you want to live a life of joy, change your agreements. In other words, change your thoughts.

The first step is to identify your thoughts. Imagine if thoughts were visible. What would they look like? Have you ever yelled at a dog? Their whole body and face droop. They shake. Their tail goes between their legs. There is no difference in the impact of the mean words you say to a dog and the mean thoughts you think about yourself.

Write down what you think about this statement: "I'm not perpetually behind. I am perfectly on time." You may write, "This is untrue. I'm behind because I'm lazy and spend too much time looking at Facebook at night, and don't get up in time to exercise, and haven't done my weekly report."

Imagine what those thoughts would look like if you said them to a child. Would you change what you would say?

Next write down the attributes of your best friend. "She listens and loves me unconditionally. I know she cares." Notice the difference in the thoughts you wrote about your friend and yourself being perfectly on time. Which ones feel better?

You may feel uncomfortable with this exercise. This is normal and to be expected. You are creating new neural pathways in your brain, and it takes practice to get them established.

As you do this, your inner critic may get louder and say things like, "This is stupid. It won't work." As I've said, your inner critic has a positive intention for you—to keep you safe . . . just in case. It doesn't want you to feel disappointed.

When you hear negative thoughts, give yourself more love and compassion, not less. It makes the learning happen faster.

Choose your thoughts carefully. Put negative ones back on the conveyer belt of thoughts that continuously runs in your head.

Check Your Alignment

Cars get out of alignment. People do too.

Wheel alignment ensures optimal drivability of your car. It helps your tires last longer and your car drive smoother. Poor alignment shortens the life of your tires and compromises key steering and suspension parts. These are very expensive fixes to make.

There are noticeable signs of misalignment. Your car pulls to the left or right, you have uneven or rapid tire wear, or your steering wheel is crooked when you drive straight.

Your internal alignment is when your values and goals align with your words and actions. If you value kindness, speak kind words to yourself. If you value fun, schedule time to have some. If you value connection, set aside time with your partner, friend, or child.

Misalignment is when you appear to lack integrity, you feel "off" inside, or are exhausted and overwhelmed.

Regular maintenance is key to smooth living.

Look for signs of "Do as I say, not as I do."

You Are Allowed

To step into your own being is scary because you are vulnerable.

"That's what I want," Susan revealed. She told her friend Marta that she wanted to start her own business. She froze midsentence. "Forget what I just said," her voice trailed off. Her head shook as she had a conversation with others who were not in the room.

Marta put her hands up. "Whoa. Stop. Breathe, Susan. Who's yelling at you right now?"

Susan curled up. Her face pinched. "My boss is going to be mad. I don't want to tell my husband either. He'll think I'm flaky. My colleagues—geez—they'll think I'm crazy and giving up. But I don't want to be on their path. I want to be on my own path."

Going after what you want can make you feel vulnerable. Fear and doubt will come up—the fear of being hurt, of what others think of you. Being vulnerable opens you up to the possibility of pain and rejection. It also opens you up to joy, deep connection with yourself and others, acceptance, and contentment.

Vulnerability is courage in action. Tell the story of who you are to yourself and to another safe person. Expect to feel uncomfortable, icky, stupid, and have a desire to take back what you said. This is normal and to be expected.

"What would you tell your daughter if she came to you and shared what she wanted?" Marta posited.

"I'd tell her to go for it. That she deserves it. Take chances. It's worth it."

"Susan—go for it. You deserve it. Take chances. It's worth the risk."

Speak your truth, feel the vulnerability, and embrace your courage.

You Get an A+!

When you give yourself permission to believe you get an A+ in all areas of your life today, you make bolder decisions and choices that lead to your heart's desires.

What's getting in the way of you believing this? Here's a sample of answers I hear from my clients:

- "I have to earn my A+. I can't just believe I deserve it."
- "It has to be hard and take a long time."
- "Doing this exercise won't work."

Translation: "I don't want to be disappointed, or feel stupid and unlovable." In other words, "I am unworthy."

We don't even realize when we stop ourselves from doing what we want, no matter what other names we call unworthiness—"I'm afraid, feel guilty or shame." "I'm selfish." "I don't deserve this."

Most people believe that worthiness is something you earn by what you do, how you look, how much money you make, or how much you weigh.

The impact of this limiting belief is significant:

- We drive ourselves harder.
- We neglect our own care—skipping meals, not getting enough sleep, overworking, over-committing, not taking vacations, or taking vacations and not being present, not celebrating our successes, doing more just to feel enough, or trying to show the world you have it all together.

People who believe they deserve and are worthy of self-love and self-acceptance experience happier lives:

- They have lower rates of anxiety and depression
- They take more risks
- They are more resilient

Worthiness is the belief that you have inherent worth and value—just as you are. No prerequisites, no qualifiers. Worthiness is an as-is, here-and-now proposition.

Answer the following question: "If I believed I get an A+ in all areas of my life—my body, friends, work, what I eat or wear—what would I do today?"

- The one requirement for this exercise is to suspend judgment and believe you have an A+ in all areas of your life.
- Write down your answers to the question.
- Remember, you already have an A+ and this allows you to write freely about your own thoughts and feelings.

Engage with the world from a place of worthiness, believing you get an A+ in all areas of your life, and see the opportunities you have been missing.

Give yourself permission to believe you get an A+ in all areas of your life today.

It Came to Me Easily and Effortlessly Under Grace

I have a daily calendar alert to remind me to set the tone for the results I want to achieve: "It came to me easily and effortlessly under grace." I apply it to what I write, teach, and think.

My client Betsy set a goal to have more balance in her life. She worked too many hours, and it was taking a toll on her health, peace of mind, and family. She put a daily reminder on her Outlook calendar that said, "What does balance look like for me today?" It popped up every morning and helped her pause long enough to make conscious choices about how she spends her time. Some days her time is spent doing all work. Other days it's 30 percent work, 70 percent family. The more she did this, the more balance she created in her life.

Awareness of her choices increased. Sometimes it was painful to realize how much time she spent working. Mostly she felt empowered and motivated to continue to choose differently.

Use a phrase to remind you of your priorities. Put it as an alert on your phone, calendar, or on a sticky note on your bathroom mirror.

Use phrases to keep you focused on the life you want to live every day.

Make Space for Better

Release anything that blocks you from your good.

Peggy tilted her head to the ceiling as she released a long sigh. "I don't know why it's not working. I'm doing everything I did the last time I made it happen." Peggy had hit a grand slam last year at work. She was focused, blocked time, batched tasks, got adequate sleep, and eliminated unnecessary distractions in order to do only those actions that would get her to the goal. She achieved the top producer award.

Her left hand rubbed her lips as her narrowed eyes focused on the computer screen. "I have to make it work again. I know I can. What am I doing wrong?" Peggy was so focused on repeating exactly what she had done before that she lost sight of the present moment and the information it gave her that would help her move forward. She clung to her past success, which blocked new ideas and techniques.

Release any experiences that you are done with—positive or negative—to have space in your life to welcome and receive new experiences and information. Release successes, memories, expectations, superstitions, judgments, things, stories, experiences, titles, failures, disappointments, fears, resentments, limiting beliefs, guilt, images, excuses, and relationships. Write them all down on a piece of paper and then burn it.

Peggy walked to a nearby coffee shop. She wrote down the all the things she did to achieve her award. She closed her writing: "I'm grateful for the actions I took and the appreciation I received from my employer. I now release it to make space for my next." She returned to her office and a grin spread across her face as she shredded what she wrote.

Release thoughts, beliefs, and experiences that have served their purpose.

Liberate Your Inner Awesomeness

Select your goals based on your inner nature and purpose.

Carl Rogers, a humanistic psychologist, believed that for a person to grow, they need an environment that provides openness, acceptance, and empathy. He believed that humans have one basic motive: to fulfill one's potential and achieve the highest level of human "beingness" possible. People develop in ways according to their personality.

Look at the following values list. Decide how to align more closely with them. Make a list of behaviors you will start doing—or stop doing.

- *Authenticity*: Getting away from defensive superficiality and being oneself.
- *Autonomy:* Moving away from what you "should" do and making your own decisions.
- *Internal locus of evaluation:* Judgment based on one's own view, rather than seeking the approval of others.
- *Unconditional positive self-regard:* Judging and accepting yourself as valuable and worthwhile, including all thoughts and emotional reactions.
- *Process living:* Recognizing that we are in a constant state of becoming and never reach a final end point.
- *Relatedness:* Seeking close and deep relationships where you can truly appreciate and understand other people.
- *Openness to inner and outer experience*: Being able to perceive and accept how you and others behave and feel.

You become more relaxed and at ease with your life as you align with your inner awesomeness.

Be where you really are.

Ask for Help and Magic Can Happen

Today, most women try to make changes alone and fail. What if you built a network of support people around you; would this stack the deck in your favor?

Recently, during one of our sessions, I asked the following question of a group of women: "What gets in the way of you asking for and accepting help?"

Here's a sample of their answers.

- "I don't want to bother people."
- "My issue is not that important."
- "I don't want to appear like I don't have it all together."
- "I should be able to figure it out on my own."
- "I feel stupid asking for help."

These simple excuses can be really translated to mean: "I don't want to be rejected, abandoned, or feel unlovable." In other words, "I am unworthy."

Another way to think about unworthiness is to listen for the phrase, "I don't deserve this." To break this limiting belief that we are unworthy, we need to ask for and accept help from others.

How to ask for and accept help:

1. Start small and build up. Pick one small action that moves you toward what you need to do or change. Send one text, or make one five-minute call. Doing this once a day helps you overcome your limiting beliefs, connect with others, and make the changes you want to make.

2. Ask others to help you celebrate your successes—**all** of them. Minimizing the courage you are demonstrating sabotages your progress. Sharing successes will also help others share theirs.

It may feel uncomfortable when you start asking for help, but it gets easier with practice.

Act as if you believe you deserve help and ask for it.

Let it R.A.I.N.

Practice R.A.I.N. to find peace from the pain of perceived deficiency.

The fear of unworthiness, or not-enoughness, dictates your behavior. You may stay busy, continuously prove yourself, or cease trying. The motivation is to avoid the fear and feelings. To heal from the sense of unworthiness, use this four-step mindfulness process to work with intense and difficult emotions.

R.A.I.N.—four steps to take to be at peace with life's hardships and stop being hard on yourself:

R: Recognition of what is happening

A: Allowing life to be just as it is

I: Investigation with kindness

N: Non-identification with the experience

R—Pause and notice that a strong emotion is present. Notice what is happening in your body. Is your chest tight, a knot in your throat or stomach, tingling in your limbs? Mentally identify it. "I feel stressed, overwhelmed, depressed." The recognition of your feelings brings you into contact with yourself and the present moment.

A—Acknowledge and accept the present moment reality. You don't have to like it. The goal is to stop the impulse to push away or ignore difficult emotions.

I—Ask, "Why do I feel the way I do?" "Are there bodily needs I'm ignoring (sleep, exercise) that are affecting my emotions?" "What do I really need right now?" These questions build a relationship between you and your emotions and thoughts.

N—You are not your mind or thoughts. Say, "My thoughts are real, but not true." Who you are is not defined by any limited sense of emotions, sensations, or stories. This is a form of detachment and love in the middle of intense emotions.

Use R.A.I.N. to create space around your default mechanisms and to steer your way through challenging emotions.

Practice the nourishing art of mindful inquiry.

Bounce Back Faster When You Miss the Mark

When you make a mistake, use the tools of self-accountability and self-compassion to move forward faster.

Self-accountability is the willingness to be accountable for the outcomes that result from your choices, behaviors, and actions. It does not involve self-criticism.

Self-compassion is being kind and supportive with yourself whenever you experience setbacks. It is not self-indulgent.

Bill downloaded the tax planning software and entered his W-2 and 1099 information. The corners of his mouth turned up. "I'm so grateful. This extra income helped me pay down my student loans." He hit the finish button. "You owe $4,987." His face turned gray and his stomach lurched. He had underestimated the amount of additional taxes he had to pay based on his increased income.

When you miss the mark:

- Say a kind phrase to yourself: "I made a mistake. It happens. No big deal. Oops. My bad."
- Remember something you love: your animal snuggling with you, a funny scene from a movie, the smell of the ocean.
- Use curiosity phrases: "I wonder how I will figure this out? I'm going to list ten ways to solve this."
- Do not make the situation bigger than it is: "I don't have to sell my home, give away my dog, or go into hiding."

Don't use self-criticism to "get yourself in line." It detracts from identifying a solution and makes you feel stupid, behind, and less than. You act against yourself through name calling, hiding, or overworking.

Bill could choose to berate himself for days, hide the information from his wife, and waste his energy. He chose self-kindness and self-accountability. "I made a mistake. This feels really bad. I want to hide this from my wife, but we made a commitment to always be honest with each other, especially when we screw up. I wish I could turn back the clock. Ugh." He called his wife and explained his situation. She responded, "Thank you for telling me as soon as you discovered it. I have a few ideas for how to pay it. We make a good team." His shoulders dropped, he took a deep breath, and said, "I love you, dear."

Identify one task with which you can be self-accountable and self-compassionate in both the process and outcome.

Do You Let Thoughts Devastate You?

Our thoughts affect our feelings. Most of us assume it's the other way around: that our feelings come first and our thoughts naturally follow.

Thinking is a habit. Just like building a habit of exercising or getting more sleep, you can develop a habit of choosing thoughts that bring you happiness and prosperity.

You may believe that you are responsible for what you *do*, but not for what you *think*. The truth is that you are responsible for what you think, because it is only at this level that you can exercise choice. What you do comes from what you think.

In the book *Evolve Your Brain, The Science of Changing Your Mind*, Joe Dispenza describes the biology of the brain and how thoughts affect feelings. Thoughts produce chemical reactions in the brain. The brain chemistry we create by our own thoughts determines how we feel.

For example, "I have to perform at 200 percent in order to keep my clients happy." This thought tells the neurotransmitters to send a chemical message throughout the brain. The chemicals produce either positive or negative feelings. In this case, feelings of anxiety, worry, and fear are triggered.

This is how we allow thoughts to devastate us.

Notice when you feel anxious, irritable, or afraid. Write down what you were thinking about before those feelings started. Have a notepad handy to keep writing down your thoughts prior to your feelings. You will notice the pattern of thoughts that trigger them. This awareness allows you to make different choices.

When you stop old thought patterns, your brain begins to prune away these unused circuits.

Retraining your brain is like potty-training a puppy. You have to keep taking it back outside until it connects the new habit with relief and happiness.

There Are Many Ways to Face Your Fear

One way to conquer a fear is to face it head on.

Jimmy Fallon is the host of *The Tonight Show*. In one episode, he filmed the experience of his guest, comedian Kevin Hart, going to Universal Studios Park to ride the new Rockin' Rollercoaster ride. Kevin is afraid of rollercoaster rides.

The filming begins when Kevin and Jimmy walk up to the ride. Kevin's smile fades. He stops, leans on Jimmy, and lets out a heavy sigh. The camera cuts to the rollercoaster's first vertical drop. Kevin decides to go and conquer his fear. The film captures his terrified expression throughout the ride.

Look for an instructor to hold your hand while you face your fear, to lead you in a way that controls your exposure to your fear, while you let go of control. Kevin had Jimmy Fallon. Jimmy wasn't scared. He liked roller coasters. Your courage to face your fear with another person strengthens your resolve to face other fears. The rollercoaster no longer controlled Kevin. He now gets to decide whether he'll ride it again. If his ten-year-old son wants him to go on the ride with him, he knows he can tolerate his discomfort instead of thinking, "I can't do this."

If you fear driving over a bridge, swimming in the ocean, heights, bugs, or public speaking, find someone to help you manage your fear so it doesn't control you.

Face your fear with friends.

Gratitude Keeps You Going, Regardless of Your Problems

Just because you don't feel serene doesn't mean you are not making progress. You only know it in retrospect. Daily gratitude is the bridge to help you keep going when you can't see your progress.

When you grow frustrated with your progress toward a goal, look at where you were a year ago. Ask a friend how they've noticed that you've made positive changes. Sometimes others can see what you cannot.

Write down evidence of how you've changed. You didn't take the bait from a colleague and get in a pointless argument. You stuck to your commitment to exercise even when you felt guilty leaving your home and family with lunches unmade and dishes in the sink. You said no to people and activities that you didn't want to participate with and in.

Gratitude helps you know and embrace the experience of being alive in each moment, whether good or bad.

In times of doubt, boost your resolve with a dose of gratitude.

Emotion Is Not the Enemy of Reason

Many people mistakenly think emotions don't mix with reason and logic. It takes more than just knowing what to do. You also need to feel it.

Emotion and reason are not mutually exclusive. Emotion is a part of the reasoning process, so eliminating it reduces your ability to make effective decisions. To make this point, think of children who have autism. They have reason, but lack the emotional capacity to grasp other people's feelings.

Your gut is symbolically connected with emotion. You may have experienced butterflies in your stomach, or a gut-wrenching feeling, your stomach "dropped" when you heard bad news, or told you not to ignore your gut feeling when making a decision. Now science has shown that your gut is your second brain via its own neural network called the *enteric nervous system* (ENS). It is a complex system of one hundred million nerves found in the lining of the gut. It developed from the same tissues as our central nervous system during fetal development. So it has many structural and chemical parallels to the brain.

Both "brains" communicate back and forth and involve the endocrine, immune, and neural pathways. The brain and gut are so connected that they seem like one system, not two.

Listen to your gut. Pay attention to the way your body reacts in different situations. Notice the twinges your gut sends you. Do not dismiss them. Identify the thought you had right before the twinge.

Next time you have that feeling in the pit of your stomach, listen to it.

Use both "brains" and improve your decision-making.

Work with Your Inner Critic

Your inner critic speaks from a place of positive intention. For example, your inner critic may say, "You're not going to eat that piece of cake, are you?" The positive intention is to keep you healthy.

Do not banish your inner critic; talk to it. Recognize it and allow it to speak up. Pushing away the negative voice in your head makes it louder and more powerful.

Use these phrases when you hear your critical inner voice:

"I hear you and I promise __________ (I will take care of you, make more money, stop stuffing my feelings, play more)."

In the example of eating the piece of cake, you can say to your inner critic, "I hear you and I know you want me to take care of myself. I promise you I am exercising and eating healthy on a regular basis. It's OK for me to have this one piece."

And . . .

"Thank you for speaking up. I hear you and I promise I am taking care of it." Reassure that concerned part of your brain that there is an adult on board and "I got this."

Identify the positive intentions your inner critic has for you.

Use phrases as a way to talk to your inner critic.

It Was Right Under His Nose

Charles Darwin conducted his famous research in the Galapagos Islands in 1831. He went there to study geology. He brought back several birds he thought were wrens, blackbirds, and finches.

He gave them to John Gould, the best taxonomist in England. John made a surprising discovery. The birds were all finches and related to each other. Their beaks were different sizes, used for different things: to crack nuts or dig out insects. There were thirteen species, matching the thirteen islands Darwin visited.

Gould was an expert taxonomist. But it was Darwin who proposed the radical notion: "Was it possible for a species of birds to split into two or more species if the birds were isolated on separate islands?" This led Darwin to the Theory of Evolution.

John Gould was unable to figure this out. He had all the pieces of information. But he associated everything he observed according to the rules of taxonomy, and so he attempted to fit what he saw into those rules. His high associative barriers got in the way of seeing what was right in front of him.

Darwin was able to figure out the theory of evolution because he had low associative barriers. He was a geologist.

Our mind makes associations unconsciously and automatically. By hearing a word or seeing an image, the mind unlocks a whole series of associated ideas, each one connecting to each other. These chains of associations are based on our own experiences.

Associative chains are efficient and effective. We can move quickly from analysis to action. They also inhibit our ability to think broadly. We don't question assumptions as readily; we jump to conclusions faster and create barriers to alternative ways of thinking about a particular situation.

High associative barriers inhibit creativity.

Low associative barriers allow for more creativity and innovation.

Enlist people who have deep and diverse backgrounds—finance, media, programming, marketing, and operations—to contribute something that is quite different and creates something quite extraordinary.

Giving and Receiving Are One and the Same

Cindy's car finally died. The repairs cost more than the value of the car, so she donated it to charity. "Now what do I do? I don't live near public transportation. I'm such a loser for not having the money to buy another car." She continued to berate herself for working at a low-paying job, having poor savings habits, and not being further ahead in life.

A few days later her girlfriend Joyce called. "My son is moving to London and doesn't need his car anymore. I'd like you to have it."

Cindy didn't understand, as if her brain short-circuited and needed a reboot. Her face flushed. "Can you say that again?"

"I want to give you a car."

Receiving feels unnatural to most people. The limiting belief is you have to earn what you receive or you don't deserve it. Receiving is a muscle. You have to exercise it to get it stronger.

How to receive:

1. Define what you would do if you believed that you are worthy of a miracle-filled life.
2. What would you do if you were free from tension, stress, and worry?
3. What would you do if you believed in your abundance and worthiness?
4. What if you believed everything you need is already given to you?
    - Take a deep breath
    - Be present
    - Never worry again
    - Dance
    - Let my light shine brightly
    - Love more
    - Gently and merrily row downstream
    - Accept gifts (time, money, love) from others

Cindy whispered, "Yes. Thank you." Joyce waited in silence and listened to Cindy's sobs, knowing that receiving seems harder than giving.

Receive and allow your heart to expand.

"What –Me Worry?"

Worry is meditation on the negative.

"What—Me Worry?" is the phrase on the cover of *Mad* magazine, said by the fictitious character Alfred E. Neuman for the past sixty years. His big ears, missing front tooth, and one eye lower than the other depicts a mischievous look, without a care in the world. His features were sculpted in ice at the Dartmouth Winter Carnival. Fred Astaire danced in an Alfred mask during a TV special. Climbers planted a Neuman flag on top of Mount Everest.

Worry is when you allow your mind to dwell on difficulties or troubles. It is a state of anxiety over actual or potential problems. Worry is a form of control, as a way to prevent bad things from happening. Excessive worry increases anxiety, triggers the fight-flight-freeze response, and may lead to relief in compulsive activities such as overworking or overeating.

The antidote to worry is to allow your emotions to come up and accept them. Watch them as if you are an outside observer, making no effort to change them. You will realize you can endure it. This is healthy emotional flow. This is called mindfulness.

Acknowledge your feelings. Express them when necessary. Take action if possible. Welcome the next feeling that emerges.

Recognize the Love that Already Exists in Your Life

When you look for one person to give you everything you want and need, you block yourself from seeing the love given to you now.

"I want a partner who reads me like a mood ring."

"Yeah. I want to be a size 0, but that's not happening either."

"So I shouldn't want the best for myself?"

"It's not that. You keep looking to this future mystery person and not seeing how much love you already have in your life. It's like you dismiss it if it doesn't come in a perfect package."

Friends, pets, coworkers, grocery clerks, other drivers, neighbors—they all provide you with love. Don't overlook what love you have now, while straining to find it in the future.

Notice and write down examples. "My neighbor picked up my trash can that got knocked over during last night's storm." "The grocery clerk told me a funny joke." "A friend shared her pain with me." This opens you to more love.

Say thank you for the love you receive today.

Every Day Is Decision Day

November 8 is National Signing Day, when high school athletes decide which college they commit to play for and sign a contract.

There's a lot of work that goes into this decision. Student athletes complete many campus tours, phone calls with coaches, and overnight trips with teams, while keeping up with their homework and their sport. It is a big decision, as many student athletes receive scholarships to attend their school of choice. Once decided, they are able to get back to being a typical student athlete in high school.

Like these student athletes, you have to make multiple decisions too. An adult makes an average of 35,000 conscious decisions each day. Some are trivial, like what to eat for breakfast; others are impactful, like taking a new job or leaving a relationship. To help make important decisions, ask yourself the following questions:

1. How long have I been thinking about this?
2. How committed am I to this change?
3. When I think about it, how does my body feel?
4. Am I feeling fear or listening to my intuition?
5. Does this decision align with my values?
6. What is the risk of doing it?
7. What is the risk of not doing it?
8. If not now, when?

You can't know the outcome of decisions ahead of time. Make the best decision and move forward.

Decide with confidence that you chose the best option with the information you had at a specific point in time.

Step into Someone Else's Shoes

Social awareness is the ability to recognize and understand the emotions of others. This skill helps you respond to the needs of others.

Brenda slumps on her desk. She ignores the phone ringing. Bill walks into her office with a report he needs her to review and approve.

"Hey, Brenda. That kind of day already?"

She sits up. Her eyes are red. Bill sits down next her. "I'm all ears. What's up?" Bill forgets all about his need for her review and approval of his report.

To increase your social awareness:

1. Notice others' body language. Crossed arms, furrowed brow, pursed lips, tapping a pen, or shoulders raised are all clues about a person's emotions. Identify your guess as to the corresponding emotion. If the person you are observing is open to feedback, tell them you noticed their body language and your guess at the corresponding emotion. This will help you increase your accuracy.

2. Practice active listening. Adjust your approach to match the other person's communication style and maximize effectiveness. One size does not fit all.

Be empathetic to the emotional drives of other people. You gain perspective and a deeper understanding of others, improve your communication, and spot problems before they grow.

Notice what someone's body language is telling you.

Participate Fully in Your Life

Success and failure are a matter of perspective. In spite of challenges, you can enjoy each day, even when you don't get the results you want.

A farmer found a magical flute. Hoping to charm his chickens into laying more eggs, he played the flute for them all day. They laid no more eggs than the usual amount. Later, when asked if he had success, the farmer replied, "Yes I did. It wasn't much of a day for egg-laying, but it was a great day for music."

Gratitude helps you be happy despite your problems. When you focus on the good around you, you reduce anxiety and increase your peace of mind.

Ask five people what they are grateful for. Then ask them about a mistake they made and how they bounced back from it. You will discover the happiest people deliberately practice gratitude and inner-forgiveness.

Increase your present-moment awareness through gratitude.

On the Other Side of Fear Is Everything You Want

Denise opened the email announcement about her favorite leadership conference. She read every word, looked at every speaker and breakout session. Her heart raced. "I belong there," she said out loud.

She called me. "There's a conference I want to attend, but it's expensive and I shouldn't leave the kids for that long, and my clients will need me during that time."

"Tell me about the conference."

Her voice got louder. "It's amazing. I would experience breakthrough ideas with my business, network with smart people, and expand my circle of opportunities." She continued gushing about the benefits of attending this conference.

I asked, "What's your decision?"

She sighed and was quiet for a few moments. Her brain danced with fear and faith.

"I'm going."

"Great. Now let's figure out how to delegate everything else, so you can be present for your miracles at the conference."

When fear comes up:

- Take three deep breaths.
- Write about your fear for five minutes.
- Call a trusted advisor and talk through your fear.
- Write a list of ten things for which you are grateful.
- Take one action.

Denise invited her sister to stay with her children and set up client sessions before and after the conference. Her business partner was her backup during the days of the conference. She bought a new journal and pen to capture her ideas, new contacts, and action steps.

When fear comes up, identify one thing you are grateful for. It shifts your energy and interrupts the negative thought loop.

Acknowledge your fear and take action anyway.

Vulnerability Takes Practice

Go to the places that scare you—tell yourself who you really are, warts and all.

I remember the first time I told a friend that I always thought I had been born the wrong gender. "If only I was born a man, then my life would have worked out so much better." Shame, grief, and intense vulnerability washed over me. Where was the rewind button? She must think I'm crazy. I think I'm crazy.

"Tell me more," she asked.

"Nope. I'm good. I'm just going to the nearest bakery and buy all the day-old treats."

It was only when I shared this belief in my late forties that a healing light pierced through my armor of protection–the mantra I said my entire life, "If only I was a man . . . "

Vulnerability is an emotion that makes you feel exposed and awkward. It's the place you avoid, push away, and protect yourself from. It requires taking a risk.

The benefits of being vulnerable are that you gain greater clarity in your purpose in life, joy, accountability, empathy, and inner compassion.

Being vulnerable allowed me to heal this wound. I love who I am—gender, warts, and all.

Shed the armor that used to protect you and now smothers your light.

National Kindness Day

Kindness is the language the deaf can hear and the blind can see.
—Mark Twain

Did you know self-kindness is a natural anti-depressant because it causes a release of serotonin in our brain? Serotonin plays an important part in learning, memory, mood, sleep, health, and digestion. It heightens our sense of well-being, increases energy and gives a wonderful feeling of positivity and self worth.

See how many times you can practice these four steps today:

- Regular deep breathing: If you're stressed, burned out, or anxious, take a few moments out to stop and allow everything to drop away. Then pay attention, breathe mindfully, and relax.
- Say NO! Give yourself permission to say no to doing things that make you unhappy and yes to the things you'd rather do.
- Ask for and accept help. Women are more successful when they ask for and accept help. We are willing to help those who ask us; now it's time to get uncomfortable and ask someone else to lend us a hand, ear, or cup of coffee.
- Laugh more. Laughing lowers your blood pressure and reduces stress hormones such as cortisol and adrenaline.

Small acts of kindness toward yourself restores a sense of humanity and belonging.

Take a kindness break every hour. Appreciate one thing about yourself.

You Are Worth Knowing

Irene sank into the chair with a bag of popcorn. She stared at the TV screen and shoveled the popcorn in her mouth until the bag was empty.

"Why are you watching *Crime Scenes*? That's a really violent show," her husband said.

Irene shook her head. "I guess I zoned out and didn't realize what I was watching."

Her exhaustion came from overdoing. She walked the dog before and after work, did all the grocery shopping, and made the meals. She volunteered regularly at her church. Influenced by others' goals and desires left no time for her to get to know herself.

Discover who you really are and what you want from life.

Suspend judgment and act as if nobody is watching you or will critique your answers to the following statements:

I dream about ____.

I'm good at ____.

I want to do more ____________________________________.

____makes me laugh.

Irene decided to consciously make an effort to find out what she really wanted. She joined a bird-watching club, had groceries delivered, and went to the library weekly to discover new authors.

Discover by doing. Let go of expectations and outcomes and enjoy the journey.

You Are Worthy

Most people believe that worthiness is something you earn by what you do, how you look, how much money you make, the number on the scale, or the car you drive. The impact of this belief is significant. To prove our worth, we drive ourselves harder. We neglect our own care by skipping meals, not getting enough sleep, overworking, overcommitting, not taking vacations, or taking vacations and not being present, not celebrating our successes, and trying to show the world we have it all together.

Jan had a cold that she tried to plow through so she could keep up her normal routine. She drank more fluids, but that was the only change she made. Her stuffy nose and sore throat kept her up at night. After a few weeks, it moved into her chest. Her colleagues confronted her about her hacking, so she went to the doctor, who diagnosed her with bronchitis and ordered her to bed rest.

She felt guilty being away from work. There was an important project and she didn't want to burden others with her workload. She did not feel worthy of taking the time to heal. Being sick is no fun. Being sick and feeling guilty about it is worse.

Guilt and blame are signals of unworthiness.

- Look for times when you feel guilty.
- Ask yourself if you intend to harm yourself or others. Ninety-nine percent of the time, the answer is no.
- Revise your definition of guilt.

Jan decided to change the way she viewed sickness. Instead of blaming herself, she said, "Everyone gets sick. When I do, I choose to stay home and care for myself."

Act as if you believe you are worthy. Ask a friend to identify three things she admires about you.

Don't Kick the Football

Charlie Brown did not learn from the past. He continued to lay flat on his back, wondering how he could have let himself fall for Lucy's football trick all over again.

The first time Lucy Van Pelt pulled the football away from Charlie Brown in the comic strip *Peanuts* was on November 16, 1952. She continued her promise to hold it, then snatched it away, until 1999. Charlie Brown never succeeded in kicking the football. He consistently ended up flat on his back, frustrated and hurt.

This reminds me of going to people for something they don't give you, whether it's time, love, or feedback. We go back to them over and over, hoping this time will be different. "If I say just the right words, in the right tone, and the right time, then they will give me what I want." People are who they are. Just because you believe someone is withholding something does not mean they have it to give.

Self-awareness is the first step. Know your story and how it affects you. Charlie Brown is the definition of insanity: doing the same thing and expecting different results.

Make peace with your past. The story you tell yourself ("this time will be different") needs resolution.

Know your relationship patterns. Identify your beliefs, emotions, and behaviors that cause you pain.

What Mindful People Do Differently

Mindfulness is focusing on your moment-to-moment experience.

Everyone experiences some level of anxiety at some point in their life. When you are about to give a presentation at work, set a boundary, or go on a date, you experience uncertainty and anxiety. A common symptom of anxiety is crazy thoughts.

Examples of crazy thoughts may include unwanted images, such as failing a presentation in front of the entire company, falling down and breaking your nose while on a first date, or someone physically attacking you. They also may be unprompted worries just before your big presentation: you think your child might be hurt or you spouse could be in a car accident.

The key to mindfulness is coming back to the present moment.

Mindful people don't believe their thoughts and they don't take them all seriously.

Imagine a recent experience when you had crazy thoughts.

1. Acknowledge your thoughts and emotions
2. Accept them
3. Pause
4. State, "This thought is real, but is it true?"
5. Take three deep breaths to come back to the present moment

Mindful people also:

- Don't try to force the thought out of their minds
- Don't try to avoid or deny emotions
- Understand that all thoughts come and go
- Do one thing at a time
- Turn everyday tasks into mindful moments
- Practice being curious
- Challenge existing beliefs
- Listen to others without trying to control or judge

Everyone experiences crazy thoughts. Make a conscious decision to develop a habit to detach from them.

Remember you are safe in the present moment.

Good Things Come in Threes

When you delegate tasks, use the Awareness Trio Questions to see if your employee understands what you expect. It will reduce misunderstandings and mistakes.

Most people aren't missing the mark on purpose or to make you mad. They are doing it because of their own mental filters. We all have filters through which we run information and what you say may be heard very differently than what you meant.

When someone does not perform a task correctly, or repeats an unskillful behavior, ask the following Awareness Trio Questions:

1. Do they know they are doing it?
2. Do they know the impact it is having on themselves and others?
3. Do they know another way?

The goal is to bring awareness to yourself and the other person. Your answers guide your next steps.

Ask the right questions and improve communication and outcomes.

Your Emotions Provide Useful Information

Most people were taught to express only those emotions considered acceptable—like happy—and suppress others labeled as bad—like anger.

Our caregivers knowingly or unknowingly sent a message about acceptable and unacceptable emotions. Fear of feeling all emotions was programmed at a young age.

Emotional avoidance is commonplace. You avoid some emotions because of their intensity and the sense of vulnerability that comes with them. You may fear disapproval from others. When you express emotions, you experience a deeply personal part of who you are.

Identify which emotions you were taught were unacceptable. Put a star next to them. Take one action to express that emotion. Write in a journal, talk to a friend, or look for others who exhibit it regularly.

Feelings Guide

Sad	Happy	Tired	Energized	Insecure	Confident	Hurt	Helped
Depressed	Hopeful	Indifferent	Determined	Weak	Strong	Abused	Cherished
Lonely	Supported	Bored	Inspired	Hopeless	Brave	Forgotten	Befriended
Disgusted	Charmed	Drained	Creative	Doubtful	Certain	Ignored	Appreciated
Angry	Grateful	Sick	Healthy	Scared	Assured	Judged	Understood
Frustrated	Calm	Exhausted	Renewed	Anxious	Prepared	Offended	Commended
Annoyed	Amused	Dull	Vibrant	Defeated	Successful	Victimized	Empowered
Discouraged	Optimistic	Weary	Alert	Worthless	Valuable	Rejected	Accepted
Upset	Content	Paralyzed	Enlivened	Guilty	Forgiven	Cursed	Blessed
Despairing	Joyful	Powerless	Strengthened	Ugly	Beautiful	Destroyed	Healed
Uninterested	Enthusiastic	Dejected	Motivated	Pressured	At ease	Hated	Loved
Disappointed	Thrilled	Listless	Focused	Forced	Encouraged	Despised	Esteemed
Hateful	Loving	Burned out	Rejuvenated	Stressed	Peaceful	Mistreated	Taken care of
Bitter	Kind	Fatigued	Invigorated	Nervous	Relaxed	Crushed	Reassured
Sorrowful	Celebratory	Blah	Animated	Worried	Secure	Injured	Made whole
Mournful	Overjoyed	Stale	Refreshed	Embarrassed	Comforted	Tortured	Saved

Emotions tell you something about your needs; they communicate what's going on inside you. Fear wants to protect you; anger means someone crossed a boundary; love signals that someone is important to you. Your emotions tell you who you are and what's important to you.

Nothing is closer to you than your emotions.

There are no bad emotions; accept them all.

Life Is Like the Game of Chutes and Ladders

If you can meet with triumph and disaster and treat those two imposters just the same . . . yours is the Earth and everything that's in it.

—Rudyard Kipling

In Chutes and Ladders, players race to be the first to the top of the board. Players roll a single dice and advance their token the rolled number of spaces. Along the way, they will find ladders to help them advance, or chutes and slides that will cause them to move backward.

Life offers us ladders and chutes. We get a promotion and our child gets accepted into their dream school. Our spouse gets cancer or we get in a fender bender.

We set goals to take us to the top of the board. It may be a new relationship, job, saving for retirement, or learning a new language. When the roller coaster of life takes us up, we are excited and happy. When we plunge down, we are scared and hanging on for dear life.

To be happy, accept what is. Learn how to be with your life as it is, not how you would like it to be. The good times don't last. And neither do the bad times.

Recover Faster from Setbacks

Resiliency is the ability to face setbacks, failures, crises, and pain, and to bounce back quickly. Without it we get stuck.

Alice was on a diet. For two weeks she ate healthfully and exercised regularly. Then friends invited her out for drinks. She joined them and drank two light beers and ate three chicken wings and some nachos. Afterward, she felt horrible and berated herself. "How could I blow my diet? I'm such a pig. I'll never be able to lose weight. I might as well eat the cake in the freezer."

How we encounter and react to life's setbacks can be broken down like this:

A: **Adversity.** We face a setback or challenge.

B: **Beliefs.** Our thoughts, feelings, and interpretation of the setback. These beliefs lead to . . .

C: **Consequences.** How we act because of our beliefs about the setback.

It's not adversity itself that creates our reactions, but our *beliefs* about our adversity. Change your beliefs about challenges.

A: **Adversity**—"I ate chicken wings and had a few beers."

B: **Beliefs**—"I can get back on track. I have two great weeks of clean eating to prove it."

C: **Consequences**—Alice practiced self-compassion, skipped the cake in the freezer, and ate healthfully the next day.

Practice your ABCs and spend more time in the solution instead of the problem.

Show, Don't Tell

Ginny is a successful realtor and works very hard to be recognized for her professionalism, integrity, and results.

Ginny shut her laptop a bit too hard and marched down to Jonathan's cubicle. She had asked him to make a flyer to send out to prospects that highlighted her expertise. He had missed the mark.

"I told you to make me look professional. This flyer makes me look like I want to invite people to a cookie swap party."

In this example, Ginny *told* Jonathan to make a flyer that highlighted her expertise. She had an image in her mind of how it would look. She did not *show* him an example. To help people be successful, show them the outcome you want.

Ginny found a sample flyer and pointed out exactly what represented her expertise. "In this flyer, it lists my years of experience, the number of homes I've sold, and that I live in the neighborhood."

Use stories, thoughts, senses, feelings, or examples to show others what you want them to accomplish.

Show others what you want. It increases success and reduces frustration and time fixing mistakes.

This Is the Worst Thing Ever!

Nothing's either good or bad except your thinking makes it so.

—Shakespeare

Recently I slipped on the ice while walking my dog and broke my ankle. Laying on the ice, I thought, "This is the worst thing to happen to me!"

I was reminded of this ancient fable.

A farmer had only one horse. One day, his horse ran away.

His neighbors said, "I'm so sorry. This is such bad news. You must be so upset."

The man just said, "We'll see."

A few days later, his horse came back with twenty wild horses following. The man and his son corralled all twenty-one horses.

His neighbors said, "Congratulations! This is such good news. You must be so happy!"

The man just said, "We'll see."

One of the wild horses kicked the man's only son, breaking both his legs.

His neighbors said, "I'm so sorry. This is such bad news. You must be so upset."

The man just said, "We'll see."

The country went to war and every able-bodied young man was drafted to fight. The war was terrible and killed every young man, but the farmer's son was spared, since his broken legs prevented him from being drafted.

His neighbors said, "Congratulations! This is such good news. You must be so happy!"

The man just said, "We'll see."

The point of the story:

- There's always plenty of evidence for the story you tell yourself (confirmation bias).
- Shift the story, and watch the evidence line up to reinforce it.

- Ditch the story and see what a moment brings.

We experience in life things we'd rather avoid. Wisdom comes from being present and working under any condition. In every obstacle lies an opportunity. How you perceive a moment and what you do with it is up to you.

These experiences teach us not to lose hope or feel utterly defeated.
Wait and see through all the pain and all the joys
and say courageously, "We'll see."

Meditate for Miracles

Every morning I meditate. It calms me down and clears my head. I am able to listen to the still, small voice inside me. This voice provides valuable guidance. When I follow it, miracles happen. My self-trust increases. I make fewer mistakes. I accomplish what's important and avoid the unessential.

After I meditate, I write down what I heard. This is a checks-and-balances system. "Is this my ego or my intuition?"

On Thanksgiving morning, I heard and I wrote down, "Text Steve 'Happy Thanksgiving.'" Ugh. No way. I'd only been divorced from Steve for a short time. This was stupid and wrong. I wanted to be right instead of happy. Finally, I surrendered and texted him. He called and we had a pleasant conversation. During the conversation the still, small voice said, "Tell him you are grateful for him." Steve had another call coming in and said he had to go. I took a deep breath, "I'm grateful for you." He thanked me and hung up.

Meditate for one minute. It is enough. Write down what you hear.

I collapsed into deep, cleansing sobs. I knew it was OK to miss him, to love him, and to feel the grief I had been avoiding. My sobs reached from my inner soul and released the pain and emotions. When I was done, I knew something had shifted. He and I were both free to live our lives. I was free to love him and bless him on his way and go on my way.

My phone beeped and he had sent a text. "I'm grateful for you too, and all the things we achieved together!"

Meditate to experience your inner wisdom.

Use Phrases to Reduce Client Worry, Stress, and Strain

Have a list of phrases to help clients and colleagues navigate choppy emotional waters. They can be used in many situations and reduce conflict and stress.

In the following example, Barb is a realtor and her clients regularly experience emotional ups and downs. Here's how she uses phrases.

"You may be right."

- Use this when clients are unable to listen to your advice. It's a sideways approach and may provide a smoother manner in approaching a challenge.
- Brent tells you the price you recommend to list it at is 40 percent below what it should be. "You may be right, Brent. Let me run the comps." This allows him to be heard without you agreeing with his point.

"That doesn't work for me."

- Use this when you get requests you do not want to participate in.
- A client asks Barb to go furniture shopping with her. "That doesn't work for me."

"People are naturally creative, resourceful, and whole."

- Use this when clients are requesting more than is reasonable, and you need to detach from them and set boundaries.
- Brent and Janice want Barb to dog sit while they are out of town. "I know Brent and Janice are naturally creative, resourceful, and whole. They will find the resources they need to take care of their needs."

"This is normal and to be expected."

- Use this when your clients are feeling afraid or uncertain, even when they experience something routine or commonly encountered.
- "Buying a home causes people to feel nervous and anxious. This is normal and to be expected."

Use phrases to guide others to emotional safety and build self-confidence.

Emotions Are Messengers

I always wished that emotions were stored in an organ. That way I could have it surgically removed. I found emotions confusing, messy, and uncontrollable. I was afraid that if I started to feel intense emotions like grief or anger, I would never stop.

I sought professional help to work through the grief I felt around my brother's death, my marriage ending, and my children going to college. I also sought the guidance of friends.

One night I had dinner with my friends Jan and Gail. They are angels in my life, who hold my hand when I walk through fear, discomfort, uncertainty, and especially emotions. I asked Jan how she deals with her emotions and where love fits into the experience of intense emotions. She drew the following on the paper placemat:

MAD + LOVE = great change

GLAD + LOVE = joy

SAD + LOVE = honoring

SACRED + LOVE = healing

She talked about the limiting belief that you should control or deny emotions. Instead, if you listen to the guidance they offer from a place of love, you make peace with having emotions and experience healing, freedom, and change.

Jan referred me to the book, *The Wisdom of 5 Messengers: Learning to Follow the Guidance of Feelings*, by Kerry Paul Altman, PhD. After I read the book and practiced a different way to relate to my emotions, I found I no longer wanted to shoot the messenger.

Make peace with your emotions.

This Moment Matters

“This Magic Moment” is a song released by the Drifters in 1960 and spent eleven weeks on the Billboard Hot 100 list. The opening line is, “This magic moment, so different and so new . . . ”

Mindfulness is being in this magic moment. It is intentionally paying attention to your experiences with openness and curiosity.

It may feel uncomfortable to stay in the present moment. This is because most people are taught that the next moment is more important than the present moment. Figuring out the future gives a false sense of being in control and of protecting yourself from being vulnerable, hurt, or victimized.

The opposite is true. You are safe in the present moment.

Practice present-moment awareness with 5-4-3-2-1.

- See five things
- Touch four things
- Hear three things
- Smell two things
- Taste one thing

This practice brings you back to the present moment. It interrupts repetitive thought loops and helps you achieve a calm, clear, and alert mind.

Mindfulness practice contributes to your ability to recognize opportunities and increases your clarity and focus.

Become aware of yourself within the present moment.

Pause and Make More Money

You can't always know the outcomes of what you are doing. But you can take time and be mindful about what you are doing before you do it.

Dagmar rubbed her forehead as she stared at the phone. "What did I do wrong? I thought I had the listing. The sellers seemed to interested in going with me." The buyers had called to tell her they chose another real estate agent.

A mindful pause is a moment of active, open attention on the present.

Take a step back from the rush of activity. Pause for two minutes before your next prospect call. Focus only on the call. Ask yourself, "What is my ideal outcome from this call?" What do I need to say to convey my ideal outcome? What is my intention in this moment?"

After the call, pause again for two minutes. Capture what you heard. Did they sigh, ask a question out of the norm of usual questions, or need additional information?

Dagmar applied this technique before her next prospect call. She paused for two minutes and identified her goal: get the listing. Her intention during the call was to be curious and open-minded. She asked for what she wanted. She got the listing. Pausing, preparing, and post-call review got her the listing and a five-figure commission.

Pause provides the necessary break from multitasking, rushing, and missing signals.

Pause to stop the flow of busyness, to see the signs, and to put two and two together.

Treat Guilt like Teflon, Not Velcro

Mindy is an executive in a marketing firm. She excels at and enjoys what she does—defining and executing strategy, direction, and culture in order for her organization to thrive. She also wants to spend her time on what matters—family, work, play, health, community. She craves to have a balance of health, well-being, and productivity.

When she tries to make time for those things that matter, she feels guilty.

- "I'm taking time away from doing day-to-day tasks to plan for the next quarter and I feel guilty."
- "I'm going to the gym this morning instead of going straight to work and I feel guilty."
- "It's Saturday and I'm going to the movies with my partner while my employees finish a big project. I feel guilty."
- "I have an unexpected opening in my schedule and I want to read. I feel guilty about wanting to do this when there are so many other things I should do."

Misplaced guilt is a reaction that you accept blame for something that does not belong to you. It is an unhealthy emotion that needs to be worked out.

Ask the following questions:

> "By choosing to ___________________ (spend time planning, exercising, playing, reading), am I intentionally trying to harm others?"
>
> If the answer is YES, describe specifically how you are intentionally harming others.
>
> If the answer is NO, then you have misplaced guilt.

Ask:

> "Why do I feel guilty for having this want or need?"
>
> "If I believe there is enough time to balance health, well-being, and productivity, what would I choose to do in this moment?"

Go with your first answer. This is your intuition speaking. It is the voice of your inherent worth and value telling you, "You deserve to have this time to meet your needs."

Mindy wrote an empowering belief. "Successful women make time for their families, work, and themselves. By consistently spending time on what matters, I am kinder to myself, more effective at work, and available to my spouse and kids."

There is enough time. Transform scarcity thinking into focused, abundant living.

Question your thoughts and beliefs and find a richer, more meaningful life.

Daydream and Discover Yourself

Henry David Thoreau wrote the book *Walden* in 1854. It's his account of simple living for two years in a cabin at Walden Pond. His conclusion from chapter 18:

"I learned this, at least, by my experiment: that if one advances confidently in the direction of his dreams, and endeavors to live the life which he has imagined, he will meet with a success unexpected in common hours. He will put some things behind, will pass an invisible boundary; new, universal, and more liberal laws will begin to establish themselves around and within him; or the old laws be expanded, and interpreted in his favor in a more liberal sense, and he will live with the license of a higher order of beings. In proportion as he simplifies his life, the laws of the universe will appear less complex, and solitude will not be solitude, nor poverty poverty, nor weakness weakness. If you have built castles in the air, your work need not be lost; that is where they should be. Now put the foundations under them."

Take time to journal what you want, not what you think you should do. Give yourself permission to write whatever comes to mind. Do not edit any thoughts as stupid or not practical.

Discover what Thoreau described:

"If a man does not keep pace with his companions, perhaps it is because he hears a different drummer. Let him step to the music which he hears, however measured or far away. By doing so, men may find happiness and self-fulfillment."

Take one step toward what you want.

Ask for What You Need

Rosa was craving connection and creativity outside of her work. The holidays were approaching, and she wanted to fill her own tanks before the demands of family obligations came knocking.

She was having coffee with her friends Barb and Karen. Waiting in line to order, Karen said, "Look at the Starbucks Gingerbread House kits. We should have a party and make them."

Rosa couldn't help but smile. She giggled as she shook her hips and shoulders, "Yes! I will host it." Her body moved to the holiday music that played in her head.

Identify ways to feed your needs:

- Connecting with friends
- Dance class
- A hot bath
- Reading
- A walk in nature
- Sleep

She invited friends with whom she connected deeply and who enjoyed playing too. Rosa delighted in finding the right kit and bought lots of extra decorating supplies. So did everyone else. The table looked like a candy store: red licorice, multi-colored sprinkles, chocolate bars, icing in a rainbow of colors. Rosa's dog happily cleaned up the occasional stray morsel that fell on the floor.

Ask the right people to meet your needs.

Receiving Is a Skill You Can Learn

But first, you need to identify what gets in the way of you receiving.

Elaine went on a weekend getaway with her friends. The group decided to get a facial the following day. She woke up and felt slightly dizzy. "I better not get a facial," she told her friend Tammy. "It may make my dizziness worse."

"They can prop you up with pillows," Tammy said.

Elainc shrugged, rolled her eyes, and let out a heavy sigh.

"This is supposed to be fun, Elaine. You're acting like you're going to be tortured."

"Fine. I'll go," she snorted. "But I don't have to like it."

Identify your obstacles to receiving.

1. Self-judgment: this may be so ingrained that you have to consciously practice noticing it.
    - "Am I going to be embarrassed for canceling? They are going to think I'm weird because I can't lay down."
    - "I should be more flexible."
    - "I should be more compassionate with myself."
2. Measuring and monitoring yourself: you were taught to meet others' expectations.
    - "Why aren't I further along in taking care of myself? My daughter would say yes immediately and yet I hesitate."
    - "I've done all this work on myself, and I'm still uncomfortable with self-care."
    - "Tammy said yes easily. What's wrong with me?"

Elaine mentioned that she had never had a facial before. She believed that spending money on it was wasteful and self-indulgent.

When the towel was placed on her face, she contracted and resisted. *You're fine,* she thought to herself. *Let it happen. Relax.* As the massage continued, she felt the tension release. *You are so tightly wound, you don't even know that you are tightly wound.* She continued to unwind and receive.

Notice your thoughts when you receive compliments, time, and invitations.

Receiving Is a Muscle You Have to Exercise

Many of us were taught that it's better to give than receive. In truth, they are one and the same. To give is no more important than to receive. But neither is it less.

Patricia hurried into the coffee shop. Deb greeted her with a hug, and Patricia relaxed into their embrace. "I'm so happy you are here," Deb said.

She gets me, Patricia thought as she ordered a coffee and muffin.

Deb started. "Tell me how you are."

Patricia's stomach growled. She picked at her muffin. Tightness ran across her chest. A knot settled in her throat. *You already asked her once to listen to your problem. She's going to think you're too needy. It's not that important. Ask her how she's doing.*

She prayed for words to come. Looking down at her feet, she mumbled, "I need help figuring out that same problem." Her checks flushed.

"I'm here for you." Deb's smile melted Patricia's frozen words.

Learning to receive involves:

1. Accepting that you have needs
2. Identify the rules you have about needs and needing
3. Asking to have your needs met
4. Receiving from others

Patricia believed she could only ask a person to meet her needs once. She craved connection and being heard. Her friend gave her love and acceptance. Through the discomfort of asking and getting her needs met, Patricia's heart opened and received.

Expect discomfort while you build your receiving muscle.

Create a Receiving Plan

As Deb and Patricia continued their conversation over coffee, Patricia settled into her chair and body, feeling solid and supported. Her chest and throat relaxed. "Thank you for listening to me. I feel so much better." Patricia gulped down her muffin.

Deb put her hands on her heart. "I'm happy to. How can I continue to support you?"

Patricia struggled with her weight and had just shared with Deb her frustration with signing up for a gym and not going. She described the roadblocks she encountered with exercising: time, stress, sleep, and competing priorities. Together they brainstormed ways she could ask for and accept help to overcome them.

When you recognize a need, identify three ways to get it met. Call a friend, write in your journal, make space for emotions to come up, or hug your pet.

"Get out a pen and paper. Let's capture these ideas," Deb suggested.

"Yes!" Patricia gushed as she scouted through her purse. With pen in hand, she wrote, "Ask Belinda if her offer still stands to join her at the gym's yoga class on Thursday evenings. Ask Barb to text encouraging phrases on Wednesday at noon. This will remind me to go for a lunchtime walk. Bookend with Patricia that I did these two activities this week."

You are ten times more effective when you plan ahead of time.

Determine three ways to get your needs met.

Emotional Intelligence, Like a Fine Wine, Improves with Age

People with a higher emotional intelligence (EI) are happier and have an easier time of forming, developing, and maintaining close personal relationships.

Think of a friend who "gets" you. They know the right thing to say when feelings are hurt or tensions are high. They listen empathetically to your problems and make you feel hopeful about life. They have high emotional intelligence.

Emotional intelligence is the ability to effectively identify, manage, and express emotions. It is understanding and managing your own emotions and influencing the emotions of others.

Think about yourself at age twenty, thirty, forty, fifty, sixty. Have your sharp edges softened with each decade of experiences? Did your empathy for others increase with each loss, failure, and disappointment you survived? Have you grown kinder to yourself as you age?

You can call it wisdom. It is also acceptance, empathy, self-awareness, social-awareness, self-management—the key skills of emotional intelligence.

Think of movie characters like Leigh Ann Touhy (Sandra Bullock) from *The Blind Side*, and Minny Walker (Octavia Spencer) from *The Help*. Think of the women supreme court justices, your mother, your grandmother, or older women you admire. Identify their EI strengths.

Enjoy one of many benefits of getting older—increased emotional intelligence.

Acknowledge how your ability to make deep personal connections with others has grown over time.

Compare and Despair

Judy's right eye twitched. She rubbed her forehead and gnawed on the end of a pencil. Forcing a smile, she said, "I'm really happy for you, Jim. You deserve the promotion. Also, congrats on your wife expecting a baby. So much joy!"

Unbelievable, she thought to herself. *I want a promotion. I want to have a baby. I want a life. What's wrong with me?* The more she compared her life to Jim's, the worse she felt.

To compare is to look at others in relation to yourself. It is a harsh form of self-torture. You never win.

When you find yourself comparing, do this:

- Check your expectations. Expectations set you up for disappointment and self-judgment.
- Compare yourself to yourself. Where were you a year ago compared to where you are now?

Judy's expectations were that she would have had two kids by now and be further ahead in her career. She released her expectations about how life should go and approached life from a place of exploration. She noted that she had made significant progress in building her endurance to run marathons and create a network of friends.

Comparison steals the energy you could use on discovering your heart's desires, your likes and dislikes, your unique skills and contributions that the world needs. If you didn't care what others thought of you, what would you do, be, and have? The answer to this question gives you clarity.

Live by your values, not by other people's expectations of what you should do and be.

Perfectionism Is Like the Game "Operation": You Get Shocked Every Time You Make a Mistake

The board game Operation is a skill-based game involving tweezers and a steady hand. It consists of an operating table, with a patient named Sam, who has a large red lightbulb for his nose. On the surface are a number of openings, which reveal cavities filled with humorously named plastic ailments, such as broken heart, wishbone, and butterflies in the stomach. The object of the game is to remove these "ailments" with a pair of tweezers without touching the edge of the cavity opening. However, if the tweezers touch the metal edge of the opening during the attempt, a buzzer sounds, Sam's nose lights up, and the player loses a turn.

Perfectionism is the same feeling as when you touch the metal edge of the cavity opening. When the tweezers touch it, you get a slight jolt, a shock.

Perfectionism is the tendency to set standards so high, they either cannot be met or are only met with great difficulty. Trying to be perfect increases stress and lowers confidence. It leads to chronic procrastination or being overly cautious and thorough in tasks, such as spending two hours on a task that should take twenty minutes. It can also be excessively checking the work you've done, redoing work to make it "perfect," or agonizing over small details.

When you find yourself in the perfectionism trap, answer the following four questions about your current challenge:

1. Does it really matter?
2. What is the worst that can happen?
3. If the worst does happen, can I survive it?
4. Will this still matter tomorrow? Next week? Next year?

Allow yourself to make ten mistakes today guilt-free.

Let Me Explain

Humans are wired to want an explanation. By making sense of an uncertain world, explanations make the circumstances of life more predictable and help reduce anxieties about the future.

Finding an explanation for an event is deeply satisfying. It creates order and coherence, which gives you a sense of stability and certainty. You are acutely aware of losing this sense of certainty when you can't find meaning in a new pattern of thought, action, or event. You look for patterns to help you explain your surroundings and circumstances. When someone says, "Jill is going to be late for the meeting," you explain, "I bet she hit bad traffic on the highway." News media explains current events, sportscasters explain the meaning of plays on the field. There is an expectation that everything you perceive means something. Even when an image means nothing more than it is, you force-fit a pattern to relieve your discomfort of not knowing.

Sometimes people act in ways that are unexplainable. Your spouse has an affair. Your dad didn't want to spend time with you when you were a kid. Your brother keeps drinking. You get fired. Your sister doesn't leave her abusive husband. Your mother tortures you about your weight.

Accept the fact that these experiences happened. Let go of the illusion that knowing the answer for others' unexplainable choices will make them less painful. "If I just knew why, I could let it go. Maybe then I wouldn't still be angry, sad, or scared." Accept that you are hurting. Allow yourself to feel the pain. The need to know why is a way to avoid the pain and hurt, and prevents you from moving on.

Let go of needing to know why.

Pain Shared Is Pain Divided

Your feelings are telling you something you need to hear. Listen and share it with others.

Kevin Hart stands 5'4" and has established himself to be a much bigger figure than his physical presence. Growing up in Philadelphia with his mom and drug-addicted father, Kevin worked hard to become a successful comedian and actor.

His comedy routine is real and relatable. He talks about his insecurities and flaws, his painful relationship with his father, his mother's fight with cancer, and his divorce from his first wife. He shares authentically, and his audiences love him for it.

It's natural to resist pain and strive for comfort. However, personal growth comes when you embrace discomfort. What you resist persists. Don't push your pain down or label it as wrong or bad. It is neither. Be vulnerable and acknowledge that you have pain that needs to be expressed. Find a safe friend and ask them to listen to you, without judgment and without fixing.

Honor your painful feelings, as they are part of who you are.

Self-Forgiveness Heals All

The Women's Ministry Group met two weeks before Christmas to swap cookies and share their gratitude and appreciation for each other.

Karen pulled out her favorite cookie recipe, bought the ingredients, and set aside the time to make them. She was about to start the process when her colleague called her. "Can you close this house sale? My daughter is dancing in the Nutcracker ballet tonight and I can't miss it."

"Sure!" Karen said, understanding that her colleague was pressed between work and family obligations. She closed the sale instead of making cookies.

Her inner dialog went back and forth. "I want to go to the party, but I feel bad not bringing anything. I really want to go. I wish I had time to make them." She decided to go empty-handed.

The women attending the party had kids ranging in age from four weeks old to twenty-nine years old. All of them had baked and brought cookies.

"Ugh. What excuse do I have? Even the woman with a newborn made cookies."

Give yourself a break.

Let yourself off the hook.

Forgive yourself for not meeting life's sometimes-impossible demands.

Karen paused, put her hands on her heart and said, "I deeply and completely love and accept myself as I am. I forgive myself for not bringing cookies to the party." She felt her guilt slip away. She confessed, "I didn't bake cookies and decided to come anyway because I wanted to spend time with you." She watched the others noodling around what she had said.

Her friend Becky groaned. "You mean I don't have to do it all? I can show up even if I don't have any food to contribute?"

Allow yourself to show up and receive love, even when you are flustered, overwhelmed, or empty-handed.

Forgive yourself for not meeting your own expectations.

Making a Mistake Does Not Mean You Are a Mistake

Recently I went to the grocery store with a long list of items to buy. I took my pen out of my purse to cross them off so I would not miss anything. As I leaned over the cucumbers and broccoli in the produce section, I dropped my pen. It landed behind a metal frame. The only way to retrieve it was to take out the produce from that section and remove the front grate.

This pen is special. It's gold plated, slim, and fits perfectly in my hand. I love the feel of it as I write.

I asked the produce manager if he could get my pen. He looked down at the metal frame, then at me, then down again. He sighed and said, "Go finish your shopping. I'll find you once I've got it." He proceeded to move all the produce into a grocery cart.

I felt really badly. I kept shopping, distracted. I didn't have my pen to cross off items on my list. I was embarrassed. I had made a mistake.

Ask for help when you make mistakes.

Say, "Oops."

Keep moving. Dwelling on the mistake longer than necessary wastes energy and focus.

The produce manager found me in the deli section. He smiled and said, "Next time, bring a Bic." Duly noted.

Mistakes are opportunities to learn. Some of us learn from other people's mistakes; the rest of us have to be the other people.

Learn from your mistakes and move past them as quickly as possible.

Your Thoughts Are Your Teachers

Practicing awareness and acceptance of your thoughts helps you overcome the tendency to get caught up in negative thoughts and feelings.

We have about 50,000 thoughts a day; that's thirty-five to forty-eight thoughts per minute.

Here are examples of my thoughts, "Add eggs to the grocery list, the fight I got in with my husband last night and trying to rewrite it, what I'm going to say to a client that will change their mind about switching to another consultant, I ate too much at lunch, I hate this cubicle."

One way to become aware of your thoughts is to practice mindfulness.

Mindfulness is a mental state achieved by focusing one's awareness on the present moment, while calmly acknowledging and accepting one's feelings, thoughts, and bodily sensations.

You can do this through active observation: noticing your thoughts, feelings, and what's going on in your body. For example, you may notice the following: "I'm sitting in a meeting and I'm acutely aware that I'm bored, my knee hurts, I'm a little hungry, I'm anxious to look at my phone, but I don't want to get the evil eye from the boss."

Accept what you notice. Judging it creates all sorts of negative thoughts and feelings. Without judgment, you can learn what thoughts bring you peace and happiness, what make you uncomfortable, and what work to support your growth.

Awareness and acceptance of your thoughts bring you more in tune with your surroundings, sensations in your body, and a way to see and choose what thoughts you want to focus on.

Practice Hands-On-Heart (H.O.H.): Place your hands on your heart and say, "I deeply and completely love and accept myself as I am." You will notice thoughts and reactions you may not have been aware of before.

The Obstacle Is the Way

Ryan Holiday wrote the book *The Obstacle Is the Way: The Timeless Art of Turning Trials into Triumphs*. In it, he shares specific strategies and techniques to take obstacles and turn them into advantages.

Everyone confronts obstacles—mental, physical, emotional, and perceived obstacles. It is what you do with them that determines success or failure.

Change how you look at obstacles. Find some benefit and use it as fuel.

- J.K. Rowling was a single mother living on welfare when she wrote her first Harry Potter book. She was rejected twelve times before selling it for $4,000.
- Maya Angelou survived poverty, sexual abuse, and racism to become a famous poet and civil rights activist.
- Oprah Winfrey was born to a single mother and grew up in extreme poverty. She created the Oprah Winfrey Show, which was the highest-rated television program of its kind in history.

Take one action today. Be deliberate and make a move. Courage equals taking action. Commit your one action to another person and follow through.

Turn every obstacle into an advantage.

Say Yes to Your Call to Adventure

Until one is committed, there is hesitancy, the chance to draw back. Concerning all acts of initiative (and creation), there is one elementary truth that ignorance of which kills countless ideas and splendid plans: that the moment one definitely commits oneself, then Providence moves too. All sorts of things occur to help one that would never otherwise have occurred. A whole stream of events issues from the decision, raising in one's favor all manner of unforeseen incidents and meetings and material assistance, which no man could have dreamed would have come his way. Whatever you can do, or dream you can do, begin it. Boldness has genius, power, and magic in it. Begin it now.

—Johann Wolfgang von Goethe, German writer and statesman

Dan had a life-long dream: hike the Pacific Crest Trail (PCT). He had a strong desire but didn't believe it was achievable. He was in his fifties, with a creaky knee, a mortgage, and kids in college.

He discovered a shorter part of the 2,600-mile PCT: the John Muir Trail, named for the famous conservationist. It is a two-hundred-mile section of the PCT and one of the most scenic parts.

He made the decision, asked his wife Karen to join him, and that's when the Universe rushed in. Every step seemed to happen just at the right time.

He got a permit, researched equipment and logistics, got in shape, and practiced hiking with a heavy backpack. Each step on its own was quite doable. The preparation for the journey was a journey.

They weren't sure if they were going to make the two-hundred-mile, twenty-day trek. Lots of people don't; sprained ankle, forest fires, altitude sickness. This made them focus on living in the moment. Every morning they would say, "We are on the John Muir Trail."

He realized his dream and completed the John Muir Trail. It all started with making a decision.

Say yes to your dream.

Make the decision and watch the Universe rush in to support you.

Do What Matters Most First

A to-do list is endless and does not necessarily help you prioritize what is most important to accomplish. Instead of writing a to-do list, write a "What Matters Most List."

Look at your list of tasks. Ask the question, "What matters most to me today?" Do those things first.

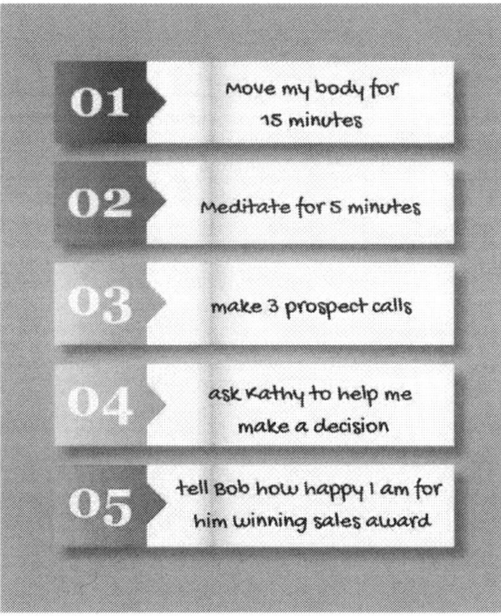

Keep the list visible. Put it on your computer monitor, refrigerator, or car dashboard. Set an alert on your phone that goes off every hour.

You will not get everything done. You will get the right things done.

Redefine success by accomplishing only what matters most.

Love Your Weirdness

My son Stevie returned from college for winter break. After he slept for twenty-four hours, we ventured out and purchased a Christmas tree and brought it home. Stevie was in charge of selecting the music while we decorated it. He loves to dance and has since he was a toddler, jumping to *Sesame Street* songs. He continues to dance freely at home to his favorite songs. As I watch him dance, my heart overflows with joy.

The first song he played was "The Time Warp," a song from the 1973 movie *The Rocky Horror Picture Show*. The song teaches specific dance steps: "It's just a jump to the left, and then a step to the right. Put your hands on your hips, and pull your knees in tight. But it's a pelvic thrust that really drives them insane. Let's do 'The Time Warp' again."

In high school, my friends and I went to see the movie. A big part of the movie experience is audience participation, so we dressed up as certain characters from the movie, joined the dancing, and recited all the lines.

When Stevie put on this song, I immediately jumped up and danced the steps and sang every word. It was as if I was sixteen again. I had my own time warp experience. So much so that I lost track of the fact that I was dancing in front of my son. "What are you doing, Moira?" my inner critic shouted. "Stop dancing in front of Stevie. You're so weird!"

Watch for the labels you give yourself. Weird, quirky, shy, and loud are examples of labels. Embrace all of you because it's all magnificent.

I shook off the inner critic and kept dancing. As I jumped to the left, I saw Stevie dancing too. We danced "The Time Warp" together.

Instead of labeling parts of yourself as weird,
maybe you can learn to call it grace.

Don't Let a Codependent Blackout Ruin Your Day

When you remember something you've done in the past and wished you hadn't, love yourself. We've all been there.

I pulled out the boxes of Christmas decorations from the garage. There was only one box of ornaments. My son Stevie carried them to the tree. "Stevie—see if there are any other ornament boxes in the garage."

"&*%@!," I mumbled under my breath. It hit me. I had given all the ornaments to my now former husband. I had kept the ones my sons made or were given to them over the years. Last Christmas, I was in the middle of getting divorced and heartbroken. I wanted the process to be over and was getting his stuff out of my house as fast as possible. I pretended to be jolly for the sake of my sons. What I really wanted to do was crawl under the covers on Thanksgiving and wake up on January 2.

As the realization sunk in, I laughed, put my hands on my heart, and said, "Moira, you did the best you could last year. I promise to buy you new ornaments the day after Christmas."

Remember that you did the best you could with what you had at the time you made a decision in the past. Love yourself and move one.

December 26 came and I rolled out of the house at 7:00 a.m. I was excited at what I might find at Macy's. I found an ugly sweater ornament, snowflakes, silver birds, and designer popcorn. I bought eighteen ornaments at 70 percent off. The cashier said, "You're all ready for next year." I beamed. Christmas came on both December 25 and December 26.

Wake up. You can handle reality.

Fly the Plane

When complexity hits, checklists help you remember what is important.

Atul Gawande wrote the book *The Checklist Manifesto: How to Get Things Right.* He describes the value of using checklists for better efficiency, consistency, and safety, especially during complex situations that require solutions that are both technical and demanding.

Checklists first came into existence in the aviation industry in the 1930s. Boeing entered their Model 299 in a competition for manufacturers that wanted to build the military's next-generation bomber. In front of a crowd of military personnel, airline executives, and reporters, the plane took off. Within minutes it stalled, turned to one wing and crashed, killing two of the five crew members.

The investigation identified pilot error as the reason for the crash. Planes were becoming bigger and more complex to fly. The amount of information needed to fly a plane was too much for one person's memory.

The pilot checklist was created. The first version was brief enough to fit on a single index card. It listed step-by-step checks to be done before takeoff, during flight, and before landing. Because of these checklists, pilots flew the Model 299 a total of 1.8 million miles without one incident. The Army ordered 13,000 Model 299s, which was named the B-17.

Checklists ensure people apply all their knowledge and expertise consistently well. Good checklists get the routine and obvious tasks out of your mind so you can focus on the hard stuff.

Now firefighters, doctors, police officers, and financial managers use checklists as a solution for extreme complexity and specialization. Applied consistently, they save lives. Doctors' checklists include hand washing. This one step done before treating a patient reduced ICU infection rates by 66 percent.

Checklists help reduce overlooking routine matters under the strain of pressing immediate demands. The first bullet on a pilot's checklist when an alarm goes off is to "fly the plane."

Develop effective checklists that help you fly your plane.

Show Off Your Buff Muscles

Character strengths provide the way for developing all other strengths.

There are five different types of strengths:

1. Strengths of talent—your innate abilities
2. Strengths of interest—what you like to do
3. Strengths of skill—proficiencies you develop
4. Strengths of resources—external supports
5. Strengths of character—attributes, an aggregate of who you are; what's inside of you

Research shows that your greatest successes are the result of using your unique strengths and that humans share the same basic twenty-four character strengths. The difference is how much you have of each one. The most commonly held character strengths are kindness, fairness, gratitude, and open-mindedness.

Practice:

- Kindness: cook a delicious meal for yourself and others
- Fairness: encourage equal participation of everyone in a meeting
- Gratitude: tell a friend three things you appreciate about them
- Open-mindedness: play devil's advocate on an issue you have strong opinions about

When you use your strengths, you increase your happiness at work and home, you increase your sense of authenticity, and learn faster.

Nurture your strengths to increase your energy, happiness, and satisfaction.

PAUSE

When Something Bothers You, Pause and Check In with Yourself

God grant me the serenity to accept the things I cannot change,
The courage the change the things I can,
And the wisdom to know the difference.
—Reinhold Niebuhr

Clarice pulled onto the highway. "It's a good thing I left thirty minutes early this morning. Traffic is lighter, and I'll have time to finish my report before my boss comes in." An ambulance sped past her. A mile later, traffic came to a dead stop. Her jaw tightened and her hands gripped the steering wheel. She felt a pain in her neck and shoulders.

Whenever something is bothering you, answer the following questions:

1. "Is this something real or something I'm creating in my own mind to upset myself?"
2. If it is real, ask, "What can I do about this as soon as possible?"
3. If it is not real, ask, "What can I do to let this go immediately?"
4. If it is potentially real or could happen, set it aside until it does become real. Worrying ahead of time is a waste of energy and keeps you out of the present moment.
5. If it is real and it's something you can't control—a serious illness, divorce, job loss—change your frame of reference about it.

Clarice took three deep breaths. She put her car in park and released her hands from the steering wheel. She stretched out her hands and recited a prayer. Her jaw relaxed. She called her boss and left a message that she was stuck in traffic and would finish the report as soon as she arrived at work.

Thoughts lead to feelings. Pause. Breathe deeply.

PERSEVERANCE

DEC 21

Don't Give Up

There was a museum laid with beautiful marble tiles, with a huge marble statue displayed in the middle of the lobby. People came from all over the world just to admire this beautiful marble statue.

One night, the marble tiles started talking to the marble statue. "Marble statue, it's just not fair! Why does everybody from all over the world come here just to step on me while admiring you?"

Marble statue answered, "My dear friend. Do you remember that we were actually from the same cave?"

"Yes. That's why I feel it is even more unfair. We came from the same cave, and yet we receive different treatment now."

Marble statue said, "Then, do you remember the day when the designer tried to work on you, but you resisted the tools?"

"Yes, of course I remember. I hate that guy. How could he use those tools on me? It hurt so badly."

"That's right. He couldn't work on you at all, as you resisted being worked on. When he decided to give up on you and start working on me instead, I knew at once that I would be something different after his efforts. I did not resist his tools; instead I bore all the painful tools he used on me."

"Mmm . . . "

"My friend, since you decided to give up halfway, you can't blame anybody who steps on you now."

Move forward despite your challenges, setbacks, and mistakes.

Recycle to Get Your Anger Out

Save delivery boxes and bubble wrap. Jump on them when you're angry. Recycle and repeat.

"Three more days, then all this madness stops," Aisha mumbled to herself.

Empty boxes piled higher than the trash bin. Disgusted by the number of gifts she'd bought and needing to feel in control of something, Aisha decided to break them down.

She jumped on a small box and heard a loud pop. "Bubble wrap." She pulled the bubble wrap from other boxes. "How is all this stuff supposed to fit in the recycle bin?"

She jumped on one sheet. Then another. She erupted in laughter, "This is awesome!" She laughed harder when she remembered a scene from a *Bugs Bunny* cartoon. Yosemite Sam forces Bugs Bunny to dance for him by shooting at his feet. "I'm Bugs Bunny dancing to the beat of the bullets," she shouted as she smashed more bubble wrap and boxes.

Anger is an emotion that can motivate change, inspire independence, or dispel illusions. Don't resist feeling angry or label it as bad or wrong. Figure out appropriate ways to get it out. Punch pillows. Scream in your car. Smash empty boxes. UPS delivers approximately 750 million boxes during the holiday season.

Breathless and beaming, Aisha released pent-up anger and frustration.

Express your anger in safe ways.

Sit with the Sadness

Holidays are emotionally loaded. Leave space in your day to feel your emotions.

Christmas morning:

"Did you hit the button on the coffee machine yet?" she mumbled. Her kids were screaming, "It's Christmas! Get up, get up!" One eye opened to see the time: 5:23 a.m.

Mug in one hand and camera in the other, Beatrice settled into her chair. Controlled chaos. A blur of wrapping paper, squeals, and crashing expectations. Cinnamon rolls and chocolate. Caffeine and gratitude warmed her body and soul.

Christmas afternoon:

"You can only bring one toy to Dad's house. That's the rule."

Beatrice scampered from room to room, packed overnight bags, favorite pillows and blankets, and put the dog in the crate. The kids slept on the drive to her former husband's house.

Feel your feelings until they dissipate. You have all the answers inside you, and your emotions are a primary vehicle for those answers.

Beatrice returned home and sank to her knees, no strength left to stand. Desolate sobs. Being alone and away from her children left her feeling intense anguish. Her body drained, she climbed into bed and slept.

Holidays have a way of bringing pain to the surface. Allow all your emotions space and express them. This too shall pass.

Hold holiday pictures, traditions, and expectations loosely.

Deep Breathing Restores Your Sanity

Holiday travel usually includes delays, whether with flights or flat tires. Pack your patience and deep breathing exercises to maintain balance, equanimity, and peace of mind.

"Delayed" the screen flashed. Tereza's skin crawled with sweat and turned clammy. Her eyes stung as she held back tears. She opened her book, the one she had saved for a month to read during her flight. She read a few pages and slammed it shut. She looked up and noticed a woman seated across from her. Eyes closed, the woman took deep, even breaths. "Hmmm. Maybe she's on to something."

Deep breathing will take your focus off emotional pain. It reduces anxiety and helps you feel safe when things seem out of your control.

Set a timer for two minutes. This allows your high-alert system to relax and to know it won't miss something important, like an announcement about your flight. Put ear buds in and play soothing music. Close your eyes and notice your breathing. Place your hands on your belly and breathe so that your belly extends your hands outwards.

The person at the counter announced, "We have an update from maintenance. The problem is fixed and we will begin boarding in thirty minutes." As Teresa's chest relaxed, she nodded to the other woman and they both breathed deeply.

Breathe deeply to ground yourself in the present moment and out of the wreckage of your future.

Gratitude Gives Perspective

It's when you feel least thankful that you are most in need of gratitude.

Helen Keller said, "Everything has its wonders, even darkness and silence, and I learn, whatever state I may be in, therein to be content."

Life is messy. In the midst of struggles, it's easy to lose perspective of who you are and what you can and cannot do, of what you can and cannot control. The furnace breaks, your son gets into a fender bender, traffic makes you late for an important meeting, you lose a document you worked on for hours. Among the daily stresses and challenges, search for gratitude. Gratitude helps you detach from your struggles.

At the end of each day, write down three things for which you are grateful.

"My son is alive. My bed is warm. My dog loves me."

After a few weeks, your perspective will shift. You will be looking for things to be grateful for. You will notice things you previously took for granted.

"My husband makes coffee for me every morning. I have a window office."

Gratitude reduces anxiety, jealousy, and scarcity thinking. It increases positive feelings and helps you bounce back faster from adversity.

Allow every problem to help you change for the better.

Interrupt Obsessive Thinking by Singing a Jingle

Hearty laughter is a good way to jog internally without having to go outdoors.
—Norman Cousins

Schoolhouse Rock! is an American series of animated musical educational short films that aired on Saturday mornings from 1973 to 1985. Topics ranged from grammar, science, and math to economics, history, and civics.

One grammar episode was titled, "Lolly Lolly Lolly Get Your Adverbs Here." The story is about a store owner who sells adverbs. This is the refrain:

Lolly Lolly Lolly, get your adverbs here.
Lolly Lolly Lolly, got some adverbs here.
Come on down to Lolly's, get the adverbs here
You're going to need
If you write or read,
Or even think about it.
Lolly Lolly Lolly, get your adverbs here.
Got a lot of Lolly, jolly adverbs here.
Anything you need and we can make it absolutely clear . . .

I use this jingle when I obsess about a situation, person, or institution, and whenever I go into the future parade of imaginary horribles. For example, "I think my biggest client isn't going to renew their contract. Then I can't pay my bills. I'll have to move out of my home. Where will I live? I better start looking for an efficiency apartment now."

I break out in a chorus of "Lolly Lolly Lolly Get Your Adverbs Here." It interrupts my obsessive thinking, my projecting of the worst outcomes. I laugh, and this allows a space for me to make another choice. "Is this thinking helping me?" No. Never. Create another thought, such as, "I know how to solve problems as they present themselves to me."

Interrupt obsessive thinking with a jingle. Then choose another thought that brings you into the present moment. Laugh.

Strengthen Your Self-Trust Muscle

Self-trust is the first secret of success. Whatever course you decide upon, there is always someone to tell you that you are wrong. There are always difficulties arising which tempt you to believe that your critics are right. To map out a course of action and follow it to an end requires courage.

—Ralph Waldo Emerson

Self-trust is a learned skill in which you rely on your inner resources—mental, emotional, physical, and spiritual. You strengthen self-trust when you:

- Practice self-maintenance (adequate sleep, healthful eating, exercise, downtime, sick time, play time, journaling)
- Keep promises you make to yourself (I'm going to bed at 10:00 p.m.)
- Live by your values (love, faith, balance)
- Express your thoughts and emotions (I feel sad)

Amy slumped in her chair, her hair falling in her eyes. She could only think about brushing it aside. She had crammed her swollen feet into her work shoes and hobbled into her office. She had promised herself to take a day off after working sixteen-hour days at a work conference. Instead, she pushed herself to go in to the office. She was no good to anyone there, especially to herself. Guilt drove her to neglect her needs, break her promise to herself, and she ended up even more exhausted.

Create a self-trust scorecard:

- List your top five self-trust actions—go to bed at a certain time, exercise, say no, participate in a hobby.
- Grade yourself at the end of each day. Green = did it! Yellow = did it a little. Red = missed the mark.
- Share your week's results with another person.

There are three reasons to do the scorecard.:

1. We do not get better without structure.
2. Repetition is the key.

3. Accountability provides the support to succeed.

Amy listed her self-trust priorities and her friend Melissa agreed to join her in completing it for a week. She discovered that what gets measured improves.

Create a self-trust scorecard. Ask a friend to join you for one week in scoring your priorities.

Play Cards

December 28 is Card Playing Day. It came about as a respite from the holiday busyness and a fun way to connect with friends and family.

While this activity may seem trivial, play is an important source of relaxation and stress reduction. It fuels your imagination and creativity and improves your problem-solving skills and well-being.

Playing cards teaches you several life lessons: Stay in the moment. Play the hand dealt you. Remain calm and think. Take responsibility for your choices and what you can control. You can't play other people's cards for them. Make the most of your hand. Enjoy the experience. Let go of the results.

Gather your friends, order a pizza, and break out a deck of cards.

Play to boost your happiness.

Use the Broken Record Approach

When you need to get a point across calmly and assertively, use the broken record approach. The broken record approach emulates repetition in situations when you want to make your point clear to another person and show that you are serious about your message. You repeat the same phrase over and over again, without getting off message.

Jessie had a difficult conversation with her employee, Mark. He was blaming his staff for mistakes that he was making. Jessie prepared to discuss this with Mark and wrote out her main message: "When you blame your staff for your mistakes, it erodes trust and confidence in your ability to lead."

Mark tried to deflect her message during the meeting. He disagreed, said facts were missing, and even brought up an example of when Jessie had blamed him for a mistake she had made.

She didn't budge. "I hear you. We can discuss that example (my behavior) at a later time. In this meeting, we are focused on your behavior of blaming your staff. When you blame your staff for your mistakes, it erodes trust and confidence in your ability to lead."

"Fine. I hear you. Now what?"

Use the broken record approach to make a clear and direct point that:

- You are serious about what you are asserting.
- You are not going to be deflected by attempts to change the subject or give a different response.
- The request you are making is reasonable.

Stick to your main point during difficult conversations.

Own Your Strengths

Dr. Martin Seligman is an American psychologist, educator, and author. He is referred to as the father of positive psychology and its efforts to scientifically explore human potential and what makes life worth living.

He developed an assessment (Values in Action Inventory of Strengths) to help individuals raise their awareness of what's best about themselves and others and to help them use their strengths to build stronger relationships, deeper happiness, and achieve life goals.

There are twenty-four core character strengths. Strengths are characteristics you use regularly, which bring a sense of authenticity. For example, you use perseverance and self-regulation to pursue a skill in music, curiosity to explore new career options, and compassion when learning new behaviors.

1. *Creativity*: New ways of thinking and acting.
2. *Curiosity*: Exploring and seeking for its own sake.
3. *Open-mindedness*: Seeing things objectively and fairly, from all sides.
4. *Love of learning*: Constantly developing skills and knowledge.
5. *Perspective*: Seeing in ways that make sense and giving wise counsel.
6. *Bravery*: Not shrinking from threat, challenge, difficulty, or pain; acting on convictions, even if unpopular.
7. *Persistence*: Seeing things through, despite difficulties.
8. *Integrity*: Presenting oneself in a genuine way; taking responsibility for one's feeling and actions.
9. *Vitality*: A zest and enthusiasm for life and living.
10. *Love*: Valuing, sharing, and caring for others.
11. *Kindness*: Doing things for others without requiring reciprocation.
12. *Social intelligence*: Being aware of how yourself and others are motivated, and acting accordingly.

1. *Citizenship*: Being socially responsible and loyal.
2. *Fairness*: Treating everyone in a similar way. Being just and without bias.
3. *Leadership*: Driving achievement while maintaining harmony.
4. *Forgiveness and mercy*: Forgiving wrongdoers rather than seeking punishment or revenge.
5. *Humility/Modesty*: Not putting oneself above others. Letting achievements speak for themselves.
6. *Prudence*: Not taking undue risks or doing what you will regret.
7. *Self-regulation*: Controlling one's emotions and actions according to one's values.
8. *Wonder*: Appreciating beauty and excellence.
9. *Gratitude*: Knowing, feeling, and being thankful for all the good things in life.
10. *Hope*: Positively expecting the best and working to achieve it.
11. *Humor*: Enjoying laughter and making people laugh. Seeing the lighter side of life.
12. *Spirituality*: Having coherent beliefs of a higher purpose and the meaning of life.

List the top five that resonate with you and build on them.

Love the essence of who you are.

I Believe in You

I discovered that my own inner wisdom is trustworthy and that it communicates to me through my natural impulses, instincts, and intuition.

I believe . . .

- In women breaking out of their cages, coloring outside the lines, and like Dr. Seuss, going to all the places they will go
- In women exploding out of themselves with fireballs in WOW moments and standing tall, powerful, and confident as they embrace their next adventure
- In women in smocks and women in pumps who roar with giddiness about what they can be, knowing they are worthy
- In group hugs, no matter how old we are, because it's great to be hugged by our communities, and know we belong
- In a world where women remember how to be as curious as a four-year-old and jump in mud puddles
- In women who feel free to ask for and accept support, and not permission, and revel in the ideas of others, and in women who embrace discomfort and welcome the next magical moment
- In colored markers, magazine cutouts, and mapping our minds, and that power comes from being playful and letting our creativity flow
- It's safe and fun to recognize your own successes and in putting our masterpieces up on the refrigerator
- In women knowing it is safe to let themselves be vulnerable and know that they can go into the unknown together and experience unexpected discoveries
- In women who want to know "X" but are thrilled to find the entire alphabet, and then make their own alphabet soup
- In women who can't stop smiling because they love how they've spent their day and grown
- In taking women to and beyond their potential and to reaching their fullest and highest power and not having to have it all together *all* of the time

- In women who proclaim, "If she can I do it, I can do it too!"
- Every women can say HELL YEAH to everything they want and no to everything else
- In enabling women to know that they are not only capable, but also worthy of love, happiness, and success

Know that there is nothing wrong with you.

About the Author

Moira Lethbridge, M.Ed., is the principal and owner of Lethbridge & Associates LLC. She draws on twenty-five years of successful organizational experience to help individuals and companies increase their productivity and improve their performance. Previously, she was president and CEO of a professional services firm, where she grew the company from five to 200 employees, increased revenue from $3 million to $35 million, and was named one of *SmartCEO* magazine's "Smart 100" in the Washington, DC, area for three years running. She is certified to administer a variety of leadership assessment tools, including The Leadership Circle Profile (TLC), the Myers-Briggs Type Indicator (MBTI), and the Herrmann Brain Dominance Instrument (HBDI). Her services include business and executive coaching, strategic planning, and leadership and personal development. Moira lives in Falls Church, Virginia and is currently embarked on a nine-month trip around the world to make time for a life that matters.

You can follow her personal journey at www.mymobileadventure.com.

Are you Ready to Live a Life of Balance and Inner Peace?

I can help you find and fulfill your own potential

My approach and method combines strategy, execution, and mindfulness. You walk away with a personalized plan of action and receive consistent support to help you Achieve Mindful Success.

- Transform yourself into what you are capable of being
- Balance health, well-being, and productivity
- Remove obstacles of negative thinking and false beliefs that block you from living in your zone of genius
- Balance achievement with enjoyment
- Find meaning and joy in work and life
- Spend your time doing what you love doing
- Achieve your goals faster and easier

I use humor, visual images, storytelling, and kindness for you to find and fulfill your potential. I create an environment of openness, acceptance, and empathy that allows you to develop in ways according to your personality.

To Get Started One-on-One

Contact me at moira@moiralethbridge.com for a free 30-minute consultation.

Or visit my website and join our Savvy Woman group

www.moiralethbridge.com